D1442901

Dirty Rotten
CEOs

Dirty Rotten CEOs

How Business Leaders
Are Fleecing America

William G. Flanagan

CITADEL PRESS
Kensington Publishing Corp.
www.kensingtonbooks.com

CITADEL PRESS BOOKS are published by

Kensington Publishing Corp.
850 Third Avenue
New York, NY 10022

Copyright © 2003 William G. Flanagan

All rights reserved. No part of this book may be reproduced in any form or by any means without the
prior written consent of the publisher, excepting brief quotes used in reviews.

All Kensington titles, imprints, and distributed lines are available at special quantity discounts for bulk
purchases for sales promotions, premiums, fund-raising, educational, or institutional use. Special book
excerpts or customized printings can also be created to fit specific needs. For details, write or phone the
office of the Kensington special sales manager: Kensington Publishing Corp., 850 Third Avenue, New
York, NY 10022, attn: Special Sales Department, phone 1-800-221-2647.

CITADEL PRESS and the Citadel logo are Reg. U.S. Pat. & TM Off.

First printing: May 2003

10 9 8 7 6 5 4 3 2 1

Printed in the United States of America

Library of Congress Control Number: 2003102014

ISBN 0-8065-2521-5

For my wife, Dawn

And special thanks to Raymond Valinoti, Jr.

Contents

Author's Note

Wall Street never likes to dwell on its fiascos. When its miscreants are caught, they usually admit nothing, yet promise never to do it again. They pay some fines, lop off a few heads, then everyone gets back to business as usual.

But the latest corporate scandals have created too much carnage to allow a quick return to normalcy. Tens of millions of investors were badly burned; trillions of dollars evaporated; hundreds of thousands of jobs vanished. Not since 1929 have Americans had their faith in corporate America rocked so severely. Don't expect them to flock back into the stock market any time soon.

It wasn't just a market cycle that caused all this damage. It wasn't the popping of the dot.com bubble. It wasn't the slowing global economy. It was the cupidity and stupidity of CEOs who were out to make themselves billionaires. Screw everyone else, from stockholders to employees to regulators, the business leaders seemed to be saying.

Like dispatches from the front, the press reports of the corporate scandals were filled with grim numbers as one major corporation after another fell dead or was gravely wounded. Enron. Arthur Andersen. Global Crossing. WorldCom. AOL Time Warner. Tyco. Adelphia. Qwest. Even Citigroup, the largest bank in the world. For months we were bombarded with stories of fraud and recklessness that involved bankers, directors, brokers, analysts, consultants, politicians, and lawyers, as well as the chief executives themselves.

It became hard to tell the players without a scorecard. (The *Forbes* List of Highest Paid CEOs could have served as one, however.) In the end, it all became a blur for many readers and investors. Newspapers, magazines, and TV hammered the scandals until they became as depressing as opening up your 401(k) statement. Readers welcomed the comic relief of Tyco's Dennis Kozlowski and his $6,000 shower curtain, Adelphia's John Rigas and his $13 million private golf course, and the laid-off Women of Enron posing in *Playboy* to pay the rent.

But the evil these men did shouldn't be simply swept into history's dustbin (the one marked "recycle") and forgotten until the next time. We need to view slow-motion replays of some of the ugliest moments in American capitalism so that they won't be repeated.

If you go beyond the headlines, it becomes clear that what happened was, sadly, inevitable. The outrageous award of stock options was the common denominator in all of these grim tales. Wave enough money in the faces of enough CEOs, and too many of them will do anything to get it. Couple that with puppet boards of directors, greedy moneylenders, ignorant investors, and sleepy regulators—and *presto!* you have the critical mass for disaster.

What can you do as a hapless investor? Read this book, remember its lessons, and in the words of the Albert Finney character in *Saturday and Sunday Morning*, "Don't let the bastards grind you down." You have stockholder rights; use them. You have brains; think before you invest. You have votes; don't waste them.

You should be mad as hell, not only because most of these dirty rotten CEOs will get away with what they did. They robbed you blind. Don't take it anymore. Stop them before they steal again.

1

Welcome to
Greed World

*It is not that humans have become any more greedy than
in generations past. It is that the avenues to express greed
had grown so enormously.*
—Alan Greenspan, chairman of the Federal Reserve, July 16, 2002

Picture a museum called Greed World, featuring the world's most
infamous financial villains sculpted in wax. It's like another Madame
Tussaud's, but starring white-collar swindlers instead of mass murderers and celebrities.

Greed World is located in Houston, naturally, home of the former Enron, now one of the museum's most popular exhibits.

A guide greets us for a quick tour. He is a handsome man in his
forties, not your typical college kid on summer break. He explains
that there are many exhibits, arranged in chronological order, but
that the most popular are the new ones representing Enron, World-
Com, Tyco, AOL Time Warner, Arthur Andersen, Adelphia, and
others from the Class of 2002. "An outstanding year for new induct-
ees into Greed World," the guide says. "We'll visit them last, in the

new wing. But I am warning you now—those exhibits are not for the squeamish."

Our first stop is the South Sea Bubble. A group of men attired in frock coats and breeches, and wearing powdered wigs, stands on a carpet-size map of the South Pacific, giggling. A sphere of clear plastic encloses them.

"Biggest investment bubble in history, until the recent collapses here," the guide says. "Almost brought down Britain in 1720. Everyone from chimney sweepers to princes owned shares in the South Sea Company. It was supposed to have a monopoly on all trade to and from the entire South Pacific. Gold, spices, slaves—you name it, the company had a lock on it, guaranteed by the Crown. Only a tiny amount of trade ever materialized, but that didn't dampen the price of South Sea shares.

"What kept propelling the stock," he continues, "were frequent rumors about more ports being opened, more ships built, more gold found in South America. They were all lies, planted by stockjobbers. Today we call them security analysts."

There is bitterness in the guide's voice, which everyone in the group picks up.

"Besides kiting the stock, the South Sea directors bought themselves a lot of powerful friends in Parliament. Key members of both the Houses of Commons and Lords were major shareholders. They saw to it that South Seas got special treatment in its complicated dealings with the government.

"Exactly how the South Sea Company was making money was a mystery. But everyone seemed to own stock in it, and everyone said its managers were geniuses.

"Is this story starting to sound familiar?" the guide asks. There are a few silent nods from the group.

"The collapse was catastrophic," he continues. "Shareholders were wiped out. The government teetered and had to take out massive loans. Investigations were launched. The public screamed for blood. Culprits had to be found.

"When auditors looked at the company's ledgers, they found

missing pages and false entries. Someone had doctored the books and destroyed evidence. Still, the greatly enriched directors and their pals in Parliament claimed innocence of any wrongdoing."

The guide pauses. "The parallels between the South Sea Company and Enron and some other companies here in Fraudville must be obvious to all of you by now. That's why I always have my groups stop here first."

He points to a quotation in a frame in the corner of the exhibit.

The South Sea project thus remains, and, it is to be hoped, always will remain, the greatest example in British history of the infatuation of the people for commercial gambling. From the bitter experience of that period, posterity may learn how dangerous it is to let speculation riot unrestrained, and to hope for enormous profits from inadequate causes. Degrading as were the circumstances, there is wisdom to be gained from the lesson which they teach. (Charles MacKay, *Extraordinary Popular Delusions and the Madness of Crowds*, 1841)

"The lesson went unheeded," says the guide, ushering us along.

"With the South Sea Company," he continues, "you had all the ingredients needed to create a bubble. You start off with a story stock—a scheme that fires the greedy imagination of the public and paralyzes its common sense. You create a buying frenzy on the stock by starting rumors and planting glowing stories in the press. You buy the influence of men in high places in government. You make deals with the bankers and brokers. You barbecue the books, then cash in your own stock. On the way out, you destroy important documents. When it's all over, you claim ignorance.

"Oh. And along the way you also screw tens of thousands of employees out of all their retirement money," he adds, sounding very much like one of those screwed employees.

A young woman in our group is moved to ask the guide the question we all wanted answered.

"Did you work for Enron once?"

In a stage German accent he answers, "I vas a cook on zee Eastern Front. I knew nozzing."

We continue on to the Charles Ponzi exhibit.

"A major historic figure," says the guide. "In 1920 he devised a pyramid scheme for taking in money from depositors, with a promise to double it in six months. He did fine as long as he collected even more money from greedy new depositors to pay off the old ones. He was done in when he had to resort to the mail to satisfy the need for new money. He was busted for mail fraud, among other things."

The exhibit shows a smiling, nattily dressed young man with a wide moustache and a straw hat, hauling in baskets of cash from eager investors. A sign over his head reads: DOUBLE YOUR MONEY IN SIX MONTHS!

The guide continues his commentary. "Eighty years after Ponzi was arrested—he eventually died broke in Rio de Janeiro—new variations of his scheme still return every year, like poison ivy. The basic gimmick is still the same, from chain letters to new public stock offerings: Promise huge returns, haul in money, postpone the day of reckoning, then cash out and run before the roof caves in."

We breeze past many tableaux depicting some of the other big swindles of the twentieth century and finally pause before the figure of Ivan Boesky. The wax likeness is remarkable, right down to his vulpine grin.

"He always wore suits of the same cut and color—black pinstripe—so he never had to bother choosing what to wear each day. Eventually, he got to wear different kinds of stripes every day, in Lompoc Federal Prison.

"Boesky's scam was crude. He bought inside information, sometimes paying with suitcases full of cash. Inside traders almost always get caught because it's easy to trace the stock trades. But almost every year, we welcome new members into Greed World for inside trading. We are now sculpting Sam Waksal, former CEO of ImClone. And we still hope to get Martha Stewart—what a draw she'd be."

We next approach the figure of Robert Brennan, still looking like the altar boy he once was. "Come, grow with us," pleads his recorded voice.

"The founder of First Jersey Securities perfected the pumping and dumping of penny stocks," says the guide. "The SEC finally put him out of business and ordered him to pay $75 million for defrauding clients. He was later convicted of bankruptcy fraud and money laundering and is now in jail."

Next stop on our tour is the Corporate Raiders display. There are the figures of Victor Posner, Boone Pickens, Carl Icahn, Henry Kravis, and others. Green light bathes all their wax faces.

"Raiders buy companies that are ripe for takeover," the guide explains. "They slash costs by firing employees and jazzing up the accounting, then resell the company, or its parts, at a fat profit. In the capitalist jungle, such predation is not only legal, it is encouraged."

The edge in his voice is getting sharper.

"But the employees who get dumped in the buy-fire-sell cycle don't see it that way. They see themselves as victims of financial games, which only benefit the raiders. Corporate raiders are in Greed World by popular demand."

We pass the figure of Donald Trump. Trump is holding a mirror, primping his hair.

"Trump was another one inducted by popular demand," the guide says. "Our board has voted him Most Obnoxious Businessman in the World, three years running."

The guide takes us next to Al Dunlap, who is wielding a chainsaw.

" The ex-CEO of Sunbeam eliminated thousands of jobs at various companies before being eliminated himself at Sunbeam, which went bankrupt. The former West Pointer started a trend."

Finally we stand before the glistening new wing of Greed World, built for the illustrious Class of 2002. The exhibits in the new wing attract the most visitors, the guide explains, because the wounds are still fresh. A lot of the visitors are ex-employees who lost their jobs, or ex-investors who lost their savings.

There is a line of people waiting to enter, and the guide huddles us together.

"Brace yourselves," he says. "These exhibits are very realistic and pretty horrifying. You see, instead of depicting these men in their boring suits, the museum board decided to portray them receiving the punishment they deserve for the deadly sins they committed. Punishment that will last for eternity, if you're a believing person."

"You mean the seven deadly sins?" the same young woman asks.

"Exactly. These men are depicted enduring the classic punishment for committing those deadly sins. Punishments that were levied since the days of Pope George the Great."

We all look at one another, puzzled. But then I am reminded that we are in the Bible Belt and that many Houstonians lost their shirts on Enron. They want to see someone suffer for it.

"Surely they were all guilty of greed," the young woman says.

"Of course. The penalty for Greed is to be boiled in oil, and all of the members of the Class of '02 qualify easily. But as you will see, there are some other punishments that are even more fitting."

We enter a very large, dimly lit amphitheater. Cut into the walls are seven exhibits, each marked with the name of a deadly sin.

The life-size figures in the exhibits are real enough to fool you at first. They seem to be made not of wax, but of human flesh.

At the first exhibit, Pride, we see a man in his skivvies, tightly strapped to the rims of a large wooden wheel. Interrogators turn the wheel faster and faster, as they shout questions at him. Occasionally they punch him as he revolves around on his endless, dizzying journey.

"Who is that?" the young woman asks.

"Jeffrey K. Skilling," the guide replies with some satisfaction. "There were a lot of contenders, but Jeffrey Skilling, ex-CEO of Enron, outclassed all the competition. His punishment is to be endlessly broken on the wheel. He was a brilliant, arrogant executive, but in the end, he wasn't nearly as smart as he thought he was. He still made hundreds of millions of dollars before jumping ship."

The next exhibit, Envy, shows a figure standing naked in a tubful of ice and water. His lips are chapped and his teeth are chattering. Occasionally, he gurgles what sounds like bits of poetry.

"The church says Envy is the second worst of the deadly sins," says the guide. "The punishment is to be kept in freezing water until hell itself freezes over. Our man in the tub here is Jerry Levin, ex-CEO of AOL Time Warner."

The young woman seems confused. "But he was never accused of any crime, and the company is still alive."

"The price of the stock dropped 80 percent after the merger with AOL, a deal that Levin put together. To cause a drop like that is a hanging offense on Wall Street."

"He's being punished for Envy?" she asked. "How's that?"

"Like the ugly girl envies the cheerleader," the guide says. "Levin envied the high growth rates and the high stock valuations of internet companies like AOL. Wall Street adored AOL but was not crazy about Time Warner. So he sold Time Warner to AOL, when AOL was at its peak."

We all look again at the man in the ice-filled tub. Through his blue lips we hear him repeating the same word: "Synergy, synergy, synergy . . ."

The guide visibly brightens as we come to the next exhibit, despite the creepy scene.

"Sloth is number four on the sin parade. Commit the sin of Sloth and you will be thrown in a snake pit from which you can never escape."

We look down beneath the glass floor and see a bald, naked man whose body is covered with the bites of the hundreds of yard-long, slimy snakes. He removes his arms from his head for a moment and looks up at us. Seconds later an adder sinks his fangs into the man's cheek. The guide is really enjoying this.

"You wouldn't think that any CEO would be slothful. Laziness is not a trait of any of them. But Sloth isn't just laziness. It's also a failure to do what you should be doing.

"No one ignored his responsibilities more than Kenneth Lay, the founder, ex-chairman, and ex-CEO of Enron. He was too busy courting politicians and playing Mr. Enron to mind the store. Had he been paying attention, he might have saved the company."

We come next to a long, deep, crowded pool, which seems to stretch all the way to the horizon. The pool is filled with boiling black oil, and the heat is intense. Through the oily mist and the gas, we spot some familiar faces.

"Welcome to the Greed pool!" The guide yells over the din of moans. "Crowded, isn't it?"

We see an oil-smeared head break the surface, revealing a few wisps of blond hair. "I've seen that face on CNBC," the young woman says.

"That's Henry Blodget, the security analyst at Merrill Lynch whose recommendations on dot.coms certainly did a lot to enrich himself and his firm's investment bankers. But ordinary investors believed him and they followed his glowing recommendations over the cliff."

The guide points to another figure bobbing in the superheated oil.

"Jack Grubman, another security analyst, from Salomon Smith Barney. He made twenty million dollars a year for being a diehard tout for WorldCom, Global Crossing, Qwest, and other telecoms that tanked. Grubman loved the telecoms as long as the firm's investment bankers got their business."

The guide peers across the steaming cauldron and shouts out another name. "James Berardino, ex-CEO of Arthur Andersen LLP, the world's most famous crooked accountants."

Up pops another familiar face from the boiling ooze. The guide grabs a long pole and pushes the figure underneath the surface.

"One of my favorites," says the guide. "Andrew Fastow, former chief financial officer for Enron. His crazy partnership deals helped sink the company, while he made thirty million on the side for himself. He was over his head then, and he's over his head now."

The young woman points to her watch.

"Yes,'" the guide says. "It's getting late. We could stay here at Greed all day. But one more man is worth singling out. There he goes, John Rigas, ex-CEO of Adelphia. He packed the board with his sons and used the company treasury as his own piggy bank. Some of the money he misappropriated went for a family golf course and the Buffalo Sabers hockey team."

We approach Gluttony. Once again the guide's face brightens at a scene that is sickening. A hefty, bald man wearing only a loincloth crouches in a large, filthy vat crawling with rats, snakes and toads. He grabs a distracted rat and stuffs it into his mouth, head first, and chews it angrily.

"The punishment for Gluttony is being forced to eat toads, rats, and snakes for eternity. You see before you L. Dennis Kozlowski, former CEO of Tyco. You'll notice that there are no pockets in the loincloth he's wearing, because he was never known to reach into his own pocket for anything."

We come to the last of the exhibits we'll see that day, Lust. A man lies buried under a pile of burning rocks. Only his face is visible—encircled in a white beard. It is Bernie Ebbers, former CEO of WorldCom.

"Being smothered in fire and brimstone is what you get for Lust," says the guide. "Ebbers lusted to create the largest telecommunications company in the world, and almost pulled it off with the help of his analyst and banker friends. But when the telecommunications business hit a wall, WorldCom decided to cook its books to the tune of about seven billion dollars in phony earnings. Poof! WorldCom became the largest bankruptcy in corporate American history.

"Ebbers wasn't only lusty and greedy, he was stupid. At one time, he was worth one point four billion dollars thanks to WorldCom stock. But he wound up owing the company over four hundred million dollars, borrowed to cover margin calls on stock he still owned."

The tour ends here, and we walk quickly toward the exit, anxious to leave the torture chamber. We thank our guide, but the young woman is persistent about his past.

"Come on, you worked for Enron, didn't you?"

"I was a vice president of public relations," the guide admits, smiling. "Can you beat that? Now I'm a guide in Greed World, doomed to talk to groups six times a day about the collapse of Enron. It's an exquisite punishment for a former flack, isn't it? Reminds me of *No Exit*."

There is no Greed World, as deserving as Houston is of such a museum. There are no guides, no exhibits. Not yet, anyway. In fact, it's surprising that some enterprising ex-Enronian hasn't put one together. There are surely millions of folks who would love to see these dirty, rotten CEOs suffer punishments only a medieval Pope could dream up.

But I wanted to give you a quick tour of who and what this book is about. On a grand scale, it's about hubris, greed, and fraud. On the human scale it's about stupid and illegal acts by individual men who made terrible choices for themselves, their shareholders, their employees, and indeed the whole economy. Trillions of dollars evaporated from portfolios. Careers collapsed. Businesses weakened. Retirements were postponed. College plans had to be changed. New businesses couldn't raise capital. The scandals rocked investor faith to the core and pushed the major markets to their lowest levels in five years.

Some of these men face long prison sentences and the seizure of their fortunes. Cheating CEOs now face even stiffer penalties for fraud. Accountants have been chastened. Regulators have been stirred awake.

But will these measures prevent financial shenanigans by future CEOs? Not on your life. Unless changes are made in how CEOs get paid, how boards of directors function, and how Wall Street banker/brokers operate, Greed World will never lack for new exhibits.

2

Follow the Money

You only find out who is swimming naked when the tide goes out.
—Warren Buffett

$\mathbf{M}$r. B. was waiting for me in a small meeting room at the Temps Perdu Golf Course in Boca Raton, Florida. Mr. B. is a retired CEO of a major bank, widely regarded as one of the world's shrewdest financial minds, and serves on a half-dozen major corporate boards. Everyone seeks his advice, from the president on down.

He is in his late seventies now, but still as sharp as ever. He has agreed to share his thoughts and observations on the Big Collapse with me, as long as he isn't quoted by name. "I speak for a lot of people," he says.

It's early evening, and we order cocktails from a waiter. Mr. B takes a mere splash of Glenlivet on the rocks. I try the same. He settles into a big leather chair, and I draw up close to him, and turn on the tape recorder.

"Do you know what parricide is?" he asks.

"Killing your father."

"In ancient Rome, there was no law against parricide because no one ever did it before. When a son finally murdered his father, the outraged Senate, responding to the mob, quickly passed a law against parricide. Of course, they already had plenty of laws against murder, and could have executed the killer without any new laws. But that's politics.

"We've been passing a lot of legislation lately that can hurt a lot of businessmen because of the previous actions of a few. They now have to swear to the accuracy of financial statements. If they're wrong, the CEOs could go to jail for twenty years.

"It was a knee-jerk reaction by the Congress. They keep voters happy by acting tough, passing redundant or silly laws, and slapping around a few rogues. Congress and Wall Street want to put this all behind us and move on, as we have moved on after other scandals like the savings and loan fiasco. But this time things are not going to be that easy to fix."

I lean forward. His voice is deep and strong, but he is keeping it deliberately low, though no one else is in the room. There is sadness in his keen eyes.

"What these guys have done is destroy investor trust. Trust isn't something you can legislate or manufacture. It is earned, and it is the cornerstone of capitalism. If you can't trust a company's CEO or board of directors, can't trust the accountants, can't trust the auditors, can't trust the analysts and brokers and banks, and can't figure out the business, why invest?"

"The bad apples spoiled the rest of the barrel."

Mr. B shakes his head, disturbing the mane of long gray hair that adorns his head like a silver helmet. A Southern senator would kill for hair like that.

"I just came back from Bohemian Grove," Mr. B said. "It's a kind of summer camp for businessmen and government leaders, off in the woods of Northern California. It's an interesting group. Maybe you read about this year's conclave in the papers. There were some protestors there. They think we're cooking up schemes to take over the world. But what we really do is drink and talk and eat a lot, and exchange ideas.

"The corporate scandals was Topic A. And if they had enough to drink, a lot of the CEOs I talked to there privately admitted to me, 'There but for the grace of God, go I.'"

"A *lot* of CEOs?"

"A lot of them have cooked their books, at least a few degrees, and shuffled cash around to dress up quarterly earnings. A lot of them have used aggressive accounting. A lot of them are guilty of overstuffing their pockets at stockholder expense, with no risk to themselves."

"So we should have a clean sweep of all CEOs?"

"The next crop would be just as bad," Mr. B said. "Probably worse. You see, the problem isn't just the CEO. Or a lack of laws. It is the whole culture. Without an economic boom, it couldn't have happened. Without widespread conspiracy among CEOs, accountants, bankers, lawyers, consultants, and brokers, it couldn't have happened. And without millions of greedy, naïve investors, none of this could have happened."

"You're blaming the victims."

"In part, sure. Most of them don't know or care what they are buying. They just want to get rich quick. They watch CNBC for stock tips from compromised analysts and cheery CEOs. Or they buy a mutual fund and forget about it, and don't even know what's in it. That doesn't amount to much due diligence."

"That doesn't excuse the bad CEOs for what they did."

"I am not condoning them, just pointing out that it was inevitable. Look. Let's play *Titanic*. The reason that story stays with us is because we all have to ask ourselves: 'What would I have done if I were aboard that ship when it struck the iceberg? Drown like a rat in the icy Atlantic? Or put on a dress, hop in a lifeboat, and live?'

"Put yourselves in the shoes of these CEOs, and ask yourself what you would have done. Your stockholders and your board are screaming about the price of the stock. Your own stock options are about to expire underwater. Your bonuses are on the line, as well as your employment contract, your career, and your reputation. Not to mention all the perks you enjoy—from company-owned penthouses and waterfront mansions to private jets. A man gets used to those things.

"At your side are high-priced consultants muttering in your ear constantly, coming up with high-tech schemes for making billions. Investment bankers are breaking down your door to loan you money to expand or buy more companies. In return for the business, they promise that their security analysts will praise your stock to the skies. They stuff hot IPO shares in your pocket, worth millions. Under that kind of pressure, you're tempted to do desperate things."

"Like make crazy acquisitions, or invent revenue, or hide debt, or fiddle with financial statements."

"Your fee-hungry accounting firm will tell you how to do the fiddling." Mr. B clears his throat and sips his scotch. "You must envision what is really at stake here. A few rosy-looking quarterly reports can mean tens, even hundreds of millions of dollars in the CEO's pocket. And in his own mind he thinks, 'We'll make it up next quarter, or next year, and we'll go back and straighten out the books then.' Restating earnings has become common."

Mr. B reached into a briefcase and handed me a typescript. "Here's something I wrote about the corporate scandals for the *Harvard Business Review*. I decided not to submit it after all, for reasons we can talk about later. But read it over, and you'll get my take on how to fix things."

I looked down at the paper. Mr. B went silent and waited for me to finish reading it before we continued talking.

Enron. WorldCom. Tyco. AOL Time Warner. Global Crossing. Adelphia. Qwest. Arthur Andersen. They were all huge, sound companies a few years ago, and are now bankrupt or very badly mauled.

The names of these companies are household words in the U.S. today, as are their former CEOs. They lost billions of dollars of stockholders' money, and cost hundreds of thousands of employees their jobs. They are as infamous as serial killers.

What happened to these companies? What on earth did their CEOs do? Why did these corporate superships founder or slip completely between the waves just because the economy got a little choppy?

Multi-billion dollar corporations are supposed to weather the occasional economic storm. Why did these CEOs sail their companies so close to the wind? Why did they take on such heavy debt loads? Why did they risk the uncharted, shark-infested waters of creative accounting?

Greed is the popular one-word answer, and it was certainly a primary cause. Without vast fortunes to be made, the CEOs of these companies would never have run their companies the way they did. By being reckless, they had billions to gain and nothing to lose—except other people's money and jobs. That is an irresistible risk-reward ratio.

"Greed is good," screams Gordon Gekko in the movie *Wall Street.*

Certainly capitalism doesn't frown on greed, and there's at least a little greed in all of us. We'd be hypocrites if we boiled these CEOs in oil for that offense alone. Look at the amount of money and power and perks we are dangling in front of them. How could they not be greedy?

To paraphrase Mel Brooks, "It's great being CEO." Chief executives of America's large corporations are the Knights of the Round Table in a world where money is King. CEOs control tens of trillions of dollars of assets, and employ tens of millions of workers. They command the armies that fight the battles of international commerce and bring home the spoils.

Their power and influence stretches even beyond the huge corporations they run. They have plenty of political clout, often right up and into the White House. They revolve in and out of cabinet posts. They have many friends in Congress and at regulatory agencies. They have clout in their states and local communities. They have clout at other major corporations, where they serve as directors on the board.

Workers depend on them for their jobs. An entire generation is betting its retirement on them. CEOs don't only run America, they *are* America.

The right CEO is as crucial to a corporation as the commanding general is to an army. Corporate wars never end, they just get bigger. Major corporations are double to triple the size they were ten years ago. The CEO has his or her hands full tending to the traditional concerns of a boss, from managing staff and operations to keeping customers happy, to growing market share, to expanding globally.

But the CEO today is being asked to do something else, too: move the stock. Dramatically and quickly. It isn't enough to run the company more productively and to increase shareholder value by making the company and its assets more valuable. That is the slow, steady way to move the stock.

Instead, many CEOs are given strong marching orders from their boards: Do anything, as long as the stock goes up. Succeed, and you will become vastly wealthy, very quickly. Fail, and you get rich anyway. The board members will make out just fine, too.

There is no shortage of people who want to be CEOs, for millions of good reasons. Compensation for chief executives has risen beyond the obscene to the simply hilarious. According to *Business Week*, in 1980, the average CEO made 42 times the average hourly worker's pay. By 1990, the CEO made 85 times as much. By 2000, it was 531 times what an hourly worker makes. And that doesn't include all the stock options, the fast track to serious money.

CEOs weren't always paid so much. They used to be paid enough to live and retire very well, but not like Arab sheiks. After all, they are supposedly employees like everyone else. Stockholders own their companies and they take the financial risks. CEOs are supposed to work for them.

But the stockholders' voices have been just a whisper in recent years, as pensions and mutual funds have become large, silent shareholders. As a result, friendly corporate boards can lavish more and more money on their CEOs, with scant complaint. The directors on the executive compensation committees—many of them CEOs themselves—then go back to their own companies and demand the same ridiculous compensation packages they just cocked up for their buddy. The audit committees do what they usually do—rubber stamp everything and go back to sleep. At work here is an old principle of wealth accumulation: Grab while the grabbing's good.

For the decade of the 1990s, when the stock market soared and many large corporations routinely managed double-digit growth each year, everyone was happy. No one was asking pesky questions of CEOs about their pay, or how they could continue growing their companies so much. After all, to grow by 10 percent a year means doubling the size of the company every 7.2 years. A 20 percent annual growth rate means doubling every 3.6 years. Not an easy task for an already huge corporation. GE managed it, but there is only one Jack Welch.

But no one was concerned. Not the stockholders, not the boards, not the regulators, not the financial press. Everyone was getting fat as long as the CEOs kept their stock moving, by hook or by crook. They often bent rules and sometimes broke them; bent some laws and sometimes broke them; paid too much for acquisitions and made horrific errors in judgment. But as long as the stock stayed high, no one cared.

But all through the late nineties, the smell of too many corporations' books began to reek. Then along came the year 2000, the economy stumbled, and the party was suddenly over. The dot.com bubble burst—as everyone knew it surely would. Earnings of the major corporations slid too, as everyone should have known they would. The business cycle—which the disciples of the New Economy had declared a relic—suddenly found a new set of wheels.

Business cycles come and go and well-run corporations survive them easily. Smart ones even know how to use downturns to gain market share. General Motors, for example, scored a coup with its interest-free loans in the fall of 2001. GM didn't make much money on the cars, but it kept the assembly lines moving, the employees on the job, and the customers in the showrooms.

But at a number of other huge corporations, something frightening happened. The relatively mild recession not only blew away the silly dot.coms. It left giants dead or seriously wounded.

As Warren Buffett wrote in a letter to his shareholders, "You only find out who is swimming naked when the tide goes out."

Huge corporations are not supposed to fly to pieces when the economy hits a speed bump, or when markets go soft, or when the competition gets tougher. They are supposed to be built to last. Like GM trucks.

But the corporate landscape has become littered with dead, dying, and badly mauled hulks. These are not tiny, high-tech start-ups, but some of the world's largest and most important corporations, in fields ranging from retailing to energy, telecommunications, and finance.

It was the CEOs of those companies themselves who inflicted the critical blows. CEOs who had been doing their damnedest to keep the stock up. The carnage is unprecedented after only a mild recession.

Here are just some of the biggest failures:

Enron, the slick energy colossus of the New Economy, is dead. It was the largest bankruptcy in American history, until outdone by WorldCom a few months later. At the start of 2001, it was the nation's seventh largest corporation. Virtually no one really knew how the company was operating or, indeed, exactly what it did to make money.

Kmart, the huge discount retailer that once had some 262,000 employees, is also in bankruptcy. It was tired of playing second fiddle to Wal-Mart, so a brash young CEO bet the entire company on a single roll of the dice—and lost. Had he won, he would have been paid a fortune. But by being wrong he still walked away with millions.

The energy and telecommunications industries are a shambles, with a number of major giants now dead or wounded after a bloody, mindless free-for-all for market share and capacity.

WorldCom, the second largest telecommunications company in the country, went bankrupt. Its collapse was Homeric, and record setting. It eclipsed that of Enron a few months earlier to earn the dubious honor of being the largest bankruptcy ever. The widely held stock went from $64.50 a share to 9 cents in two years. The books were simmering for at least that long.

Global Crossing and **Qwest,** two other sprinters in the telecom race to disaster, were also allegedly cooking their books. Global is in bankruptcy and Qwest is on the ropes, its stock having fallen over 90 percent. **Adelphia,** a cable and telecommunications company, is in bankruptcy after its CEO was caught allegedly robbing billions from the treasury.

Tyco International, a multi-billion-dollar conglomerate with an insatiable appetite for almost any kind of business, is suffering from life-threatening indigestion: too much debt. Its value has dropped by over two-thirds. Its ex-CEO has become a poster child for corporate greed.

AOL Time Warner, the media behemoth, is awash in debt and without a rudder following their $106-billion merger in early 2000. A year later, the company took a $56-billion write-off in a single quarter. In effect, that meant that AOL bought Time Warner for nothing. Its stock price has fallen over 90 percent.

Merrill Lynch, once the most respected name on Wall Street, has been skewered by regulators, has had to pay huge fines, and faces countless stockholder lawsuits. It will survive, but has been badly scarred.

Citigroup, the largest bank in America, and **J.P. Morgan Chase,** the second largest, were hauled before Congress to justify fishy billion-dollar loans they made to **Enron** and **WorldCom.**

Arthur Andersen LLC is no more. Its punishment was swift and drastic once it came out that their auditing seal of approval was for sale. An Andersen sign-off on financial statements became a red flag to investigators. Andersen accountants did more to sell American investors down the river than the crooked CEOs who paid them.

As these companies collapsed, or their stocks swooned, long-silent stockholders, including the formerly passive pension funds, started screaming "Off with their heads!" In most cases they've gotten their wish, too late.

Yet the men who ran these corporations were once heroes to their stockholders and boards. They were lionized by Wall Street, academia, and the financial press for their management skills and vision, but mostly for their ability to move the stock.

They are now vilified. They're called greedy crooks for playing fast and loose with other people's money. They're blamed for playing footsie with Wall Street and for allowing a lot of financial shenanigans to go on in their companies, from barbecuing the books to exaggerating revenues. They're blamed for cruelly firing workers just to make quarterly earnings estimates and for making critical errors of judgment.

They aren't just scapegoats. Stockholders and regulators are wringing the right necks. The CEOs are indeed the folks responsible for damaging or killing their companies. They deserve the blame. That's what they get the big bucks for.

But they got a lot of help and encouragement from their boards, security analysts, investment bankers, accountants, lawyers, consultants, mutual fund managers, pension funds, and other silent stockholders, as well as clueless regulators. No one complained when they seemed to be making money.

Few people are willing to cut these CEOs any slack now. They screwed up their companies but still became very, very rich. They earned astronomical salaries, pocketed fat bonuses, and cashed in short-term stock options worth hundreds of millions of dollars. What's more, they didn't risk a dime of their own money. When the stock went up, they cashed in their options. When it went down, they still had their fat pay, and a new set of stock options, at a much lower stock price.

Meanwhile long-term stockholders got mauled, and hundreds of thousands of their employees lost their jobs and retirement savings.

How do we make sure this doesn't happen again? We have passed tougher laws to punish errant CEOs, we have put boards on notice to tend to business, and we've fined and chastened Wall Street and the banks for being eager enablers.

But the one surefire way of reducing the risk of corporate fraud to near zero is simple.

The document ended there. I looked up at Mr. B. "There seems to be a page missing," I said.

There was an impish grin on his face. "I'm holding on to the last page until you do your own homework. We'll talk again later, and see what you think."

"Where should I start looking?" I asked.

"Follow the money. Take a look at how much CEOs have been making over the last few years, often for doing poor jobs. It will make you sick. That's where to begin."

3

Those Stunning
CEO Paychecks

But it takes a lot of money to live freely by the sea.
—Albert Camus

In his first novel, *This Side of Paradise,* F. Scott Fitzgerald has his young hero, Amory Blaine, engage in a discussion on capitalism.

The time is the early 1920s and the hero is walking along the road, back to his alma mater of Princeton, when a Locomobile stops to give him a lift. Blaine, peeved at having lost a job as an advertising copywriter, and at the world in general, turns his frustration on the occupants of the car, a business executive and his flunkie, both wearing goggles in the open-air car as it breezes through the countryside.

Blaine is in a mischievous mood, and turns an inquiry about his job status into a defense of socialism, which shocks the other two men, just a nine-iron shot away from Princeton. Enjoying their discomfort, Blaine carries on, and after putting down the American ruling class, suggests that wealth is overrated, anyway.

"Money isn't the only stimulus that brings out the best in a man, even in America," he says.

"That's the silliest thing you have said yet," says the mogul.

Blaine makes a more eloquent pitch to sell the theory.

"Let me tell you if there were ten men insured against either wealth or starvation, and offered a green ribbon for five hours' work a day and a blue ribbon for ten hours' work a day, nine out of ten of them would be trying for the blue ribbon. That competitive instinct only wants a badge. If the size of their house is the badge, they'll sweat their heads off for that. If it's only a blue ribbon, I damn near believe they'll work just as hard. They have in other ages."

"I don't agree with you," says the mogul.

Today's CEOs certainly wouldn't agree with Amory Blaine, either. They want a lot more than ribbons for their efforts. They hope to become at least centimillionaires if they hold down a major CEO job for just a few years.

One hundred million dollars is well beyond what all but the most jaded could possibly spend in a lifetime, let alone during one's retirement years. How many waterfront mansions and Manhattan penthouses and Paris flats can you live in? How many yachts, cars, horses, and other amusements can you play with? Executive pay isn't supposed to launch dynasties or bankroll financiers. CEOs are hired help, after all.

CEOs compete like schoolkids playing King of the Hill, vying to be the one who makes the most money each year. Not to assure themselves a very comfortable life; they already have all that. They want to be Number One in their industry, period. As Bernie Ebbers, former CEO of WorldCom, said, "Money is the way to keep score."

Each year, *Forbes* and *Business Week* publish the CEO scorecards, listing the earnings of the top five hundred CEOs in the country, for all to see.

There was a time when CEOs complained about those lists. Who wants his salary printed in a magazine? When I was an editor at

Business Week in the mid-seventies, public relations people would call me all the time, complaining that we had overstated their bosses' compensation. In those days, CEOs weren't starving, but they would be lucky to earn as much as major league second basemen. But there was still no shortage of applicants for the executive suite. The pay, perks, power, and prestige were reward enough.

But those complaints faded after a while. CEOs began to realize that it paid to advertise. The information is public anyway—revealed in the company's proxy statement sent to all shareholders. That's where the magazines themselves get their numbers. CEOs felt that if you had a great year, why not flaunt it? They wanted everyone to know how valuable they were.

The lists were useful to CEOs in another way, too. They helped them boost their compensation packages ever higher. Every year, CEOs could go to their boards, magazine in hand, and demand to get more than so-and-so, whose company didn't do as well as his. And so the compensation packages for all CEOs spiral upward. Thus, it is ironic that the lists—which were intended for stockholders to see how much they were actually paying the bosses of their companies—had the effect of boosting their compensation.

Headhunters also helped sweeten the kitty for CEOs. Corporations hire executive search firms to find top outside talent. The headhunters work on commission. The more pay the CEO gets, the more the headhunter gets—up to 30 percent of the executive's total compensation for the first year on the job. Headhunters naturally do everything they can to ratchet up pay and benefits.

Table 3.1 shows what, according to *Forbes,* the top twenty-five CEOs made in 2001 and what they earned over the preceding five-year period.

(You can check out how much all five hundred CEOs earn each year at www.businessweek.com and www.forbes.com.)

The average CEO of the largest five hundred corporations in America made between $11 million and $15 million in 2001, depending on which magazine you read. Discrepancies arise

TABLE 3.1

CEO	Company	2001 Total Compensation ($ million)	5-Year Compensation ($ million)
Larry Ellison	Oracle	$706.1	$799.5
Michael Dell	Dell Computer	201.3	445.7
Jozef Strauss	JDS Uniphase	150.8	n/a
Howard Solomon	Forest Labs	148.5	197.1
Richard Fairbank	Capital One	142.2	n/a
Eugene Isenberg	Nabors Industries	123.8	212.2
Richard Fuld, Jr.	Lehman Bros. Hldgs.	115.6	194.5
Joseph Nacchio	Qwest	101.9	296.3
Landon Rowland	Stilwell Financial	93.3	121.0
Thomas Siebel	Siebel Systems	88.4	153.3
Steven Jobs	Apple Computer	84.0	84.0
Ralph J. Roberts	AT&T Comcast	69.1	154.4
John Gifford	Maxim Integ. Prod.	60.2	185.3
William McGuire	UnitedHealth Gp.	58.1	146.2
Dan Palmer	Concord EFS	43.4	67.6
Henry Silverman	Cendant	40.5	298.1
Kenneth Freeman	Quest Diagnostics	35.0	29.1
Sanford Weill	Citigroup	34.6	728.3
Bernard Ebbers	WorldCom	34.6	72.4
Albert L. Lord	SLM Corp.	33.7	48.1
Bruce Karatz	KB Home	32.7	56.5
Lee Raymond	Exxon Mobil	32.7	82.1
Timothy Donahue	Nextel Comm.	32.6	n/a
David Komansky	Merrill Lynch	31.2	120.5
David Mott	MedImmune	30.2	n/a

Reprinted by permission of Forbes magazine, May 23, 2002 © 2003 Forbes, Inc.

because the compensation packages can get very complicated, and the methodology used to total them up differs. It's safe to say that if the brain trusts at these two magazines cannot agree on how to add up all the numbers, the CEOs would be hard pressed to do it themselves.

CEOs took a little bit of a haircut in 2001, as paychecks were down 6 percent from the previous year. But Table 3.2 shows what the top twenty-five made in the year 2000, before the economy soured.

Executive pay packages grew like marijuana all through the 1990s. The average annual income of CEOs rose more than five and a half times in the decade. Compliant boards of directors found it easy to be generous with the stockholders' money as long as the stock was rising. Directors kept on increasing CEO salaries,

TABLE 3.2

CEO	Company	2000 Total Compensation ($Million)	5-year Compensation ($Million)
Michael Dell	Dell Computer	236.0	245.8
Sanford Weill	Citigroup	216.2	785.2
Gerald Levin	AOL Time Warner	164.4	209.6
John Chambers	Cisco Systems	157.3	313.7
Henry Silverman	Cendant	137.5	281.4
Louis Gerstner, Jr.	IBM	103.4	282.5
Joseph Nacchio	Qwest Comm.	97.4	194.2
Walter Sanders III	Advanced Micro	92.2	120.5
Steven Jobs	Apple Computer	90.0	90.0
Jeffrey Skilling	Enron	84.4	n/a
Philip Purcell	Morgan Stanley DW	77.1	205.4
Jack Welch	General Electric	76.4	324.8
Larry Ellison	Oracle	75.2	112.5
Michael Eisner	Walt Disney	72.8	737.7
Jack Gifford	Maxim Integ. Prod.	61.4	132.5
Maurice Greenberg	Amer. Int'l Gp.	59.2	128.6
Arthur Levinson	Genentech	59.1	89.9
Edward Whitacre, Jr.	SBC Comm.	56.1	118.6
William McGuire	Lehman Bros. Hldg.	54.0	84.52
Thomas Siebel	Siebel Systems	53.7	65.1
Ronald Zebeck	Metris Cos	51.2	59.2
Wilfred Corrigan	LSI Logic	51.1	56.3
William Esrey	Sprint FON	49.03	144.3
James Morgan	Applied Materials	48.1	81.6

Reprinted by permission of Forbes magazine, May 14, 2001 © 2003 Forbes, Inc.

bonuses, and perks, but most important, kept piling on the stock options.

Go back to 1990, and the executive pay packages look puny. Table 3.3 shows what the 25 best-paid executives made that year.

In 1990, America's top 25 CEOs averaged annual incomes of a mere $9.1 million. (That excludes Steven Ross, who hauled in a one-

TABLE 3.3

CEO	Company	1990 Total Compensation ($million)
Steve J. Ross	Time Warner	78.1
Stephen M. Wolf	UAL	18.3
John Sculley	Apple Computer	16.7
Paul B. Fireman	Reebok Int'l.	14.8
Dean L. Buntrock	Waste Management	12.5
Israel Cohen	Giant Food	11.5
Martin S. Davis	Paramount Communications	11.3
Michael D. Eisner	Walt Disney	11.2
G. Kirk Robb	Genentech	9.2
Joseph D.Williams	Warner-Lambert	8.8
Michael L. Ainslee	Sotheby's Holdings	8.7
Richard K. Eamer	National Medical	8.6
Herbert J. Siegel	BHC Communications	8.4
George V. Grune	Readers' Digest Assn	7.5
Rand V. Araskog	ITT	7.3
P. Roy Vagelos	Merck	7.1
Richard D. Wood	Eli Lilly	7.1
Bram Goldsmith	City National	7.1
Louis V. Gerstner Jr.	RJR Nabisco	7.1
Leon C. Hirsch	US Surgical	7.1
Roberto C. Goizueta	Coca-Cola	7.0
Richard A. Manoogian	Masco	7.0
Daniel B. Burke	Capital Cities/ABC	6.7
William S. Edgerly	State Street Boston	6.5
Robert P. Luciano	Schering-Plough	6.5

Reprinted by permission of Forbes Magazine, May 27,1991 © 2003 Forbes, Inc.

time gain of $75.3 million due to the merger of Warner Communications and Time, Inc.) Yet by the year 2000, the average annual compensation of these corporate chiefs was $46.5 million. Is the job five times as difficult?

CEOs used to carp that they didn't even make as much as baseball players. But they surpassed them a long time ago. The average baseball player made $600,000 in 1990. A decade later, the average was $1.9 million. The top CEOs average 25 times that amount. In some cases CEOs earned more in a year than entire teams were paid.

CEOs are indeed captains of industry, but they are paid a lot better than any military captains. U.S. Navy captains (the equivalent rank is colonel in the army or Marine Corps) receive a base pay of $7,625.20 per month.

The highest-ranking military officers in the land, the generals and admirals on the joint chiefs of staff, receive $13,598 monthly, as long as they have over twenty-six years in service. Other generals and admirals get a maximum of $12,324 per month.

At the very bottom of the military pay scale is the raw recruit, who makes $1,105.50 a month. After four months, his pay goes up to $1,239.40.

So a four-star general makes less than 10 times the pay of a lowly, slick-sleeve private. In 2000, the average CEO made 531 times what the average hourly worker in his company made.

But does the military have trouble attracting qualified men and women when the maximum pay is a mere $147,888 a year? Hardly. (It is accepted wisdom that anything run by the government, from mass transit to the postal system, will be inefficient and expensive. Yet the government has struck a very good bargain for taxpayers on military pay.)

What drove CEO compensation to such levels? The stock option, of course. Costing the CEO nothing, options allow him or her to buy shares at a fixed price, which is usually below the current price of the stock. The option typically lasts three years, after which the CEO can exercise the rights to buy stock at the option price, which is presumably much lower than the current price.

CEOs love options, and will fight to the death to keep them. No wonder. They create fast, riskless fortunes. We'll take a close look at options in Chapter Four.

Spend just a few years as a CEO, and thanks to options, it's even possible to make the biggest list of all—the *Forbes* Rich List. The 2001 list of the four hundred richest Americans is thick with entrepreneurs who became billionaires: William Gates III ($54.3 billion) and Paul Allen ($28.2 billion) of Microsoft; Larry Ellison ($21.9 billion) of Oracle; John Kluge ($10.6 billion) of Metromedia; Sumner Redstone of Viacom ($10.1 billion); Michael Dell ($9.8 billion) of Dell Computer; Ted Turner ($6.2 billion) of AOL Time Warner; Rupert Murdoch ($7.5 billion) of News Corp; Gordon Moore ($5.3 billion) of Intel; Micky Arison ($4.6 billion) of Carnival Cruise Lines; Michael Bloomberg ($4 billion) of Bloomberg Media and New York's City Hall (the first billionaire mayor in history); Charles Schwab ($4 billion) of the brokerage that bears his name. And the list goes on.

Men like these founded their own enterprises out of thin air, and risked everything they had to get them going. They put everything on the line to create their corporations, and in most cases still have all or most of their fortunes invested in their companies. For the jobs they provided, and the wealth they created and the services and goods they created, they deserve to be on the Rich List.

But the *Forbes* Rich List now also abounds with custodial CEOs. They are just employees of the companies they work for, not their founding geniuses. Microsoft CEO Steve Ballmer is worth the most of any manager ($33.2 billion). Citigroup's Sanford Weill ($1.6 billion), is also on the list, and there are dozens of other "employees" who are worth at least $600 million, *Forbes'* cut-off point for the four hundred.

Even Bernie Ebbers, disgraced ex-CEO of WorldCom, made the Rich List at one time, reaching the rank of 174 in 1999, with an estimated worth of $1.4 billion at the time.

The *Forbes* Rich List is the unofficial scorecard of wealth in America, and still makes big news when it is published each year, despite all the spin-offs and knock-offs. It rates some commentary here. (Full disclosure: I was an editor at *Forbes* for seventeen years.)

The idea for identifying the four hundred wealthiest people in America came from Malcolm Forbes himself and caused a lot of grief at the magazine when he proposed it. Editors tried to talk him out of it, pointing out how difficult and expensive it would be to compile. And to what end? Prurience?

Malcolm seldom pulled rank on James Michaels, his legendary chief editor, who thought the idea was lame. But Malcolm insisted and the Rich List was born. Michaels installed a full-time editor and a platoon of researchers to work year 'round on the project. The first Rich List appeared in 1983 and was an instant success. Malcolm was not the only one who wanted to know who really owned America. (*Forbes* magazine also owns the Social Register, which lists the four hundred most socially prominent Americans, but net worth counts more than pedigree these days.)

Uncovering and then verifying people's wealth is a difficult and dicey business. *Forbes* researchers pore over real estate records and stock ownership lists for candidates; they trace the ownership of trusts and foundations; they unravel the ownership of offshore corporations; they snoop around in wealthy enclaves like Palm Beach; they watch the big-ticket auctions at Sotheby's; they keep an eye on rapidly rising entrepreneurs.

The researchers have to develop thick hides pretty fast. A former researcher, Evan McGlinn, describes what it was like working on the List. "I spent every waking moment pissing people off by asking them how much they were worth. People hung up on me, pleaded with me to get off the list, threatened, moaned, sighed, and yelled that I was scum. Others begged to get *on* the list. They lied, claimed false assets, promised me trips, and yelled that I was scum. It was a fun job."

McGlinn adds that the job also had its entertaining moments. He once had to verify some numbers with David Geffen, the former mailboy from Brooklyn who became a billionaire when he sold his music business.

McGlinn told Geffen that the magazine estimated he was worth just over $1 billion. He didn't deny what he was worth, in fact he said that he was a lot richer than other people who outranked him on the list, because he had a lot of his money in cash, not stock.

"How many people in America do you think have more cash than I do?" he asked. "There aren't many."

Geffen chose wisely when he wrote his checks. One of them was to DreamWorks SKG, the Hollywood movie studio in which he partnered with Steven Spielberg and Jeffrey Katzenberg in 1994. The studio's hits—including *Gladiator, Shrek, American Beauty,* and *Saving Private Ryan*—have helped to boost Geffen's net worth to about $3.5 billion in 2002, making him the forty-seventh wealthiest person in America. Geffen still has bragging rights among his own Hollywood set. He outranks Katzenberg ($820 million), who is No. 316 on the list; Spielberg ($2.1 billion), ranked at 90; and his old friend Barry Diller ($950 million), ranked at 272.

Donald Trump is another Rich Lister who pays close attention to the rankings. He is aware that bankers look at those numbers, too, and Donald needs to be friendly with his bankers. He would often argue with *Forbes* researchers, claiming they were ranking him too low.

That didn't stop the magazine from printing a cover story on Trump in 1989 asserting that the Donald was on the edge of financial collapse. But the Donald bounced back, and returned to make a lot more Rich Lists. In 2002, he ranked number 110 on the *Forbes* list, with an estimated worth of $1.8 billion.

Trump disputed that, too, claiming he was worth a lot more. "Five billion is the real number," he told *Forbes*. He bragged about his plans for putting up the world's tallest building in Chicago; and Europe's tallest building in Frankfurt. He said that construction had started on the fifth high-rise tower on an 80-acre site in Manhattan, where a total of eighteen are planned. His new Trump World Tower, located near the UN Building, is a big success: a single apartment sold for $38 million, believed to be highest price ever paid for a Manhattan apartment.

But *Forbes* was not persuaded by Trump, and stuck to its numbers. He was listed as worth $1.8 billion, not the $5 billion he claimed. "Ah, if only there weren't all those partners and debt obligations," the magazine noted.

There are a lot more folks who would prefer not to be on the Rich List at all, however, especially those who have inherited their wealth—about a third of those listed. Most silver-spooners like to keep quiet about their wealth.

I once attended an engagement party in Bucks County, Pennsylvania, at the country estate of a silver-spooner, who was the father of the bride-to-be. The home sat atop a hill overlooking acres of rolling meadows and pastures. This was prime horse country, and the silver-spooner had his own stable a few hundred yards from the main house. Some people at the party wore pinks, having ridden the hounds earlier. How colorful. But the champagne was Korbel, and the white wine poured by the liveried servants was jug Gallo.

At one point the host ushered me into his indoor pool house and sat down with me at a wicker table and chairs. He had discovered that I wrote for *Forbes*, and he lit into me for ten solid minutes about the Rich List. He insisted that it was no one's business but his own what he was worth. He cursed Malcolm Forbes and his lineage. (He was especially angry because Malcolm fudged on what he himself was worth.)

He complained that once his name appeared on the Rich List, he had to worry a lot more about kidnapping and robberies. Bad guys could read *Forbes*, too.

He carried on about the onslaught of folks looking for handouts, and the weird looks he got at his country club after being listed among the Richest 400 Americans. He spattered his wine. He got loud. He got my goat.

I felt like Amory Blaine, riding in that Locomobile. Blaine rebelled at the mogul's assumption of superiority. I now recognized the feeling.

I wanted to lace into this rich twit whose only claim to anything was his birth certificate. He hadn't done anything worthwhile with all his money. He simply lived off his portfolio. The only jobs he created were for grooms and groundskeepers.

I wanted to tell him that being on the Rich List was a very small price to pay for being rich. I wanted to tell him that if he didn't want to deal the consequences of being born wealthy, he could give his money away. I wanted to tell him that he was a lazy, idle wastrel and a cheapskate, to boot, serving such cheap champagne and wine at his own daughter's engagement party.

But I managed to hold my tongue, probably because I didn't drink that lousy wine. If I'd had a few, it could have been ugly. I hemmed and hawed and told him to write a letter to the editor. Then I left.

It is futile to try to hide your wealth in America. We live in a capitalist society where money is power, and folks want to know who has their capital and who has the power.

Just as movie fans think they have a right to know about the private lives of stars, Americans feel entitled to know who the rich really are, how they got their money, and what they are doing with it. And what the people want to know, journalists will uncover.

4

The Stock Option:
The CEO's License to Steal

The abuse of stock options has been enormous.
—Paul Volcker, former chairman of the Federal Reserve

During a relaunch of *Esquire* magazine some years ago, Clay Felker and his editors decided that the signature story of the new, revamped *Esquire Fortnightly* would be a profile of Curt Flood, the former baseball star for the St. Louis Cardinals. He was a hero who dared fight the system, and he was pictured on the cover like Gary Cooper facing his destiny in *High Noon*. He was the poster boy for the new *Esquire*, a Man with Principle.

In his struggle with the lords of baseball over free agency, Flood became almost as famous off the diamond as he was on it. In Flood's day, players couldn't ever negotiate with other teams, no matter how long they had been in baseball. The teams owned the players, period. Flood went to court—all the way to the U.S. Supreme Court—and lost.

But he stirred up so much dust along the way that baseball veterans did win the right to become free agents, and were able to sell their services to the highest bidders after their original contracts were up. By the late 1980s, baseball players were making more money than CEOs.

Flood's belated victory did even more for CEOs that it did for ballplayers, however. Corporate boards didn't need much persuading that their top executives should make more than a weak-hitting shortstop, and so the era of the Big Pay for CEOs quietly began.

The means of payment wasn't just cash. CEOs wanted to get paid in something a lot more valuable than cash—the stock option.

The stock option is such a great deal for the CEOs and such a lousy deal for stockholders, it is a wonder that it's legal at all. But it was signed into law by none other than Harry S. Truman, when he signed the Revenue Act of 1950. Attached to the act was a provision that made the stock option legitimate. So the stock option is legal, but it certainly isn't fair.

Consider the wacky way it works: A stock option is a right to buy a given number of shares at a given price, after a minimum of two or more years.

Most options are granted with an exercise price well below the current price of the stock. In a typical example, say a stock is trading at $10 per share, and the CEO gets an option to buy a million shares at $5 per share, which can be exercised after a certain period, usually a few years.

If the stock goes from $10 to $20, the stockholders are happy—the value of their shares has doubled. But no one is happier than the CEO—the value of his option has tripled. If he exercises his option at $5—costing him $5 million—and then sells the shares at $20, he pockets $15 million.

If the stock rises to $30, the stockholders triple their money; but the option-holding CEO will increase his fivefold; his $5 million cost will net him $25 million. The stock option is thus a leveraged, legal license to steal for the CEO and other officers lucky enough to receive options.

And what if the stock goes nowhere, and stays at $10 a share for years? The CEO still nets $5 million. It is only if the stock drops below $5 a share that his options are underwater. But the CEO has ventured nothing, so he has lost nothing.

What's more, if his options sink underwater, his company will probably reprice the old options at lower stock prices, or grant new options using the new, current market value. It's win-win for the CEO all the way around. It's easy to see why CEOs love stock options so much, particularly after a steep decline in the price of the stock. About 80 percent of all compensation paid to CEOs in 2001 was in the form of options. Executives who took small pay cuts were quick to ask their boards for a lot more new stock options, at a lower exercise price.

Take Charles Schwab, for example. The CEO of the huge financial services firm took a 93 percent cut in his 2001 salary and bonus. The stock sank from a high of $30 to $15 a share during that year. But Schwab was given 1,116,000 options, almost four times the number he received a year earlier.

Does Schwab really need more options? If the stock returns to its previous high of $45, Schwab will realize over $31 million. But that is pocket change for Schwab, who is worth about $4 billion and ranked forty-second on the *Forbes* Rich List in 2001. Still, when it comes to options, even the richest CEOs can't resist getting their hands on more of them.

According to *Business Week*, in 2001, a year of collapsing stock prices, more than two hundred boards of directors rewarded CEOs for doing poor jobs by swapping their old, underwater options for fresh, lower-priced ones.

The basic idea behind the option, in the words of Alan Greenspan, is "to align the long-term interests of shareholders and managers." In other words, give the guys who run the company a share of the rewards if the stock goes up. Common sense dictates that a CEO with skin in the game is going to watch the stock like a hawk. Besides, without them you won't attract or retain top talent. Or so the myth goes.

But long before the advent of options, CEOs were still paid well enough to assure plenty of applicants for the job. *Business Week* first began tracking executive pay in 1950. At that time, the best-paid CEO in America was Charles Wilson, the chairman of General Motors, who earned $4.4 million in today's dollars. The top-paid executive in 2001 was Ralph Ellison, CEO of Oracle, who made 175 times that amount. All because of Curt Flood and Harry Truman. Flood allowed CEOs to become free agents, and Truman gave them options.

Executives were a bit shy about asking for large amounts of options until the 1990s. I'd like to think they were a less greedy bunch in those days, and were in their jobs for more than money. Hank Paulson, CEO of Goldman Sachs, still insists that "most CEOs I have worked with . . . are driven by wanting to do well, a sense of honor and purpose. They don't need huge megapackages."

But as the economy and the stock market revved up for a record run, CEOs started to lose their shyness about asking boards for tons of options. Their justification? The overnight fortunes being made in the tech industries. Everyone wanted to get paid as if they were running Microsoft or Intel or Dell.

Headhunters told compensation committees that in order to woo or retain talented CEOs, they had to grant large amounts of options. Otherwise the CEOs would jump to high-tech corporations or other startups where they could make fortunes in only a few years.

Corporate boards paid no attention to the serious flaws in that argument. First, CEOs of tech companies usually take a big risk with their careers. And new companies often lack the cash to pay high salaries. So options become the equalizer. There's high reward for the high risk.

For large, established corporations, however, there are no such similar risks to the CEO's job. If he gets fired, he will walk away a multimillionaire because of the golden parachute in his contract. So why reward him with so many options?

The second flaw in the argument is subtler: Why would a major corporation want as its CEO someone hell-bent on making himself rich so quickly? Why hire someone so greedy? If he's that greedy, maybe he'll cook the books, or rob the place blind. Apparently, such questions never arose. They should have.

Nonetheless, CEOs garnered ever-larger options packages. In 1980 the average pay of a CEO running a large corporation was 42 times that of the average working man. The ratio rose to 104 times in 1991, to 305 times in 1997, and to 531 times in 2000, thanks to options. Is the CEO worth more than 531 other employees? Perhaps in the eyes of the CEO and the board, but not in the eyes of the workers.

As the market reached new heights through the 1990s, the logic of awarding lots of options appeared sound. The stocks of almost all companies were going up, and the CEOs of almost all companies had barrels of options. *Post hoc, ergo propter hoc.*

But when the economy soured with the new millennium and most stocks went down instead of up, CEOs were still hauling in tens and hundreds of millions of dollars as they exercised their old options. The CEOs were cashing out while the stockholders were going down with the ship.

The first problem with stock options became as apparent as the sliding Dow: Exorbitant pay didn't really buy better CEO perform-ance after all. It may have bought better *temporary* performance, but not long term.

Second, a lot of the gains in stocks were due to a roaring econ-omy, itchy 401k money, and "irrational exuberance." P/E ratios went off the charts; the rising tide floated all boats. The market became unsustainably overvalued.

"The abuse of stock options has been enormous," says Paul Vol-cker, former chairman of the Federal Reserve. "An instrument that was rationalized as aligning the interests of management with the stockholder has, in my opinion, too often become an instrument for aligning the stockholder with the interests of management."

According to *Fortune,* in the five years from 1996 though the year 2000, the five highest-paid executives in the land made a total of $1.4 billion, or $274 million on average, largely through exercising stock options. Yet four out of the five companies run by these CEOs underperformed the market and underperformed their peer companies: Walt Disney, Cendant, Computer Associates, and Apple Computer.

In the year 2001, *Forbes* evaluated all top CEOs on the basis of pay vs. performance. Presumably, the best-paid CEOs would turn in the best performances, especially in a bad year.

Of course it didn't work out that way. The best value for the stockholders was Warren Buffett, the CEO of Berkshire Hathaway. As CEO, he earned a total of just $500,000 over a five-year period, but his company had a five-year total growth rate of 26 percent. (Of course, Buffett owns a big chunk of the company, and profited from that increase.)

The worst values for stockholders were Michael Eisner and Sandy Weill, who both took home well over $700 million over a five-year period. Citigroup stock did well for that period but Weill did a lot better. (At least until the stock dropped about 40 percent in the wake of disclosures about its unsavory dealings with Enron and WorldCom.) Disney stock unperformed its peers for that period, and was still sliding while Eisner became one of the four hundred richest people in America, ranking #379 on the *Forbes* list for 2001.

Other CEOs whose pay was in the hundreds of millions while their companies' stock sank include William Esrey of Sprint and Joseph Nacchio of Qwest. Meantime, companies like Qualcomm and Solectron, among the fastest-growing for that period, paid their CEOs rather modestly.

There appeared to be little rhyme or reason to the award of options. And there were obvious cases of overkill. Dell CEO Michael Dell received more than 38 million options from 1996 though 2000, for example, even though he already owned 353 million shares as the company founder. Over the same period, Larry Ellison of Oracle received options on 20 million shares, although he already owned 700 million shares. Both men are multi-billionaires. Did the directors think awarding even more options would make

Michael Dell and Larry Ellison focus even more on the stock price than they already had?

In addition to this kind of empirical evidence that superior pay doesn't buy superior performance, an important study emerged in the summer of 2002. The study, written by four professors who track executive pay and performance, put fear in the hearts of CEOs everywhere. It found that the amount of stock that CEOs own has nothing to do with how well the company does.

"There's no relationship whatsoever," said one of the paper's four authors, Dan R. Dalton, dean of Indiana University Kelley School of Business.

The study was broad and deep, encompassing over two hundred previous studies dating back over thirty years and involving more than two hundred companies. It found that the relationship between executives' stock holdings and their company's performance is statistically zero. Writing about the study in the *New York Times,* David Leonhardt observed: "This means that an alphabetical ranking of companies is as apt to predict their performance as a ranking based on an executive's holdings." Ouch.

"You have to step back and ask yourself who is attending to the long-term interests of an organization?" asks another of the study's authors, Catherine M. Daily, a professor at Indiana. She answers her own question. "No one."

Of course, the authors did not go a step further: to measure whether excessive stock options did any *harm* to stockholders. The answer to that question is Enron, WorldComm, Adelphia, Tyco, AOL Time Warner, Qwest, etc.

The study came out just at the peak of the corporate scandals in mid-summer of 2002, when stock options were being attacked on a different front. Stockholders were finally beginning to understand who gets stuck with the tab for all those fancy options: *They* do.

When a CEO exercises an option, he is getting stock from the company valued at the current market price, but costing the CEO his original, much lower option price. The stock dilutes the value of shares held by other stockholders. Say there are one million shareholders owning 100 million shares. If the CEO exercises an option on 10 million shares, meaning there are now 110 million shares in the company, earnings have to be spread over more shares, and stockholders wind up with a thinner slice of the pie.

Usually, corporations will buy back stock to replace the optioned shares, but this is a raid on the corporate treasury to make up for the options that were exercised. Either way, the stockholders pay. Even for mediocre performance.

Just how many shares of America are sitting in CEOs' option plans? Over 15 percent of all shares of America's largest corporations are reserved for the CEOs and other officers. In other words, CEOs and other option holders own 15 percent of the companies they work for. But they didn't have to put up a nickel, and have nothing to lose if the company tanks.

Most stockholders don't know how many options are held by company management, or the potential liability of those options, unless they pore over footnotes in financial records. The cost of options does not appear as an expense on the profit and loss statements. The cost is only counted as expense when the options are exercised. And when they are exercised, the cost can be deducted from corporate taxes.

The net result of this odd soup of bizarre tax law and goofy accounting is to keep stockholders in the dark about a huge liability. If you subtract the cost of options from earnings, some corporations' earnings would drop from positive to negative, especially high tech companies that give out lots of options and often post only skimpy profits, if any at all.

In all, Patricia McConnell, an accounting analyst at Bear Stearns, estimates that earnings at major corporations would have dropped 9 percent in 2001 if options were deducted as an expense. (McConnell based her findings on 287 of the five hundred companies in the S&P 500.)

At Microsoft, famous for sharing the wealth, options expense came to $3.3 billion in 2001, almost one third of the company's entire net income. But none of that showed up in earnings statements.

Sophisticated investors and institutions like pensions and mutual funds have known all about this options scam for many years, and factor in the cost of options when they do their own stock analysis. But the average investor is blind to the true picture.

In 1994, the Financial Accounting Standards Board tried to put a stop to the three-card monte game that hid the cost of options. The powerful accounting board, which decides on generally accepted accounting rules, proposed a rule change that would have required corporations to deduct the estimated value of the stock options against their annual earnings. In other words, tear the fig leaf away from earnings, and show them as they really are—minus options costs.

But a funny thing happened on the way to adoption of the new rule. Congress stepped in and stopped it. Pressured by lobbyists representing CEOs, especially those in the high-tech sector, legislators voted on a bill that stopped the FASB in its tracks, and preserved the old way options were accounted for. The vote was a major victory for lobbying groups like TechNet, which represents giants like Microsoft, Hewlett-Packard, and Cisco Systems; and the Information Technology Association of America.

One of the senators who sponsored that legislation to protect the status quo was Barbara Boxer (D-Calif.). Her actions would come back to haunt her seven years later, when she grilled ex-CEO Jeffrey Skilling about Enron's accounting tricks. "The most egregious, or the one that is used by every corporation in the world, is executive stock options," Skilling said of accounting tricks. "Essentially, what you do is, you issue stock options to reduce compensation expense and therefore increase your profitability."

Skilling reminded Boxer that she played a key role in keeping that old trick alive. "I think FASB tried to change that," he said to her, "and that you introduced legislation in 1994 to keep that exemption." Boxer didn't reply.

Since 1973, the Financial Accounting Standards Board, nicknamed Fasby, has been the designated organization for establishing standards of financial accounting and reporting in the private sector. Those standards govern the preparation of financial reports. They are officially recognized as authoritative by the Securities and Exchange Commission and the American Institute of Certified Public Accountants. In other words, Fasby set the rules for corporate accounting. They are the guys in the white hats. Fasby didn't like the way options were being expensed, and wanted the rules changed so that the real costs were obvious.

But the (then) Big Six accounting firms, knowing the wishes of the CEOs who paid their lavish fees, balked and fought Fasby over the proposed change. They were the guys in the black hats. Fasby and the Big Six were at loggerheads. Warren Buffett, America's favorite investor, describes what happened next, in a droll piece he wrote for the *Washington Post*: By an 88–9 vote, the U.S. Senate declared that option grants were expense-free. "Darwin could have foreseen the result," Buffet writes. "It was survival of the fattest."

Over the next six years, CEO pay tripled.

In mid 2002, in the wake of the accounting and compensation scandals at Enron, WorldCom, and elsewhere, the question of how companies should account for stock options again arose. This time, however, CEOs faced a tougher battle holding on to the status quo.

One of the nation's biggest institutional investors, TIAA-CREF, finally got out of its crypt and started complaining about the elephant under the rug. For decades, TIAA-CREF, which manages some $265 billion of pension money, only worked behind the scenes to urge corporations to do right by their stockholders. Now it decided to take off the gloves. The public was clamoring for more transparency. In accounting-speak, that means clearer, more truthful numbers. John H. Biggs, chairman of TIAA-CREF, wrote letters to 1,754 major public corporations, urging them to treat all employee stock options as expenses.

Already there had been grumbling in Congress about requiring such a change, but intense lobbying again stymied passage of bills that would have required it. Once again, legislators from high-tech states like California, where options are as common as surfboards, opposed the change.

But Biggs's efforts came at a fortuitous time, as CEOs were seeking to restore investor confidence. A few corporations volunteered to expense options in the future—including Coca Cola, the Washington Post Co., General Motors, Procter & Gamble, and AMB Property Corp. (Of course, they had far less options money to account for than high-tech companies like Microsoft and Cisco.)

In his letter, Biggs wrote that "voluntary expensing of options contributes to clear, straightforward and high quality financial reporting, enhancing credibility that surely will be highly valued in the post-Enron market."

Singly, then by twos, and then by groups, dozens of major corporations agreed it was prudent to make the accounting change. One influential group that signed on was the Financial Services Forum, made up of twenty-one CEOs from the biggest financial companies in the country, including Allstate Insurance, American Express, AIG, Bank One, Bank of America, Bank of New York, Citigroup, FleetBoston Financial, Goldman Sachs Group, Household International, JP Morgan Chase, Merrill Lynch, MetLife, Morgan Stanley, Prudential Financial, State Street, and Wachovia. General Electric, part of the group, had already agreed.

The CEOs of these companies, the most powerful financial institutions in the U.S., were major beneficiaries of stock options.

Did they give up the fight without a struggle? Hardly. Lobbyists had succeeded in keeping Congress under control, and measures to force the expensing of options had been routinely defeated. Even the president's new corporate governance law omitted any attempt to monkey with the sacrosanct status of the option-as-is.

But there was pressure being brought on other fronts, too. Standard & Poor's had announced that it would begin reporting businesses' stock option grant expenses to determine the core earnings for companies in the entire S&P Compustat database. In effect, this meant that the cost of options would be visible for the entire world to see in S&P's widely used financial data.

S&P estimated that the total option expense for fiscal 2002 for all companies in the S&P 500 amounts to 17 percent of estimated 2002 earnings. That is a mighty large liability to bury in footnotes.

Further, the International Financial Accounting Standards Board had already announced that it was going to insist upon options being expensed on all financial reports issued around the world. Companies that did business out of the U.S.—which is to say nearly all of them—would have had to conform to the new standards anyway.

Still, the protectors of the Magic Option were not really caving in. They were making a preemptive strike. For if there was one thing worse than having to expense options, it was being forced to share them with the troops.

In 1993, Senator Joseph Lieberman (D-Conn.) had introduced a bill that would have forced corporations to distribute half their available options to rank-and-file workers, or lose tax deductions for the options. The CEOs went into a panic. It was okay to throw a few crumbs to the troops, but half the options pie? No way. Lobbyists saw to it that the bill got nowhere.

But Lieberman was back in 2002 with another plan, and it was no less frightening. It amounted to virtual wealth transfer from rich executives to ordinary workers. The name of the bill bordered on obscenity: The Rank and File Stock Options Act.

The bill called would have required the following:

- In order to claim tax deductions, companies must offer at least half of the total available stock options to employees making less than $90,000 a year.
- The SEC must finalize rules requiring majority stockholder approval of every stock option plan or stock purchase plan.
- The SEC must recommend rules requiring top executives to hold their stocks for a set period of time and forbidding them from selling their shares while still employed with the company.

As far as CEOs were concerned, the only thing missing from the bill was a picture of Karl Marx. The Lieberman bill bordered on seizure of private property. The stock options had always been their baby, and no one in Congress had the right to tell them how to divvy them up. What would be next? Limits on the amount of money a chief executive can make? Would they be held to 20 times the salary of the average worker, as Plato had suggested?

Lieberman, who was always considered a friend of the deductible stock option, had clearly gone too far. So the timing seemed perfect for a number of major corporations to volunteer to expense options, rather than have Congress entertain any egalitarian notions of wealth transfer. Note: The Lieberman bill never got off the ground.

Some corporations even whined that figuring out the cost of options each year would be too tricky. "That's nonsense," wrote Buffett. "Believe me, CEOs know what their options grants are worth. That's why they fight for them."

Buffett pointed out that options have cash value the instant they are granted. "If my company, Berkshire Hathaway, were to give me a ten-year option in one thousand shares of A stock at today's market price, it would be compensating me with an asset that has a cash value of at least twenty million—an amount the company could receive today if it sold a similar option to the marketplace."

Indeed, Buffett pointed out that executives can turn options into cash long before the options can be exercised. "The day an employee receives an option, he can engage in various market maneuvers that will deliver immediate cash, even if the market price of his company stock is below the option's exercise price," he wrote.

The precious stock option survives, more or less intact, and will continue to be doled out—"in wildly disproportionate amounts to the top dogs," in Buffett's words—for another generation of CEOs.

The cost of options won't be hidden away from shareholders any longer.

The main thing is, however, that the stock option—which made knaves into multimillionaires at Adelphia and WorldCom and Enron and elsewhere—survives to enrich a new generation of CEOs. Investor beware.

✸　✸　✸

While fat salaries and stock options would seem like compensation enough for top CEOs, most also receive a lot more, all paid for by you, the shareholder, whether you know it or not. They can get performance bonuses, low-interest loans that are sometimes totally forgiven, tax reimbursements, special bonuses, and rock-star perks.

What's more, if they fall on their faces and get canned, they have golden parachutes—severance and contract guarantees to assure they still walk away with millions. Even bumbling CEOs who never manage to get the stock high enough to exercise a single option are still taken care of. Is there any other job in America that pays you a fortune because you fail to do your job?

It is Disney's hapless CEO, Michael Eisner, whose name pops up so often when it comes to excessive compensation. The arena of bonus payments is no exception.

If you look at the company's proxy statement for 2002, you will see that Eisner is entitled to a performance bonus. Not based on the stock price, or even on revenues, but on an "adjusted net income." There are at least seven critical items that don't count against Eisner's bogey. Laying off more staff, for example, will not affect his bonus. Neither would closing down a business—such as the ill-fated Go.com, which cost Disney $1.5 billion in 2001, according to *Forbes*.

What can be even more valuable than performance bonuses, however, are loans made to CEOs by their employers. At least the performance bonuses are linked to goals. The low-interest loans are not. CEOs request them, and directors grant them, simple as that. Stockholders have no say.

The loans are sometimes totally forgiven, i.e., turned into gifts of cash. What about any taxes due? Some companies will pay the CEO "gross-up" payments for the taxes. John Legere, CEO of disgraced Global Crossing, which went bankrupt in January 2002, was forgiven a $15 million loan by Asia Global Crossing. He collected another $4.7 million to pay the taxes on the forgiven loan. No wonder the payments are called gross-ups.

These loans can sometimes be enormous. Take the case of Bernie Ebbers, former CEO of WorldCom. He not only drove the company into bankruptcy, costing tens of thousands of jobs and billions of dollars of losses to stockholders, he also walked away from the company owing it $408 million. He used some of the money to buy WorldCom stock, meet margin calls, and make some other investments. The interest rate is a mere 2.3 percent. Ebbers has said that he will repay the loan, but he will not be required to if he declares personal bankruptcy. If Ebbers chose to pay the loan back in monthly installments, it would cost him about $1.57 million per *month*, for a period of thirty *years*.

John J. Rigas, CEO of Adelphia, outdid even Ebbers. He borrowed some $2.3 billion, guaranteed by the company. Some of the money went for a private golf course as well as other privately owned cable companies. It will be hard to repay that loan from prison. But if he were to attempt it, at the same interest rate Bernie Ebbers got, Rigas would have to pay about $12 million a month—$144 million a year—for thirty years.

Another big borrower was Stephen C. Hilbert, the former CEO of Conseco. He was forced out of the company owing it $162.5 million in 2000, and has not kept up on the interest payments since he left.

Many CEOs borrow money from their corporations to pay for homes; others simply let the companies buy their homes for them, and live in them rent free. We are not talking split-level ranches and pieds-à-terre here. Many large corporations buy mansions and penthouses for their CEOs to live in.

In 1999, Tyco spent $18 million on the New York apartment for its CEO, L. Dennis Kozlowski, on which he has never paid a dime in rent. At the time, the CEO personally was busily raking in some $300 million in salary, bonuses, and sale of Tyco shares over a three-year period. Kozlowski set new highs—or lows—in extracting such perks from his company. More on that later.

If you own shares in a major index fund, or one that invests mainly in large corporations, walk a little slower the next time you are in New York City's premier neighborhoods. You might feel a sense of pride and sophistication as you stroll the canyons of Fifth and Park avenues, lined with some of the most expensive apartments in the world, which you helped to buy. PepsiCo maintains two luxury apartments in Manhattan; Toyota Motor North America bought a $6.8 million pad for its CEO, Toshiaki Taguchi; Vivendi bought a $17.5 million duplex on Park Avenue for its ill-fated chairman, Jean-Marie Messier. The list goes on. "Corporations have been buying apartments in Manhattan for as long as I can remember," says one real estate agent.

Do you own any shares of GE, one of the most widely held stocks in the world? Pause when you pass the Trump International Hotel and Towers on Central Park West. Glance upward and you will be looking at four luxury apartments where present and former GE executives live for free. Their park-view pads were bought and paid for by you and other stockholders. One of the apartments—which cost $11.3 million—was until recently reserved for GE's CEO, Jeffrey Immelt. But he moved out, saying he didn't need it.

Another of the GE apartments is used by Robert Wright, head of GE-owned NBC. Former GE CEO Jack Welch occupies a third apartment occasionally. Or, I should say, he used to occupy an apartment. It was Welch's bad luck that his post-retirement perks came to light in the middle of the corporate scandals. He was immediately tarred with the same brush as L. Dennis Kozlowski, John Rigas, Bernie Ebbers, and other infamous CEOs.

The perks, made public by Welch's estranged wife, Jane, in the course of their divorce battle in 2002, were truly imperial. In addition to the rent-free penthouse, GE paid for fresh flowers, wine, laundry and dry cleaning services, a cook and wait staff, a housekeeper, toiletries, newspaper and magazine subscriptions, even postage. GE also paid some of Welch's bills at Jean Georges, the pricey restaurant that is located in the building.

GE paid for Welch's country club memberships, including Augusta National, and made available VIP tickets to New York Knicks basketball games, Yankees and Red Sox baseball games, the

French Open, Wimbledon, and the US Open tennis tournaments and the Olympics. Welch was also accorded unlimited use of a corporate Boeing 737 jet, a limo and driver in New York, bodyguards when traveling abroad, and satellite TV installations in his New York apartment and his three other homes in Massachusetts, Connecticut, and Florida. GE also provided appliances, security systems, and sophisticated computer and telecommunications equipment.

The revelation of these benefits sold a lot of newspapers and did a lot of damage to the image of Welch, widely acclaimed as the best CEO of the modern era. In twenty years under his reign, GE grew from a manufacturer of electrical gear, light bulbs, and appliances into a global conglomerate. Revenues went from $25 billion to $130 billion. The price of GE's stock rose 2,786 percent over the same time span.

Welch had negotiated the perks in 1996, in lieu of more income. He should have taken the additional cash then. To stifle the critics and get himself off the evening news, Welch decided to turn back all the perks or pay for those he does use. "In this environment, I don't want a great company with highest integrity dragged into a public fight because of my divorce proceedings," Welch wrote in the *Wall Street Journal*. "I care too much for GE and its people." And his own reputation, of course. If Jane Welch had intended to embarrass her soon-to-be ex by detailing his post-retirement perks, she certainly succeeded. Hell hath no fury.

Probably the hardest of all perks to justify are golden parachutes, which reward even the most incompetent CEOs just for having been there. Unlike most other mere mortals, CEOs cannot simply be fired, even for gross incompetence. You, as a mere white-collar stiff, can often get canned for any reason at all, aside from discrimination, and you don't have any recourse whatsoever. (I witnessed an editor fire a reporter by fax, while he was on vacation. The reason? Because *his* boss told him to "stage a public execution" to shake up the staff. Gestapo tactics didn't die with Hitler. But the fired reporter had the last laugh; he has a very successful career with an arch-rival publication.)

CEOs face no such rude treatment—they have contracts that protect their salaries and other perks, even if they screw up. In some cases, they get their packages even if they are convicted of felonies. Nice work if you can get it.

5

"The World's Leading Company"

Live fast, die young, and leave a good-looking corpse.
—John Derek

Cynics will tell you that in the end, Enron was like Frankenstein's monster—a fiendish creation that was out of control. Who needed it, except the people who got rich from it?

The virtual company is virtually gone now. In the year 2000, Enron was ranked as the seventh largest corporation in America by *Fortune*. But by the end of 2001, Starship Enron had crashed into bankruptcy and ignominy, as the nasty little secret about the company finally met the light of day: It simply wasn't making enough money. Its financial statements were dream sheets; its earning projections were fantasies; its success story was a myth. Kenneth Lay, Jeffrey Skilling, and their cohorts had made monkeys out of presidents, investment bankers, investors, accountants, security analysts, politicians, academicians, financial journalists, regulators, and most

Enronians (that's what employees at Enron called themselves). The stock sank from a high of $90 to pennies a share in eighteen months, wiping out billions of dollars of investors' money.

There are a lot of folks who would like to forget there ever was an Enron, from George W. Bush to Joe Berardino, former CEO of Arthur Andersen LLC; to thousands of employees; to millions of investors; to hundreds of millions of electric, gas, and water customers from California to Argentina to England to India.

They all bought the company line that Enron was the world's most successful energy company and that it was making an elegant leap to the absolute pinnacle—the biggest company in the *world*. In case you didn't get that message, it was emblazoned on a banner that hung in the lobby of the company's headquarters at 1400 Smith Street in Houston: THE WORLD'S LEADING COMPANY. Say it long enough, and people will believe it.

The fact is, Kenneth Lay and Jeff Skilling really had something going. Too bad they let it all get away from them. The tale of Enron is a tragedy, made all the more painful because its villains were among our best and brightest, and its victims were in the millions.

How did it happen? Why did it happen? Who is to blame? How can it be prevented from happening again?

Like all classic tragedies, Enron's featured extraordinary people with extraordinary ambition who took an extraordinary fall. But the story begins humbly.

Kenneth Lay, the co-founder and architect of Enron, was born on tax day, April 15, 1942, in a dot town in southern Missouri called Tyrone. But the Lays didn't have to worry much about paying taxes. Ken's parents, Omer and Ruth Lay, were Ozark people—sober, hard working, God fearing. They were poor farmers without even a farm to work.

Omer Lay hired out to work in the fields and also ran a grocery store, but there were five mouths to feed—Kenneth had an older sister Bonnie, and a younger one, Sharon.

Omer lacked education but not ambition. He picked up the family and moved to Mississippi, where he managed to get a sales job, but only briefly. He moved the family again to Rush Hill, in north-east Missouri, in the late 1940s. He had work on his brother-in-law's farm, and also took a job selling tractors and other farm equipment. In his spare time, he was minister of the Rush Hill Community Church.

Rush Hill was a very small town without a single paved road. The population was under 200. Omer Lay never even earned enough money to afford a house for his family—they rented all the time—but he earned a lot of respect in the community, and served on the PTA and the Planned Progress Committee.

Young Kenneth Lay did not take long to display the work ethic he inherited from his father. From the age of twelve he worked on farms every spare moment, cultivating fields and bucking bales.

"It's hard for me not to think Ken was an adult when he was a child," Sharon Lay recently told the *Kansas City Star.* "He worked every summer, every holiday, every opportunity he had to work."

Omer Lay eked out a decent life for himself and his family in Rush Hill, but he always lived with a nagging question: What would his life have been like if he had gotten a college education? He didn't want his kids to wind up asking themselves that same question when they were adults.

Omer determined that all three of his children would go to the University of Missouri in Columbia. But with Omer's limited resources, he couldn't afford to send his kids away to Columbia, even if they could manage to raise the relatively modest tuition for state residents.

So Omer packed up the family once again, bade farewell to family and friends in Rush Hill, and moved to Columbia in 1957. He figured his children would then be able to commute to college from home, and save the cost of board.

The kids went to Hickman High, while Omer and his wife, Ruth, found work, fittingly and deliberately, at the University of Missouri.

Omer worked as a security guard at the university library while Ruth worked in the campus bookstore.

Bonnie, Kenneth, and Sharon all graduated high school and all entered and graduated the University of Missouri, just as their parents had dreamed and sacrificed for. Omer Lay had lived a poor life, but he had given his children the keys to unlock doors that had been closed to him. Bonnie became a psychologist. Ruth owns a corporate travel agency—which once was the agency for Enron in Houston. (Kenneth Lay didn't forget his sister, or any of his family, in later years.)

Growing up in tiny towns and working hard in the fields from an early age didn't dull Kenny Lay's curiosity about the world beyond the horizon. Like many a farmboy, he daydreamed as he baled, and fed his resolve to get away from such a dreary life.

Of all things, the world of business fascinated young Lay. Maybe it was the notion of working with his head instead of his back that most appealed to him.

"I spent a lot of time on a tractor and had a lot of time to think," Lay told the *Houston Chronicle*. "I must confess I was enamored with business and industry. It was so different from the world in which I was living."

Thirty-five years later, Lay would do his thinking from the plush seat of his Gulfstream IV, and he was still enamored of business and industry.

Lay graduated tenth in his class at Hickman High out of a class of 276. He was short, with a slight build, and not the type to hang around with the jocks. Classmates recalled him as very smart, very decent, and very serious. He sang in school choirs, was vice president of the French Club, and was in the National Honor Society. He was a nerd, but a likeable one.

In 1960, he enrolled at the University of Missouri, where Dad was watching the library and Mom was selling textbooks. Young Kenneth was still interested in business, but he chose to major in economics rather than business administration. He wanted to study the big picture, not the dull mechanics of running a company. He was an excellent student and caught the eye of a brilliant professor with the improbable name of Pinkney Walker. Without Walker, there might never have been an Enron.

Walker was already a legend on campus when Lay took his first economics course. He had been teaching at MU since 1940 and had earned a solid reputation on and off the campus. He had his bachelor's degree from the University of Texas and his MBA and Ph.D. from the University of Pennsylvania. In his teaching career at MU, which ended in 1975, Walker introduced more than 40,000 students to the importance of gross domestic product. None were more memorable, and few much brighter, than Ken Lay.

"He was a brilliant student," Walker told the *Kansas City Star.* "He took my first course in economics and did extremely well in it."

Walker took Lay under his wing, and even gave him a job as his assistant during the school year. During the summer, Lay painted houses and managed to save enough to buy his first car, a used Pontiac convertible. He also joined a fraternity, Beta Theta Pi. But he was no campus Romeo. He had a girlfriend, Judy, who later became his wife.

Lay did extremely well in his economics studies, earning a bachelor's degree with distinction, an honor shared by only two other students in the prior history of the school.

Retired economics teacher John C. Murdock recalled that Lay cared more about economic theory than ordinary finances. He told the *Kansas City Star* that "his interest in economics and finance was an intellectual kind of interest. Even today, I don't believe that what motivated him ever has been the money. It has been the idea of doing something big and new and different."

But Lay was far from indifferent to money. Walker recalled Lay telling him "I've got to get out and make some money," when Walker asked Lay to stick around MU another year to earn a master's degree. "He had a real motivation to get ahead in the world." However, Lay cooled his ambitions long enough to earn that advanced degree and in 1965 headed for Houston. It was a city he would come to love, and to which he gave a lot of money and support in later years.

His first job was as a senior analyst at Humble Oil, though he then knew very little about the energy business. That was all to change. Ken Lay would come to know the energy business as well as anyone in the world, and to have visions for it that no one else could foresee.

He began courses for his Ph.D. at the University of Houston, and nailed down a position as an economist in corporate planning at Exxon. But in 1968 he took a career break. With the Vietnam War at full tilt and students rioting in Chicago, he joined the U.S. Navy at the age of twenty-six. He was originally stationed in Newport, Rhode Island, and had a cushy job as a supply officer. But Lay chafed to do something more significant. He wound up in Washington, still working for the Navy. He undertook the task of doing something about the government's financial forecasts, which were woefully off the mark and led to bad timing and wrong decisions as the economy skidded. Lay vowed to find out what was wrong, and was given access to the right people in the Navy, the government, and even the Council of Economic Advisers. Lay immersed himself in the work, and he delivered.

In his 200-page report, which was also his Ph.D. thesis, Lay wrote: "One significant element was the poor quality of official projections of the costs of the Vietnam buildup." He suggested accounting changes for the nation while at war, and some of these were adopted. Already, Lay knew that accounting could work wonders.

The new Ph.D. also began teaching courses at night at George Washington University, in macro and micro economics. In 1971, a familiar face would grace the scene in Washington—Pinkney Walker, Lay's mentor at the University of Missouri. Walker was appointed by President Nixon to be a member of the Federal Power Commission and immediately hired Ken Lay as his chief aide. The seeds of Enron were planted.

One of the FPC's most vexing responsibilities was overseeing the nation's vast electric power system. What had long been a quiet, sleeping industry was wobbling into all kinds of difficulties. A few years before, there had been a three-day blackout in the Northeast that affected a third of the population of the U.S. Power prices were rising even faster than inflation. New power plants weren't getting built on time, if at all, because of environmentalists. Problems were emerging with the nuclear power plants that had been built, yet the industry had committed to building many more.

Walker left the FPC in 1973 after a two-year stay, but before he left he put in a good word for Lay with the Interior Department, and Lay became undersecretary for energy at the age of thirty-one.

As first a student and now an overseer of energy industries, Lay would have known well the name and the saga of Samuel Insull. Depending on your sympathies, Insull was either the true father of cheap electricity for the masses or a greedy robber baron who wanted to control all the electric power in the United States. Lay would later be compared to Insull, and it's easy to see why.

Samuel Insull came to the U.S. as a young immigrant from England in 1881. He had an interest in electricity, and soon met and impressed Thomas Edison, the man who actually did put lightning in a bottle. He began working for Edison as his secretary and confidant, and in 1892, Edison made Insull head of his fledgling Chicago Edison Co., the company that became General Electric.

In those early days, only direct current power was available, which meant that the power generators had to be located fairly close to the customers who used the power. After a distance of only about a mile or so, the flow of direct current drops to a trickle, due to losses over the power lines. Yet Edison was wedded to the idea of direct current, and his fledgling power companies therefore had to be smack in the middle of whatever communities they served. And there had to be a lot of them if electric power was to be available to everyone.

Insull had a different view. He envisioned building a few, very large powerhouses, which could supply an entire city. The trouble was the loss of power over the lines using direct current. George Westinghouse, Edison's nemesis, who was promoting alternating current, provided the solution. Power generated at AC does not dissipate nearly as much over the power lines as power generated at DC.

Insull wanted to build large power plants, and AC was the only way to go, so he broke with his mentor and bitter rival of Westing-house to achieve his vision. Edison's old DC systems soon faded away.

Insull kept on ordering larger and larger generators from the company he co-founded, GE. The bigger the powerhouse, the more homes that could be served, and the cheaper the unit cost of churning out the power. Insull was bringing cheap electricity into a lot of homes in Chicago and elsewhere, and he was also making himself very rich. By 1907 Insull had acquired some twenty other power companies around Chicago, and renamed his company Common-wealth Edison.

Insull's strategy was quickly copied in major markets around the country and each city or region soon had a single, large power company instead of dozens of small ones. Power was cheaper, and no one objected. The marketplace was working.

If the story ended there, Samuel Insull's name would be on a lot of public schools, and his stature in the history books would have been assured. Edison may have invented methods of producing and using electricity; Insull made electric power cheap and abundantly available.

But electricity had barely begun replacing gas lamps across America before agile financial minds saw ways to exploit the new industry. Insull had an inspiration that was to lead to his demise: the holding company.

Basically, a holding company is an umbrella company that controls a bunch of smaller companies. It gets control by acquiring a controlling share of stocks and bonds issued by the operating companies. Investors liked the idea—it gave them diversification—and so it took off. Pretty soon almost all the operating utility companies in the U.S. were controlled by holding companies. So far, no harm, no foul.

Insull, through his own holding companies, eventually controlled hundreds of electric utilities and other businesses in thirty-two states, having assets of some $500 million. Yet Insull's own investment was only $29 million.

The public bid up the stocks of these holding companies far beyond the value of what lay beneath. Investors loved holding companies, but the general public was growing suspicious of what was happening to their electric bills. Suspicion turned to outrage when there was a spate of newspaper stories about how some holding company executives were robbing the operating companies, with the ultimate patsy being the ratepayer.

The stock market crash in 1929 and the resultant collapse in the value of holding company shares spelled big trouble for Insull. Everyone from stockholders to customers was screaming for his scalp, including president-to-be Franklin D. Roosevelt, who knew a good election issue when he saw one. He condemned "the Insulls, whose hand is against everyman's."

Insull was forced to surrender his investments to creditors, and was tried three times for securities fraud, each time winning acquittal. But Insull couldn't hold up his head anywhere in the U.S. and retired to Paris, where he had a heart attack and died in a Metro station in 1938. He was stone broke.

Ken Lay, visionary that he was, could not have foreseen in 1973 that the course of his own life would have parallels with Insull's. But his own path to infamy was just about to begin.

Lay was thirty-one, an undersecretary in the Interior department, and highly thought of in Washington. What he was not, however, was anything even near well-to-do. It was time to make some money. Where better to look than the energy industry, in which Lay had become expert? He wound up taking a job in Winter Park, Florida, as vice president for corporate development of Florida Gas Company. It wasn't much of a position of power, but pleasant enough. Lay stayed six years, and is recalled fondly by former colleagues as a "super leader."

He returned to Houston in 1979 to work at Transco Energy—minus his wife, Judy, but with a new bride, his former secretary, Linda Phillips. The man who hired Lay was Jack Bowen, the same man who had hired him at Florida Gas Company. "Ken enjoyed getting out on the pipeline, going to compressor stations, talking to people, and making sure he really listened," recalled Bowen in the *St. Petersburg Times.*

In 1981, Lay became president of Transco Energy and stayed three more years before seeing the opportunity he was waiting for. He left to join Houston Natural Gas Company, and merged it with InterNorth of Omaha, creating one of the largest gas pipelines in the U.S. Kenneth Lay was forming his vision. He changed the name of the company to Enron. Let the games begin.

By 1985, the second leg of the Reagan era, the issue of energy deregulation was getting more and more support. "Deregulation" simply means that the government stops regulating, gets out of the way, and permits the market to determine rates. The government had deregulated natural gas; now it was working on deregulating electric power and telecommunications.

Just as Sam Insull had done with big generators, Lay knew that deregulation of electricity should save consumers money, and improve efficiency. He also knew that it would create the need for a huge, space-age exchange to trade energy. And that created opportunities for hedging and other forms of very profitable strategies. Lay aimed to run that exchange and to make money on every single kilowatt and btu of gas that traded over it.

To help things along, he began a courtship with Washington and local politicians. Enron contributions went mainly to Republicans, and friends were taken special care of. According to the Center for Public Integrity, Enron and its CEO, Ken Lay, donated more than $550,000 to George W. Bush alone since 1993, making the company his top career patron. Enron made a total of $5.8 million in campaign contributions to members of Congress since 1989. It was the company's best investment.

In his years in Washington, Lay had learned his way around the corridors, and he became Enron's best lobbyist. Ultimately, it was Ken Lay's Washington connections as much as anything else that allowed Enron to become the largest energy company in the world, and later, the largest bankruptcy on record.

6

The Man Who Knew Too Much

We're the world's coolest company.
—Jeffrey Skilling, former Enron CEO

Jeffrey Skilling was born on November 25, 1953, in Pittsburgh, Pennsylvania, the second of four children. His father, Tom, was a mechanical engineer who sold valves to water companies and electric utilities. The family moved to New Jersey for a while before settling in Aurora, Illinois, a middle-class suburb of Chicago.

Skilling was a daredevil as a kid, always taking physical risks.

"Jeff spent half his life in a cast," his brother Tom told the *Houston Chronicle*. "He was breaking his bones, or he fell out of a treehouse. He ran down the hill on the Indiana dunes and went headfirst into a tree. I remember we worried about him because he had partial amnesia.

"He always seemed to come back, but I always thought it instilled in him a special drive not to be put down again—to do things right and make something of his life."

Skilling never lost his appetite for risk. He would later go on adventure trips with executives at Enron—dirt-bike trips across Mexico, racing in SUVs across the Australian outback. On an African safari he once said he would like to take a trip risky enough for someone to get killed.

He was a very good student in high school, and earned membership in the National Honor Society, just as Ken Lay had years earlier. He also worked on the school yearbook.

In his spare hours, Skilling and his brother Tom worked at a local community access TV station. Tom did some on-air announcing, and became very good at it. Today he is a TV weatherman in Chicago. Jeff preferred to run the control room. Naturally.

He had excellent grades, and had a good choice of colleges to attend, but chose Southern Methodist University, which awarded him an engineering scholarship. In 1971, he headed for Dallas with a group of friends also recruited by SMU.

He joined Beta Theta Pi fraternity, the same one Ken Lay had joined in Missouri. Beta is a large, conservative, prestigious fraternity, the first west of the Alleghenies. It is not a party frat. In fact, pledges are not even allowed to drink during recruitment. But the roster of prominent Betas is long and deep—from politicians to university presidents to jocks to businessmen to actors (James Arness) to writers (Ken Kesey). Close to two hundred senators and congressmen were Betas, as were twenty-three governors. The fraternity claims more Rhodes scholars than any other fraternity, with eighty.

Beta Theta Pi, which is founded upon a concept called Men of Principle, also boasts of dozens of former and present CEOs among its brothers, including Sam Walton, founder of Wal-Mart, and Hugh McColl, former chairman of Bank of America.

But nowhere on the current roster of successful Betas will you find the names of Kenneth Lay and Jeffrey Skilling. These men who once ran what was the largest energy company in the world no longer make the cut of illustrious Betas. Infamy doesn't cut it.

While working as a mechanical engineering intern one summer, Skilling made an unsettling discovery. He was working at an asphalt company in Chicago and saw up close what mechanical engineers actually do for a living. He didn't like it.

He earned his degree in applied science but before graduation he added some more business credits. In 1975, he took his first grown-up job with First City National Bank in Chicago. He also took a bride, Susan Long, a coed at SMU who was also from the Chicago area.

It was not a great time to be launching a career. The economy was the weakest it had been since the Depression. Gerald Ford was in the White House, a dead man walking after pardoning his predecessor, Richard Nixon. Inflation was in double digits, unemployment was high, urban crime was at record levels, and business found capital too expensive and too hard to come by to grow. Taxes and inflation were strangling everyone, as the bills for the guns and butter policies of Lyndon Johnson were now being delivered to the doorsteps of American corporations and wage earners. The maximum tax rate was 98 percent.

To add to the damage, the OPEC oil cartel was choking the world economy, having succeeded in doubling the price of crude after it imposed embargoes on shipments. Long lines and high prices at the gas pumps resulted in some shootings.

A new word entered the American vocabulary—"stagflation." The economy was stagnant while inflation raged at double-digit rates, which sent the stock market into a decade-long swoon. In 1973, the Dow Jones Industrial Average peaked at 875. It would not hit that level again until the 1980s. Small investors fled the stock market for bonds and almost anything tangible—real estate, gold, art, antiques, even baseball cards. At least seven million small investors abandoned the stock market. The sad state of the market was

exemplified by a *Business Week* cover story of Aug. 13, 1979, entitled "The Death of Equities." The cover illustration was a photo of
a crumpled paper airplane made out of a stock certificate.

Federal, state, and local governments were all running large
deficits. In 1975, New York City went bankrupt, though the rest of
the country didn't give a hoot. The city's appeal to the federal government for financial help fell on deaf ears, prompting the famous Daily
News headline:

FORD TO CITY:

DROP DEAD.

In Texas, where there was plenty of oil, there was serious talk
of breaking away from the union. President Ford's solution to the
problems with the economy was pitiable. He started a campaign
called Whip Inflation Now, and become its biggest cheerleader.
Ford urged everyone to wear a WIN button on his lapel, and try not
to pay too much for things. It didn't do much for the economy, nor
for Ford's hopes for staying in office. In 1976, he lost to Jimmy Carter, whose economic policies were even worse than Ford's. By the
time Carter left office, the interest rate on six-month Treasury bills
was over 18 percent.

Jeffrey Skilling decided to take a breather from the stagnant business scene, and in 1977 he applied to the Harvard Business School,
which was no easier to get into then than it is now. Its MBA program
had 4,695 applicants in 1977; only 789 were accepted. Skilling was
one of them, and his intelligence stood out even in that select company.

"The general impression of Jeff in school was that he was one of
the brightest people we'd ever met," said Ryan Kuhn, a classmate
and friend of Skilling's at the B school. Kuhn now engineers mergers
and acquisitions for Kuhn Capital in Chicago. "It was clear that if
merit drove success, this guy would succeed."

Skilling impressed classmates and professors alike with his com-
mitment to free-market principles. One professor, Jeffrey Sonnen-
feld, who taught management, told a reporter that he recalls Skilling

holding court in The Galley, a student hangout. Even then he had an interest in electric power, and railed against the government for its role in subsidizing electric power to rural communities. Skilling insisted rural electrification should have been left to the free market. (In the 1930s, the government created the Rural Electrification Administration, to help farmers and other people in rural areas get electric power by forming their own power cooperatives. Major power companies bypassed isolated communities at first. It wasn't profitable to run miles and miles of wire to serve only a handful of customers. But as time went on, private power companies were ready and able to serve those customers, and it became harder and harder to justify the government-subsidized co-ops.)

Skilling would later take a much more keen interest in electric power and the role of the federal government in energy regulation. He would do all he could to end it—and with the help of Ken Lay, would largely succeed.

But at Harvard, Skilling is most remembered for his comments in class one day, in a course called Productions and Operation Management, taught by Dr. Chip Bupp. John LeBoutillier, the conservative writer and former Congressman, was a student in that class and recalled the incident in one of his columns. The professor asked the students what the CEO should do if he discovered that his company was producing a product that might be harmful, or even fatal, to consumers.

Skilling's hand shot up. "Jeff was one of the brightest members of Section A," writes LeBoutillier. "With thinning blond hair and wire-rim spectacles, he had a mature persona to go with a slight Southern drawl. He often expressed disdain toward any government intervention. One of the natural leaders inside Section A, when he talked, as the commercial said, 'Everyone listened.'"

Skilling didn't miss a beat with his answer: "I'd keep making and selling the product," he said. "My job as a businessman is to be a profit center and to maximize return to the shareholders. It's the government's job to step in if a product is dangerous."

LeBoutillier, who wrote the book *Harvard Hates America*,

recalled that several other students nodded their heads in agreement. "Neither Jeff nor the others seemed to care about the potential effects of their cavalier attitude. What if this product harmed consumers? How about the company's employees? Were they in danger during the manufacture of this product? And what could happen to the company if the CEO made the wrong decision?

"Few in Section A that day dared to raise these questions. At HBS—and business schools nationwide—you were then, and still are, considered soft or a wuss if you dwell on morality or scruples."

Skilling certainly wasn't voicing any radical notion. Business schools—even Harvard—are supposed to develop business leaders who act in the shareholders' interests first.

In 2001, the Aspen Institute surveyed 1,978 new MBAs from thirteen leading B-schools including Carnegie Mellon, Columbia, the University of Pennsylvania, and Northwestern. They were asked what a company's top priorities should be. As reported in *Business Week,* three out of four said the most important goal was to maximize value for shareholders. Seventy-one percent said satisfying customers was most important, while only 33 percent put a high priority on producing high-quality goods and services.

Only one fresh MBA in twenty thought the environment was worthy of being a top corporate goal. Just 25 percent thought creating value for their local communities ought to be a top priority.

But if Skilling had stuck to the mantra of "shareholder value," Enron would never have wound up in bankruptcy court. Skilling, Lay, and other top Enron managers wound up putting their own interests before those of the shareholders. They took their hundreds of millions out of Enron while taking the stockholders on a dizzying ride to disaster. Under the cloak of capitalism, they turned into princes of darkness. You can't blame the HBS, or capitalism, for that.

As William F. Buckley observed in a column, "To believe that capitalists will behave honorably just because they are engaged in capitalism is akin to believing that no priest will engage in pedophilia simply because he is a priest."

Skilling graduated in the top 5 percent of his class at HBS and went off to conquer the world. But his ties to Harvard—and Harvard's ties to him—would endure. Indeed, Enron would become the most important corporation in America to Harvard, and vice versa. Four members of its seven-person governing board, the Harvard Corporation, had direct links to Enron. Enron paid the school to do research on its pet projects like energy deregulation.

Harvard Watch, as its name implies, is a watchdog organization made up of Harvard students and alumni concerned with corporate governance at Harvard. In a report dated May 2002, *Harvard Watch* identified some of the people sharing significant Enron and Harvard links.

Robert Belfer, patron of Harvard's Belfer Center for International and Strategic Affairs and Harvard's Environmental and Natural Resource Program, and a holder of a number of Harvard posts. *Enron link:* Enron's largest stockholder, former Enron director since 1985.

Ashley Brown served as executive director of the Harvard Electric Policy Group (HEPG). *Enron link:* HEPG received Enron funding; publicly promoted energy deregulation.

D. Ronald Daniel, a member of the Harvard Corporation. *Enron link:* Managing director of McKinsey & Co. when Jeffrey Skilling was a McKinsey consultant to Enron, presumably reporting to Daniel.

William Hogan, professor, Kennedy School of Government; research director, Harvard Electric Policy Group (HEPG). *Enron link:* HEPG received Enron funding and promoted proposals for energy deregulation in California and elsewhere.

Robert Rubin, member of the Harvard Corporation, former director of the Harvard Management Company, and former secretary of the U.S. Treasury. *Enron link:* Chairman of the board, Citigroup (Enron's largest creditor); established relationship with Enron CEO Kenneth Lay in late 1980s while at Goldman, Sachs, a major Enron financier.

Jeffrey Skilling, Harvard MBA; presented two papers promoting deregulation in California and elsewhere through the Harvard Electricity Policy Group (HEPG) in 1994; worked with HEPG's William Hogan to design and promote deregulation in California. *Enron link:* Former Enron CEO; former Enron director.

Lawrence Summers, Harvard University president and member of the Harvard Corporation. *Enron link:* As U.S. Treasury Secretary, promised Enron CEO Kenneth Lay that "I'll keep my eye on power deregulation and energy-market infrastructure issues."

Herbert "Pug" Winokur, former member of Harvard Corporation and director of Harvard Management Company; patron of the Herbert S. Winokur, Jr., Public Policy Fund at Harvard's Kennedy School of Government. *Enron link:* Former Enron director since 1985; chair, Enron finance committee; former chairman, Azurix Corporation (Enron subsidiary). (Note: Winokur resigned from the Harvard Corporation in June 2002.)

Skilling never forgot the HBS and made sure there was a steady stream of Harvard MBAs flowing into Enron. At its peak, Enron was hiring 250 MBAs a year, including as many as it could get from Harvard. There were plenty of takers.

Upon graduation, Skilling didn't want to join the ranks at a major corporation, having to scramble and scratch for years to get to a position of power. He had no patience for corporate gamesmanship.

He accepted an offer from McKinsey & Co., the elite management consulting firm. He wanted to be a business mastermind, not a management trainee. Consulting would allow him to be just that. If he proved himself a success at consulting, corporate job offers at the top levels would come his way. Corporations routinely wound up hiring their McKinsey consultants. One of them, Louis Gerstner, once a McKinsey partner, became CEO of three major corporations. In 1958 Gerstner left McKinsey to run American Express. He later became CEO of Nabisco, and then a very sick IBM, which he brought back to life before retiring a hero. A very rich hero.

McKinsey had established itself as the best and brightest consulting firm in the country, although new competitors like the Boston Group and others were nibbling at its substantial pie. At their best, consultants provide a brain trust to help CEOs solve business problems. They parachute in, investigate the problem, and offer solutions. At their worst, they are fee-hungry charlatans, whose "solutions" can be disastrous. If their advice fails, consultants can always blame the company for botching the implementation of their suggestions.

In Houston, Skilling concentrated on the energy and chemical industries. Eventually he began doing work for the recently retitled Enron. It was the beginning of a beautiful, tragic friendship.

As soon as Skilling met Ken Lay their minds meshed. They shared a similar vision. Between them, they had a lot of intellectual horsepower to put on the same track, and the results would be world-shaping. The energy business in the United States, and elsewhere around the world, would never be the same. Neither would a lot of other things.

Skilling and Lay together would create a new kind of company, and new kinds of businesses. They were hailed as geniuses. Of course they would wind up being cursed as crooks and liars. But the business models they crafted are Topic A at the nation's business schools. Look out. There are more Enronesque companies on the horizon.

Skilling was working for McKinsey in 1987 when Ken Lay sought his council. Enron was in poor financial shape, weighed down by debt from acquisitions. What's more, the value of its huge natural gas holdings was dropping. Enron faced being squeezed into bankruptcy as the cost of servicing debt ate up more and more revenue.

The natural gas industry had recently been deregulated, which Ken Lay had long hoped and worked for. But the natural gas industry, long accustomed to regulated rates and established ways of doing things, was not coping well with the change to free-market pricing. Prices fluctuated wildly on the spot market, causing chaos for both producers and consumers. Major gas buyers like gas companies and industrial users wanted consistent, long-term prices instead of dealing with sudden spikes on the spot market.

Skilling saw what was needed—a national gas market. And Enron was perfectly positioned to create it. Enron could supply gas on long-term contracts at fixed prices, which its customers wanted. But Enron went a lot further than that. Enron would also sell options to buy gas later, at a fixed price. Customers liked options, because they provided hedges.

For example, a gas company might buy an option on a supply of gas instead of committing to a fixed contract. If the price of gas fell, it would let the option expire, just like options on the stock market, and buy natural gas on the open market. If gas rose in price, it would exercise the option. Enron also arranged swaps for customers, and variations on those strategies including "swaptions."

In creating what became known as the Gas Bank, Skilling was quick to employ all the latest Wall Street financial tricks to tweak profits out of its trading. Overnight, the nature of Enron began to change. It had taken its first giant step from a pipeline company to a worldwide finance and trading company. Skilling saw that while producers could make money selling gas, and their customers could make money reselling it or burning it to make their products, the middleman could have it both ways without having to make any major capital investment.

Enron could buy at volume discount from producers, then sell long-term contracts to users at a premium, because of the service value added. It provided a marketplace for the options and swaps so customers could fine-tune their own costs. Enron made money here, too. In short, it made a lot of money on gas every time it was bought, sold, or traded. The Gas Bank was a huge success. It only whetted Skilling's appetite for more innovation.

In 1990, Skilling finally left McKinsey and joined Enron full time as head of Enron Gas Services, later called Enron Capital and Trade Resources. Skilling surprised colleagues at McKinsey when he left, because he had little management experience and no apparent taste for it. And McKinsey had been good to him. He was head of its Houston operation. At one time, Skilling worked on a team for

Thomas Peters, who would later write the best-seller *In Search of Excellence*. "Skilling could out argue God," Peters recalled.

But the prospect of joining Enron as a top executive became irresistible. Skilling was thirty-seven, bristling with ideas, and had the friendship and confidence of the CEO, Ken Lay. He could be Cardinal Richelieu to Ken Lay's King Louis XIII. And there was no telling how much money could be made.

Enron had become the most important broker and trader of natural gas in the country. Skilling and Lay both knew that was just the beginning; their gas model could work across a whole range of other industries.

But Enron was still operating at a handicap, compared to other pure brokers and traders on Wall Street. They were not allowed to use the same accounting.

Since Enron was indeed a broker and trader, Skilling went to Washington and asked that Enron be allowed to use the same accounting methods that brokers and traders on Wall Street use. Known as mark-to-market, the method permits brokers and traders to record the value of their securities at the end of each trading day.

If the regulators had not ruled in Enron's favor, and disallowed the mark-to-market accounting for the company, Enron could never have grown the way it did. There's no question Skilling and Lay would have done something special with Enron, but they would never have been able to prop up the bloated colossus that it became without mark-to-market accounting.

Some SEC staffers objected to Skilling's request, but he managed to win approval anyway. As Tom Peters said, he could out-argue God. According to the *Washington Post*, the day he received word of the approval, Skilling let out a loud yell and cheers went up around the office.

The use of this accounting method was the cornerstone of the new Enron. And yet Skilling would later tell members of Congress, "I am not an accountant," in defending himself against Enron's accounting fraud.

The non-accountant was ecstatic because the method allowed the company to count revenue from long-term contracts, and to book most of the profit the same day a deal is made, even though the revenues and the profits could be many years in coming.

So, for example, if Enron built a power plant and sold its production for five years for $1 billion, that revenue and the estimated profit would be recorded right away. In some cases, even before the facilities were completed.

Mark-to-market accounting makes sense for the Wall Street brokers and traders who are dealing in securities, which have a well-known value. The stocks and bonds it holds are priced every day on the major exchanges. Likewise, any profit or loss is obvious—the difference between the cost of the stock and its current price.

Mark-to-market accounting was not at all common practice for old-industry firms, like energy companies. But Enron took the ball and ran with it. Who was to say exactly what the value was of the contracts in Enron's portfolio? How do you price them every day? There is no ticker tape crawling along the bottom of your television screen reporting price movements.

In short, Enron valued its portfolio pretty much the way it wanted to. And the accountants didn't seem to mind. The increased revenues and earnings bumped up the stock, which gave Enron more borrowing power to create long-term deals that it could instantly book. These deals, in turn, increased revenues and earnings, which bumped up the stock, which meant Enron could borrow more, and on and on. But like a shark that will drown unless water constantly flows over its gills, Enron would die if the stream of new deals dried up.

The appetite for new deals and new ventures was insatiable. Skilling needed bright, hungry entrepreneurs to keep the water flowing over the shark's gills and hired MBAs by the score. They would milk existing businesses, start new ones, revolutionize old businesses over the Internet—-whatever it took.

Enron evolved into a strange duck of a company. Its entire life rested on the ability to come up with more and more deals. The strategy succeeded at first because there was a fat, easy prey handy—the electric power business. Thanks not a little to Kenneth Lay, electric power was finally being deregulated. Much larger than the natural gas business, electric power sales would be in the tens of billions of dollars annually. The target was perfect for Enron, and it attacked with speed and precision. Its success with the Gas Bank gave them a leg up over the competition.

But there is a big difference between electricity and gas, which posed both problems and opportunities for Enron. You cannot stockpile electricity as you can with natural gas, and just turn a valve from a storage tank to get more. Electricity has to be created the instant it is needed. So if Enron was going to be able to offer the same kinds of contracts and other deals as it did with natural gas, it would have to have guaranteed sources of instant supply, as needed. So, besides contracting for "spinning reserves" from other power companies, Enron started buying and building power plants to add to their available pool and bolster reserves.

Again, the mark-to-market accounting method played a role. It allowed Enron to instantly book the revenue stream from a power plant over its entire lifetime, on the day the contract was signed. The costs of the power plant would be added to long-term debt.

Enron began building and buying power plants and other power facilities all over the globe, to keep the water flowing over the gills. In 1992, it bought *Transportadora de Gas del Sur*, a big South American pipeline company. A year later, responding to government deregulation in Britain, Enron began operation of the Teesside power plant, in the northeast of England. As soon as these plants were approved, Enron booked their decades-long revenue streams.

Keeping the shark alive meant taking on increased risks, however. It's doubtful any other company in its right mind would have built a $2.9 billion power plant in India, for example.

On paper it looked great. Skilling's risk analysis team of 180 sharp men and women went to their computers and ran all the numbers. The team gave its approval and the plant, which also received U.S. government assistance, was soon built.

But there is a lot more than numbers involved in building a massive project in a poor country. The construction alone had an explosive impact on Indian politics, where accusations of bribery caused a change in administrations. The new party in power was forced to be anti-Enron because it came to power itself by charging the opposition with being Enron-cozy.

The plant was delayed. There were ugly demonstrations and arrests, and there were protests about power costs. Enron had a major problem on its hands, and it fell to Rebecca Mark to solve it.

Mark was the CEO of Enron International, and no screenwriter would dare leave her out of this movie. Mark was a dangerous cocktail of brains, ambition, and great looks. In other words, she was like most people at Enron, except she was much better looking.

She was smart enough to use her appearance to her advantage at Enron and elsewhere around world, where she was constantly flitting to make deals. She made no apologies for her miniskirts and high heels. Business was business and you use whatever advantage you can. All dolled up in her power suit, the honey-blonde Mark was a dazzling presenter. She was known as Mark the Shark.

But her heels and minis didn't go over well in India, where women walk around wrapped up like mummies. To put shocked local officials at ease, Mark switched to local dress. It is hard to say which outfit was more effective, but Mark managed to sweet talk authorities into resuming the project—or pay a $2 billion fine. Construction resumed and Mark returned home a hero.

She later told a reporter from *Business Week*: "We were extremely concerned with time, because time is money for us. People thought we were pushy and aggressive. But think of the massive bureaucracy we had to move. How do you move a bureaucracy that has done things one way its entire collective life? You have to be pushy and aggressive."

Mark's arm-twisting—allegations of bribes were never proven—succeeded in getting the project underway again. But the plant was a disaster for Enron. Enron's accountants may have been booking revenues and profits from the Dabhol plant for decades, but those revenues were never to be.

The plant was finally mothballed in June 2001 after its sole customer, the Maharashtra State Electricity Board, claimed the plant's rates were too high and they refused to pay. So much for computer models.

Gas, electricity, what was next for Enron? Water was the logical choice. The analogies to gas and power were obvious, were they not? So Enron decided to make a huge plunge into the world's water business, in places where the price of water was not government regulated.

Enron created a new company to conquer the world of water and called it Azurix. It would revolutionize water supply throughout the world, and make tons of money in the process.

To run it, Enron chose Rebecca Mark, whom they knew would be fast out of the blocks to secure water contracts and buy facilities around the world. The new company went public in March of 1999, and raised $695 million. Mark went shopping.

Her biggest purchase was Wessex Water, a major water company in England, where water had recently been deregulated. Mark planned to use the Wessex plant as a model for how Azurix would capitalize on the world's water needs. The cost of the plant was $2.2 billion.

But Mark immediately ran into a problem here, too. When Wessex Water raised rates, customers howled to the politicians, who responded accordingly. They decided to re-regulate water and lowered the rates Azurix could charge. Any potential profits from the plant vanished.

Mark made other bad deals. She spent almost half a billion dollars on a thirty-year concession to supply water to areas of Buenos Aires before realizing the might of local labor unions. Then contaminated water got into the system and cost Enron $5.4 million to repair it.

Mark wasn't having much luck back in the U.S., either. The company had been trying to get the state of Florida to privatize its water supply. Azurix would become a major player, buying water as it became available at favorable prices, and then banking it in underground aquifers, to be pumped up when needed. It was a daring plan, and Florida wasn't ready for it, especially when voters heard about it. They feared higher water rates if the state got out of the water business.

Rebecca Mark had been quick out of the gate at Azurix, but also very quick to stumble. Only eighteen months after Azurix was launched at $19 a share, it was absorbed by Enron, which paid $8.375 a share for the stock. Azurix was out of business.

Enron quietly disposed of whatever Azurix assets that it could, and absorbed huge losses in the process. It sold Wessex Water, which originally cost $2.2 billion, for $777 million. Enron wound up with $900 million of Azurix debt, which helped speed its trip to bankruptcy court.

Rebecca Mark blamed the failure of Azurix on the fiasco at Wessex Water. But she was through at Enron. At 42, she'd had enough. Instead of spending any more of Enron's money, she went home to count her own. For her efforts at Dabhol and Wessex, Mark was amply rewarded. She walked away clicking her heels with Enron shares then worth about $82 million.

The losses on Azurix, and on other plants and investments and trading schemes at Enron had a strange way of not appearing on financial statements. Quarter after quarter, earnings improved and revenues magically grew, and so did the stock price.

In 1990, when Skilling joined Enron full time, shares traded at about $8. When he was named president six years later, the stock was about $20. By the end of the year 2000, when he was named CEO, the stock was at $90 and Enron was ranked by Fortune as the seventh largest company in the U.S.

A year later it was broke, and Jeffrey Skilling had been gone for months.

7

How Enron
Held Up the West

*Wisdom is like electricity. There is no permanently wise
man, but men capable of wisdom, who, being put
into certain company, or other favorable conditions,
become wise for a short time, as glasses rubbed
acquire electric power for a while.*
—Ralph Waldo Emerson

In 1998, California power officials had some grim news for electric customers in the state: By the year 2000, there would be a major energy shortage in the state, and blackouts were likely.

At the Enron offices in Houston, executives began licking their chops. Enron was the biggest power trader in the world, and could stand to make huge profits if California ran short of power and had to scramble to buy it on the open market. In effect, Enron controlled that market.

Eager young Enronians in the company power division played with their computers, devising strategies to maximize Enron profits if the predicted energy shortage came about.

❖ ❖ ❖

The threat of a power crisis in California was nothing new. For decades, the utility companies in the state had lagged badly in building new power generating plants to meet expanding demand. Some of this had to do with geography, some with environmentalists, some with fear of nuclear power. The state shared blame, too, for its terrible job at regulating the industry, and the utilities themselves for poor public and consumer relations.

Electric utilities were tradition-bound to build power plants in their own operating areas. Southern California Edison Co. built plants in southern California, and Pacific G&E built its plants in northern California, for example. But giant power plants can't be built just anywhere. They require large amounts of water to cool the huge steam generators, whether they use coal, oil, or uranium. In California, with few major rivers, that means the ideal location for steam-powered plants is smack on the Pacific Ocean, where water is abundant for cooling, and the sea provides easy access for fuel delivery.

Utility companies also prefer to build new plants near their major load centers—major cities like Los Angeles and San Francisco. This saves on transmission costs. And for years, that is just what they did.

But Californians didn't like to mess up their coastline with ugly power plants, especially nuclear plants. In the 1960s, environmentalists took to the courts to fight them, and the Sierra Club was often a more than worthy opponent. These court battles were usually long, arduous affairs, and even when utility companies prevailed, the years of court delays meant they could never get ahead of the state's growing demands for power.

The first major setback for a California utility was the proposed Bodega Bay nuclear plant upwind from San Francisco. Opponents insisted that it lay atop an earthquake fault and sued Pacific Gas & Electric Co.

The utility produced six eminent geologists who said the site was safe; six eminent geologists for the environmentalists said the site was unstable and dangerous. The decision went to the Sierra Club and the plant was shelved.

The shaky ground defense often proved effective in a state crisscrossed with earthquake faults. Besides Bodega Bay, the utilities lost siting battles over five other planned coastal plants: Point Arena, Davenport, Nipomo Dunes, Point Conception (Little Cojo Cove), and Malibu (Deer Creek Canyon). All were nixed because of citizen protest or proximity to earthquake faults. Pacific G&E finally did succeed in siting one nuclear plant, but only after a split in the Sierra Club ranks. Some hardcore members were opposed to all new development of power plants, especially nukes, on ideological, no-growth grounds. But the Sierra Club insisted it was not anti-growth, and proposed a compromise site for the plant, which PG&E accepted. The new plant was built at Diablo Canyon.

But the costs of the delays were enormous. The two units that PG&E hoped to have operating in 1972 and 1974 didn't begin to operate until 1985 and 1986. The estimated cost grew from $320 million to $5.8 billion—a seventeenfold increase. Ratepayers didn't realize it, but they would have to foot that bill.

California wasn't the only place where utilities had a hard time getting approval to build new plants. The nation had come a very long way from the days of Thomas Edison, barely a century before, where the sight of a power plant rising in their neighborhood was met with cheers from residents eager to get electric light in their homes. Electricity had gone from being a modern miracle to a necessary nuisance. No one wanted a power plant in his backyard anymore.

In New York, Consolidated Edison Company planned to build a pumped storage plant atop historic Storm King Mountain, a magnificent outcrop overlooking an historic region on the Hudson River, in Westchester County. The plant, which would pump water uphill during the day when demand for power was low, and then reverse the flow to drive turbines and generate power for the evening spike in demand, was elegant in its engineering. But it would have put a giant hole atop Storm King Mountain.

The Federal Power Commission approved the project in 1963, but a small group calling themselves the Hudson River Preservation Conference appealed the FPC ruling and went to court. The group contended that the FPC had not adequately considered all the factors that were of interest to the public, namely, the beauty and historical significance of Storm King Mountain.

This was the first time a power plant had been challenged largely on aesthetic grounds, but the courts ruled for the Preservation Conference, and environmentalists all over the country had a powerful new weapon to fight land-use battles. Beauty and history were now on the side of the enviros.

Each year, California slipped further and further behind in meeting the state's growing power needs. Frustrated in their attempts to build new plants, the utilities had to import power from out of state to make up for the shortfalls.

Most of this extra power came from the hydroelectric plants in the Northwest, where the dams would be filled with runoff just when California's power demands were the greatest. But the costs of importing the power were a lot higher than the home-made electricity and Californians' power bills soon ranked among the highest in the country.

In the year 2000, the state power authorities ran into the equivalent of the Perfect Storm. It caused rolling blackouts throughout the state, enormous increases in the price of wholesale power, the bankruptcy of the state's largest power companies, and a $10 billion tab for taxpayers. It also made Enron hundreds of millions in profts.

There were five key elements that came together to create the storm:

Weather. There was drought in the Northwest the previous summer and winter, meaning much less runoff behind the power dams. So there was less hydroelectric power available to sell to California.

Relentless power consumption. Electric power demand had been growing at the rate of 6 percent per year for the past five years, reflecting the state's economic growth, especially the large number of digital and Internet companies headquartered in cities such as San Jose and San Francisco.

No new power plants. No major power plants were built in

California in a decade. A few were finally under construction, but were years away from completion, and still would not make California self-sufficient in energy.

A botched deregulation scheme. In 1996, California became the first state in the country to deregulate the sale of electric power. The state Public Utility Commission would no longer set rates, and existing power companies would no longer have monopoly rights to service areas. Free market economics would reign. Presumably, competition would mean more companies would generate and sell electricity, resulting in cheaper, cleaner, more reliable electric power.

It was a major victory for Kenneth Lay and Jeff Skilling, who had lobbied so vigorously for deregulation of the power business. It was fitting that California, the largest state, should be the first to let the marketplace determine power costs.

Every state in the nation was watching how California would handle deregulation, as they would soon follow suit. There was quite a lesson to be learned—in how *not* to deregulate.

Regulated consumer prices. After deregulation, wholesale energy prices rose dramatically in California, especially during the year 2000. But politicians prevented utility companies from passing along those increases to their residential customers. No matter how much the power companies had to pay for power, they could only charge their customers the old, cheaper rates. Thus the deregulation process was never completed. The ultimate user was getting electricity at an artificially lower rate than the market dictated. Power consumption didn't go down, and the utility companies lost more and more money with each new kilowatt they sold. Buy high and sell low is not the way to run a business.

In the winter of 2000–2001, California almost ran completely out of power and was buying electricity at any price—and still demand didn't slacken and the threat of blackouts grew. Finally, the state engaged in rolling blackouts, deliberately cutting off power to whole neighborhoods at a time, to prevent the whole system from collapsing. Manufacturing plants closed down for lack of power. There was even speculation that the entire state would plunge into darkness when football fans turned on their TV sets to watch the NFC Championship Game.

The state was in a panic as power demand and power costs kept rising. The price of a megawatt-hour of electricity jumped from under $50 to $1,200 in some cases. PG&E and other utilities that were unable to pass along their meteoric price hikes screamed for relief. They were losing tens of millions of dollars a day.

Eventually, California was able to impose a $250-per-megawatt ceiling on power sold in the state, and after a while, the crisis eased. But not without a very heavy price. In the end, California's two largest electric utilities were bankrupt, and the state was left with tens of billions of dollars in power bills.

Throughout the crisis, the whiz-kids from Enron were manning the power switches, playing the disaster for all it was worth. They had cute names for the different strategies they used to maximize profits during the shortage. One was called Death Star, which took advantage of congestion on the state's transmission grid. Enron could relieve that jam by bargaining with other power traders to reschedule their power deliveries or by using less congested power lines. But the state had to pay Enron to do all this reshuffling. The "congestion payments" ran as high as $750 per megawatt-hour. Sometimes the lines were congested, and sometimes they were not. All Enron had to do was create the *appearance* of too much congestion on the grid, and the state would pay.

In some cases Enron bought and sold power at a loss, just to be able to take advantage of the congestion charges. By manipulating the congestion on the grid, and increasing the congestion payments, Enron and the other energy traders upped the cost of power for everyone in the entire region.

Another one of Enron's little games came into being when California capped power prices at $250 per megawatt hour. Meanwhile, the price for power in neighboring states was five times that price. So Enron bought power in California and sold it out of state at five times its cost. The tactic did nothing to help California's power shortage, but it did a lot for Enron's bottom line.

Ricochet was the name given another of Enron's trading tactics, also known as "megawatt washing." Sellers could sometimes charge California more than the cap price of $250 per megawatt hour, as long as the seller could justify the higher costs—if the power came from out of state, for example. Enron would buy power in California at $250 and ship it out of state to a friendly trader, who would then pass it back for resale in California at five times the original price.

The details of these and other tactics only came to light in May, 2002, after federal regulators released internal Enron documents describing them. The internal legal memos describe "dummied-up" power delivery schedules, giving "false information" to the state, and "knowingly increasing congestion costs." The memos, which were between Enron lawyers, were devastating evidence that Enron had manipulated the power market during the crisis. But they left unanswered a more important question: Was the manipulation illegal?

Still, the memos also helped vindicate Governor Gray Davis, who sounded like a madman in the middle of the crisis, blaming the rocketing price of power in California on market middlemen. "About thirty billion dollars was extorted from this state," he told a reporter from the *New York Times*. "Those who claimed that there was no price manipulation were just plain wrong."

Of course the memos were too little, too late to help California get any money back from Enron. It had long since gone bankrupt. California taxpayers will foot the bloated power bill for many years to come.

Skilling denied that Enron or the other trading companies or power producers did anything improper during the power crisis, and maintained that they were not responsible for any price gouging. In fact, he went into the belly of the beast to explain where the blame should be placed.

On June 21, 2001, he spoke before a public affairs organization at the Commonwealth Club of California in San Francisco. He put the blame for the crisis not on Governor Davis, whom many were fingering, nor on Enron or the power producers. Instead, he pointed to the members of the state Public Utilities Commission, who had refused to allow the utilities to enter into long-term power contracts, which would have prevented the price spikes. For his trouble, Skilling was nicked on the face with a berry pie, thrown by a protester.

Jeffrey Skilling was named CEO on December 13, 2000, effective February 12, 2001, just as Enron was working its black magic on the California power system.

His ascendancy to the top executive position was not surprising, given Skilling's close relationship to CEO and Chairman Ken Lay. Skilling had been president and chief operating officer, and had served on Enron's board, since December 1996.

Enron gushed about Skilling's achievements in an announcement: "Under Skilling's leadership, Enron pioneered the use of risk management products and forward contracting structures in the natural gas industry and has since applied similar concepts in electricity, bandwidth, metals, and a range of other commodity products."

The one commodity not mentioned was water. The subsidiary company Enron had created to control the world's water, Azurix, had just gone down in flames, within eighteen months of its creation. The financial liability was yet to be accounted for.

Instead, the press release described its financial health in typically gauzy prose. "The company, with revenues of $40 billion in 1999 and $60 billion for the first nine months of 2000, markets electricity and natural gas, delivers physical commodities and financial and risk management services to customers around the world, and is developing an intelligent network platform to facilitate online business."

That's quite a bag of tricks. But investors, analysts, and the press bought the whole act. In the year 2000, *Fortune* magazine named Enron "America's Most Innovative Company" for the sixth year in a row. *Fortune* also named Enron the top company for "Quality of Management" and the second best company for "Employee Talent."

Rival *Business Week* was also handing out laurels to Enron management. In 1996 and 1999, *Business Week* named Kenneth Lay one of the nation's twenty-five top corporate managers.

Among his other numerous honors, including the Horatio Alger Award, Lay had also been inducted into the Texas Hall of Fame ("Greed World" would claim him later. See Chapter One.) Lay had become a legend. He was the guru of the New Economy, who had grown Enron ninefold in less than a decade.

At a meeting of top energy executives in London in June 2000, Lay was asked how he could top that record.

"We'll do it again this coming decade," he answered cockily. At the time, Enron was on track to produce $80 billion in revenue that year. If the company were to increase ninefold again in the coming decade, it would be the largest corporation in the universe.

A reporter from the *Economist* was at that meeting, and later spoke to Lay about the arrogance at Enron. Lay compared Enron to Drexel Burnham Lambert, the investment bank headed by Michael Milken in the junk-bond era of the eighties.

Drexel and Milken were accused of arrogance, Lay said, but were just being "very innovative and very aggressive." Lay called Milken a friend.

Of course Milken went to prison for breaking the law, and his investment banking firm, Drexel Burnham Lambert, went belly up. *The Economist* did not quite predict that the same was in store for Ken Lay and Enron. But it did remind its readers that "hubris can lead to nemesis." (That's British for "Pride goeth before a fall.")

Anyone looking at the Enron annual report for the year 2000 would have found a lot more Enron hubris. In the letter to shareholders signed by Kenneth Lay and Jeffrey Skilling, they threw out growth projections that were totally off the charts. They were setting their sights on markets worth trillions, not mere billions. Enron planned to have its fingers in every tasty pie, all over the world:

As energy markets continue their transformation, and non-energy markets develop, we are poised to capture a good share of the enormous opportunities they represent. We believe wholesale gas and power in North America, Europe, and Japan will grow from a $660 billion market today to a $1.7 trillion market over the next several years. Retail energy services in the United States and Europe have the potential to grow from $180 billion today to $765 billion in the not-so-distant future. Broadband's prospective global growth is huge—it should increase from just $17 billion today to $1.4 trillion within five years.

Taken together, these markets present a $3.9 trillion opportunity for Enron, and we have just scratched the surface. Add to that the other big markets we are pursuing—forest products, metals, steel, coal and air-emissions credits—and the opportunity rises by $830 billion to reach nearly $4.7 trillion.

Lay and Skilling were predicting Enron would become the world's first trillion-dollar company. But "hubris can lead to nemesis."

In early 2001 Enron seemed to be delivering on its promises, and was enjoying its final moments in the sun. Investors, money managers, regulators, and the press were still unaware of the off-the-books partnership deals that Enron used to hide debt, hedge investments, and create phony profits.

The stock was trading in the range of $70 to $80 a share, up from less than $40 the year before. During the previous summer of 2000, the stock had hit an all-time high of $90. The price/earnings ratio was about was as high as 70, unheard of for an energy company. But then again, Enron was more than an energy company. And a lot less, too.

Yet the arrogant new CEO, Skilling, insisted that the stock was still undervalued and should be trading at about $126 a share. Skilling seldom took his eyes off Enron's stock price. After all, there was his barrelful of stock options to consider. And Enron stock was also the collateral for a lot of the company's partnership deals.

"Ken and I have worked together since 1990, and we don't want to break up a team that has delivered superior returns to Enron's shareholders," Skilling said in accepting his promotion to CEO. Within a year, those stockholders would see the stock drop to pennies a share, wiping away billions of dollars without a trace.

But Enron was still bragging and strutting its stuff. In April 1999, Kenneth Lay had spent $100 million for the naming rights to the new ballpark for the Houston Astros, calling it Enron Field. The way the deal was structured was pure Enron.

The company agreed to pay the Astros $100 million over a period of thirty years. But in return, the Astros signed a contract with Enron to supply its energy needs. The power contract was worth $100 million. Enron immediately marked that contract to market, booking all the revenue the first year. Cool.

Everything about Enron was cool. Skilling said Enron was the coolest company in America; Lay had said that Enron was "a New Economy company before it was cool." They even talked about wrapping a huge pair of sunglasses around the fifty-story Enron Tower. Cool.

Jeffrey Skilling was forty-seven, and CEO of the world's most innovative company, which he had done much to shape. But attention to Enron had taken its toll on his marriage, which ended in divorce after twenty-two years.

Skilling was upset at the failure of his marriage, and took responsibility for it. At a class reunion at Harvard, instead of listing his accomplishments, he wrote about the toll his career had taken on his wife and three children.

But he soon had a new love interest. As his mentor Ken Lay had done many years earlier, Skilling fell in love with his secretary, Rebecca Carter, and they planned to get married. In the spring of 2001, Skilling appeared to have the world by the shorts.

Then the company's stock price started to slide. When Skilling was officially installed as CEO on February 12, Enron was trading at around $80 a share. By mid-April, it was trading around $60, and had dipped as low as $53.

The stock drop was partially due to the general slide in the market after the internet bubble burst. But some of it was due, too, to increasing apprehension about Enron's ability to meet its numbers. The economy was slowing, and yet Enron made no changes in its earnings forecasts. Where were those earnings going to come from?

To be sure, the energy business appeared stronger than ever. There was surprisingly little anti-Enron sentiment because of its market manipulation during the California power crisis. Enron had dodged a public relations nightmare thanks largely to the Bush administration, which blamed the power crisis on the state's inability to get enough power plants built, and the state's faulty deregulation plan. The administration said nothing about market manipulation.

In the first three months of 2001, Enron continued to do a lot of energy business, announcing long-term energy contracts with Owens-Illinois, Quaker Oats, Eli Lilly, JCPenney and Saks Incorporated, all marked to market, adding handsomely to Enron's revenue.

On April 17, 2001, Jeffrey Skilling held his first conference call with security analysts since assuming the title of CEO. He would announce the company's eagerly awaited quarterly earnings, and announce whether or not Enron was on course to meet its predicted annual results.

Wall Street had become mesmerized with quarterly earnings, although very few companies' revenues come in neat, quarter-slices. But if a company has a bad quarter, its stock gets pummeled, even if the next quarter more than makes up for it. Analysts say they don't like surprises.

So companies became adept at meeting their earnings projections, even if it involved some juggling of the books. The aim was to grow consistently, with no negative surprises.

No one was better at this than Jack Welch, who managed to expand GE's earnings for twenty consecutive years while he was CEO from 1981 to 2000. It is a record that is likely to last a lot longer than Joe DiMaggio's fifty-six-game hitting streak. Each year, GE grew 10 percent to 17 percent, for two solid decades. And Welch called almost every shot beforehand. In the last decade of his tenure, the company missed estimates only twice in forty quarters. To do that, it helps to have some flexibility with your accounting.

In his book, *Jack: Straight from the Gut,* Welch describes the agony GE executives went through each quarter when GE still owned Utah International, the vast mining company.

"As a sector chairman and then vice chairman, I had sat in meetings with my peers, listening as we all told how valiantly we worked to make the quarter's or the year's numbers," he writes. "Then the executive in charge of Utah would stand up and unknowingly overwhelm those contributions one way or another.

"'We had a strike at the coal mine,' he'd say, 'so we are going to miss our profit projection by fifty million dollars.' Or he would just as easily come to the meeting and say, 'The price of coal went up ten bucks, so I have an extra fifty million to toss into the pot.'"

Welch decided to sell Utah International, which had been the biggest and most prized acquisition of Welch's predecessor, Reginald Jones.

"I felt the cyclical nature of Utah's business had made our goal of consistent earnings impossible," Welch wrote.

Jeff Skilling had no such troubles ironing out earnings spikes and dips at Enron. For as it turned out, earnings could be almost anything the company wanted them to be.

It was a cocky Skilling who read the numbers out during the conference call on Tuesday, April 17. The call was also webcast over Enron's website.

- An increase of 18 percent in earnings for the first quarter of 2001 from a year ago;
- an increase of 281 percent in revenues to $50.1 billion;
- an increase of 20 percent in net income to $406 million;
- an increased 65 percent in energy volumes;
- an increase of 59 percent in new retail energy services contracts to $5.9 billion; and
- an increase of seven-fold in broadband network services delivered.

The numbers were extremely impressive, but Skilling had even more to cheer the analysts. He increased the expectation of earnings for the year, from $1.75 to $1.80 per share. In the spring of 2001, there were few companies revising earnings upward as the sagging market and softening economy took their toll. Enron seemed not only unsinkable, but incapable of taking in any water at all. The stock rallied.

After announcing the numbers and offering more details about the quarter's revenues, Skilling fielded questions from the analysts and money managers on the conference call. Skilling always hated answering questions, especially those he perceived as dumb, whether from analysts, money managers, or the press. It was not prudent to anger any of these groups, but Skilling couldn't help himself. He liked being a smartass. He thought it was cool.

One money manager, Richard Grubman of Highfields Capital Management in Boston, asked a dumb question. He wanted to know why he couldn't see Enron's balance sheet. Skilling testily explained that Enron was not required to provide a balance sheet until it actually filed its statement with the SEC a few weeks later. This was common practice at Enron. Enron actually filed its quarterly statement on May 15, 2002.

Grubman still groused about not seeing more numbers. "You're the only financial institution that cannot come up with a balance sheet or a cash-flow statement after earnings."

Skilling had lost his patience with the man. "Well, thank you very much," he said sarcastically. "We appreciate that, asshole."

There was a long pause. It isn't every day that a CEO insults a money manager on a conference call that is being webcast all over the globe. There was no doubt about what he'd called Grubman. And Skilling was hardly ashamed of his rudeness.

He later said that he liked to let people know "when he is exasperated," and that Grubman was a short seller in the market. Short sellers make money when a company's stock drops—they sell shares borrowed from a broker and replace them later at what they hope will be a lower price. At the time Skilling called Grubman an asshole, Enron was trading at $60 a share. By the end of the year 2001, Enron's stock was trading for less than $1 a share, meaning short sellers who stayed the course made a huge score. A seller who was short 100,000 Enron shares at $60 in April, and replaced them in December with shares bought at $1 a share, netted himself $5.9 million. Some asshole.

8

Running Out of Tricks

*I know it would be devastating to all of us, but I wish we
would get caught. We're such a crooked company.*
—Enron executive, 2001

On May 14, 2001, Enron's co-chairman and the third highest
ranking executive, L. Clifford Baxter, suddenly resigned. His resignation made no sense. Baxter was just forty-two years old, happily
married with two kids, popular at the company and seemingly des-
tined for even loftier status.

He was a Yankee transplant to Houston and found Texas to his
liking, as so many ex-northerners do. He was born in Amityville, a
quiet suburb of New York City made infamous by a horror movie.
Baxter would eventually star in a horror show of his own.

After graduating from New York University, he served in the Air
Force from 1980 to 1985, achieving the rank of captain. He returned
to New York and got his MBA from Columbia in 1987.

After a brief stint in investment banking, he joined Enron in 1991 and found a home. He became part of the team responsible for transforming Enron from a gas company to a stealth company. It was Baxter who engineered Enron's trading operations. He held the title of chairman and CEO of Enron North America and was later named chief strategy officer and then vice chairman of Enron itself. But he stayed out of the limelight that followed Lay and Skilling.

There was not a lot that went on at Enron that Baxter didn't know about. And one of the things he knew about bothered him a lot. Andrew Fastow, Enron's chief financial officer, had cooked up "special purpose entities" that Fastow was profiting from, at the expense of Enron. Furthermore, the deals were borderline insane.

Baxter complained to Skilling about LJM, another of the off-the-books partnership deals designed to hedge risk, hide Enron debt, disguise losses, or pump up revenues. There was nothing new about the SPEs, as they were known. Although they were very complicated in their construction, the SPEs boiled down to this: robbing Peter to pay Paul.

Andersen's round-heeled accountants initially raised objections to the deals, but eventually signed off on them. Enron was paying Andersen about $1 million a week for its auditing, accounting, and other services. Given Enron's growth rate, Andersen figured that would rise to $2 million a week in a year or so. The client got what he wanted.

In a typical deal, Enron would "sell" an asset, record the sale on its books, and then buy it back later at a profit to lenders. But the obligation to buy back the asset never appeared on the balance sheet. Poof—the debt seems to vanish.

Because of the complex nature of the deals, some private individuals had to be involved. Those private individuals in the partnership stood to profit handsomely on the deals once Enron bought the asset back.

The major lenders in the deals consisted of big banks like Citigroup, J.P. Morgan Chase, and Merrill Lynch, as well as pension funds like CalPERS, the California Public Employees Retirement

System. It is ironic that California pensioners, who suffered power blackouts and enormous price jumps in the cost of gas and wholesale power because of market manipulation by Enron and others in 2000, also profited from off-the-books gas deals with the same company. Money has no conscience and no memory.

Baxter didn't like the smell of the new SPEs, which Fastow cheekily code-named LJM—the first initials of Fastow's wife, Lea, and two children. Fastow and some hand-picked associates made millions on these deals. CFOs are not supposed to make killings at their companies' expense, even if the deals passed muster with the accountants from Arthur Andersen as well as Enron's lawyers, Vinson & Elkins.

The Enron board also okayed the deals and appointed Fastow general partner, despite the possible conflict of interest. It's still not clear if the board really understood the license it was handing Fastow.

Baxter took his concerns to CEO Skilling, more than once. According to Sherron Watkins, an Enron executive who later turned whistleblower, "Cliff Baxter complained mightily to Skilling and all who would listen about the inappropriateness of our transactions with LJM."

But nothing happened. The deals that he complained about continued. Baxter resigned in mid-May, using the lame excuse that it was for family reasons. Skilling issued a statement on Baxter's resignation: "While we will miss him, we are happy that his primary reason for resigning is to spend additional time with his family, and we wish him the very best."

Baxter didn't leave empty-handed. He had been cashing in his Enron stock options since October 1998, and records show he cashed in more than 500,000 shares of Enron stock for $35.2 million. His last reported stock sale was January 31, 2001, when Enron stock was still selling at $80 a share, near its all-time high.

But Baxter was not through with Enron. In November of 2001,

with the company on the verge of collapse, Baxter was named along with Ken Lay and eight other senior company officials as defendants in a lawsuit filed by shareholders in U.S. District Court in Houston. The suit accused the executives of concealing Enron's true financial state while cashing their options while the stock was near its peak.

A few weeks later, on January 11, 2002, Baxter appeared on the radar screens of two congressional committees. The Senate's Permanent Subcommittee on Investigations, led by Michigan Democrat Carl Levin (D-Mich.) had asked for documents from Baxter, and House Energy and Commerce Committee investigators were also planning to meet with him. They didn't finger him for any wrongdoing. One source said he was "a bit player, not a big fish in the frying pan," but they wanted to talk to him because his name was mentioned in an eight-page letter written by Sherron Watkins the previous summer to Kenneth Lay. It was clear that he knew about, and had complained of, the shady partnership deals.

Baxter sank into a deep depression and had trouble sleeping. Would he be required to provide evidence that could put Skilling, Lay, and Fastow, and others behind bars? Would he have to surrender some or all of his own $35.2 million haul? Would he ever be able to hold up his head again?

On January 23, Baxter went to see Dr. Kirk Lee, who gave him two prescriptions, one for Celexa, an anti-depressant, and the other for Ambien, a powerful sleeping pill. His wife, Carol, told police that on the evening of January 24, Baxter went to bed at 9:15 p.m. in their home in Sugar Land, an affluent Houston suburb.

When Carol went to bed two hours later she found him snoring and said she was glad to see him getting a good night's sleep. But Baxter woke up at about 2:00 a.m., never to sleep again.

He slipped out of bed, and arranged the pillows to make it appear to his wife that he was still asleep. He then wrote a brief suicide note, printed in block letters, sealed it in an envelope, and left it on his wife's car.

Leaving the house wearing only a T-shirt and sweatpants, with no shoes, he got into his Mercedes and drove a few blocks away down Palm Royale Boulevard. He parked the car, took out his Smith and Wesson .357 Magnum five-shot revolver, held it to the right side of his head, and pulled the trigger.

His troubles with Enron were over.

Though the police originally called his death a suicide, there was—and still is—speculation that foul play might have had something to do with Baxter's death. Could someone have killed him because he knew too much and was about to talk to government investigators?

Baxter's suicide note, which was finally released by his wife after a legal battle, seemed to put that theory to rest for all but hardcore conspiracy addicts.

Carol, I am so sorry for this. I feel I just can't go on. I have always tried to do the right thing but where there was once great pride now its [sic] gone. I love you and the children so much. I just can't be any good to you or myself. The pain is overwhelming. Please try to forgive me. Cliff.

It was short, sad, and convincing. The Houston police were satisfied and officially labeled Baxter's death a suicide.

On August 14, 2001, Jeff Skilling, at the age of forty-eight, decided that he, too, wanted out at Enron. Ken Lay tried to talk him out of resigning. Lay had managed to change Skilling's mind earlier in his Enron career, when Skilling temporarily left the company complaining of fatigue, only to show up a few days later nearly mad with boredom. But Lay had no luck this time. Skilling shocked Enron employees and the investment community when he said he was resigning "for personal reasons."

Skilling had been CEO for just six months, but it had been largely downhill for Enron's stock. When Skilling took over as CEO on February 12, 2001, Enron's stock closed at $79.80 per share. When he resigned on August 14, it was $42.93, a drop of 46 percent, and far worse was yet to come.

Investors were finding Enron just too opaque to figure out. It was hard enough to grasp exactly how it was making money in the energy business. It was a genuine mind-breaker to decipher its other businesses, which were being added all the time. Analysts had to trust Enron's numbers, and couldn't apply the computer models they usually used to make forecasts. They relied on Enron, which they hated doing.

Most analysts still recommended the company as a buy, but those analysts worked for the big banks with lucrative investment banking ties to the company. The big banks helped arrange the SPEs. They didn't want to see the stock price slide. The stock was Enron's underpinning for the deals.

The financial press was getting weary of being baffled by Lay and Skilling, however, and was beginning to smell blood. One *Fortune* writer, Bethany McLean, dared to pull away the fig leaf first, in a piece titled "Is Enron Overpriced?" dated March 2001, when Skilling was just getting used to the view from his top-floor CEO office.

"It's in a bunch of complex businesses. Its financial statements are nearly impenetrable. So why is Enron trading at such a huge multiple?" the article dared to ask. At the time, Enron was trading at 55 times trailing earnings, while a competitor like Duke Energy traded at only 22 times earnings.

"Start with a pretty straightforward question: How exactly does Enron make its money?" McLean asked.

It was a question no one seemed able to answer, not even veteran credit analysts, who have no axes to grind. "If you figure it out, let me know," said Todd Shipman at Standard & Poor's.

The Enron myth was finally being questioned.

Meanwhile, Skilling and other top Enron executives, including Kenneth Lay, were exercising stock options and selling stock at a steady clip, even as the price of the stock dropped. Since 1998, Lay had unloaded $201.6 million worth of Enron stock, pocketing a total of about $119 million. Skilling sold a total of $190.4 million worth over the same period and netted a profit of $112 million. In all, Enron Corp.'s executives and directors sold about $1.3 billion worth of stock in 1999, 2000, and 2001. Eighteen Enron officers and directors executed at least sixty-four sales of the company's stock in 2001, according to filings with the Securities and Exchange Commission.

And many of them took the money and ran. Lou Pai, chairman of Enron Energy Services, left Enron after selling more than $270 million in shares. Thomas White left to become secretary of the Army after selling Enron stock for $12 million. Kenneth Rice, chairman of Enron Broadband, left in August 2001, after cashing in 1.1 million shares for $72.7 million.

Investors and analysts couldn't ignore the widespread insider selling. It's a very bad sign when so many insiders sell stock that is on its way down. Enron's multiple began to fall to earth. On the day Skilling resigned, Enron stock was less than half what it fetched a year earlier.

Skilling—who bragged that he had never failed at anything he had ever run—was heading out of Dodge City as fast as he could, with his saddlebags loaded. But like the outlaw who holds up the bank at gunpoint and tells the frightened teller to put only big bills in the satchel, Skilling left some money on the table when he left—or so it appeared. By quitting, he abandoned a $20 million severance package and also had to repay a $2 million loan that would have been forgiven at the end of 2001.

Skilling will have a very hard time ever convincing anyone that the reasons for his hasty departure were "personal"—unless you count self-preservation and wealth-preservation as personal.

Enron had consumed Skilling's life, and he could never free himself from it. Even his new fiancée was an Enron insider. After his bitter divorce, Skilling had begun dating Rebecca Carter in 1998—after having sought permission to do so from the Enron board of directors.

Carter, known to Enronians as "Va Voom," was very easy on the eyes and her career at Enron took off after she began seeing Skilling. She became a senior vice president and company secretary, earning $600,000 a year. Her name even appeared on Enron stock certificates.

Carter chose not to follow Skilling into his peculiar early retirement in August 2001. She certainly didn't need her Enron paycheck, as hefty as it was, to pay grocery bills. Skilling was now very rich, and the couple was soon to marry. Skilling had just finished building a new, Mediterranean-style mansion in tony River Oaks. But Carter chose to stay on at Enron, and remained through its final gasps.

To the thousands of fired Enron employees who also stayed to the end, and who soon found themselves struggling to make mortgage payments, Rebecca Carter will always remain someone special. And not because of her looks, or her infamous husband.

After Enron collapsed in the summer of 2002, a pool of $28.8 million was set aside to partially satisfy the severance pay claims of the 4,200 Enronians who had been fired. Under terms of the deal, every ex-worker would get a maximum of $13,500. It was a lot less than they were entitled to under Enron's compensation policies, but at least it was something. Since Enron was in bankruptcy, its creditors didn't have to make a dime available to anyone. The payments, minus taxes, would be paid almost immediately.

But of the 4,200 affected employees, a small group of executives refused to sign off on the deal, postponing or even threatening any distribution. Most prominent among those former executives was Rebecca Carter. The new bride refused to accept the proposed package and demanded that she be paid exactly what she says she was owed, $875,000. She refused to go along with the settlement, endangering the payout to all 4,200 of her former co-workers.

"If you're married to the person who helped ruin the company, it takes some gall to turn around and want more money out of it," Nick Tubach, a former employee, told the *Houston Chronicle*. "It's almost like killing somebody's family and going back to plunder the house."

In announcing Skilling's departure, Ken Lay tried to reassure Enron employees in an e-mail that all was still well, and that Skilling's resignation "was for personal reasons and is voluntary. I regret his decision, but I accept and understand it."

Few others did. In fact, the SEC later admitted that it was Skilling's sudden resignation in mid-August that finally stirred investigators to poke into Enron's books.

Lay, the avuncular chairman whom most Enron employees idolized, said that he was resuming the title of CEO, and sounded positively bubbly about Enron's future.

"I want to assure you that I have never felt better about the company. All of you know that our stock price has suffered substantially over the last few months. One of my top priorities will be to restore a significant amount of the stock value we have lost as soon as possible."

Lay's next sentence would return to haunt him: "Our performance has never been stronger; our business model has never been more robust; our growth has never been more certain; and most importantly, we have never had a better nor deeper pool of talent throughout the company. We have the finest organization in American business today. Together, we will make Enron the world's leading company."

Nonetheless, Lay systematically continued selling his stock, through a loan-repayment scheme that kept the sales from public view for months. He took loans from the company, exercised his options, and then repaid the loans with the stock. Yet he urged his own employees to hold on to their shares and buy more. Later, the company would even change administrators of its 401(k) plan at a critical time in Enron's collapse, preventing employees from selling, even if they wanted to. It is estimated that Enron workers lost about $1 billion in their 401(k)s when the company collapsed. Most employees had loaded their plans heavily with Enron shares because the company had a matching policy with the stock.

Just a few days after Ken Lay's soothing e-mail to employees, he received a very disquieting letter from Sherron Watkins, an eight-year veteran of the company and vice president of corporate development. The forty-two-year-old executive, who had worked as an accountant at Arthur Andersen before joining Enron in 1992, wanted to talk to Lay about some accounting problems. Watkins was not in Enron's inner circle of decision-makers, but had a lofty enough position in the company to warrant serious listening. She had been working for CFO Andrew Fastow that summer, looking for Enron assets to sell, and started poking around in Fastow's off-the-books deals to see if there was anything worthwhile selling. What she found stunned her: huge losses that had not been reflected in company financial filings. Her husband, Rick, told *Time* that "she always had a flair for numbers." Lay scheduled a meeting with Watkins for August 22 and asked her to bring in whatever information she had.

Watkins, who was born and lived in and around Houston and graduated from the University of Texas, alerted Arthur Andersen's head man on the Enron account, David Duncan, and two other Andersen partners, of her concerns. She outlined what they were in a seven-page memo addressed to "Mr. Lay." She didn't pull any punches.

"Has Enron become a risky place to work?" she began. "For those of us who didn't get rich over the last few years, can we afford to stay?"

Watkins raised fears that Skilling's abrupt departure "would raise suspicions of accounting improprieties and valuation issues."

Citing the LJM partnership deals and other questionable practices that inflated revenues by hundreds of millions of dollars, she wrote, "I am incredibly nervous that we will implode in a wave of accounting scandals."

She didn't buy Skilling's excuse for bailing out, either. "I would think he wasn't having fun, looked down the road and knew this stuff was unfixable and would rather abandon ship now than resign in shame in two years."

Watkins didn't just point her finger at problems, she went to suggest how Enron might extricate itself from the mess it was in, by fessing up to the hidden losses, ending the shady deals, and restating earnings.

Things were getting beyond control. She quoted one manager from the principal investment group as saying, "I know it would be devastating to all of us, but I wish we would get caught. We're such a crooked company."

Watkins suggested to Lay that Enron should conduct an inquiry using new lawyers and new accountants because Arthur Andersen and Vinson & Elkins had already passed on the deals and therefore had conflicts of interest. Lay said he would use different accountants and lawyers, according to Watkins, and she left his office feeling that he would. Watkins assumed Lay had been unaware of all these problems and had been duped by those around him. Could Kenneth Lay, the founding genius of Enron, have strayed so far out of the loop?

Ken Lay did launch a probe, but used the same accountants and lawyers. When Watkins learned of this, she said she was "sort of surprised." But it seemed to her that "Mr. Lay was not making these decisions." At least, that is what she preferred to believe.

Watkins could simply have been covering her own rear end with the detailed memo, which she could wave later at investigators as proof of her own innocence in any shady deals. But she didn't resign in high dudgeon after her meeting with Lay, nor go charging off to authorities with what she knew. Still, when the memo resurfaced after Enron's collapse, she was hailed as a selfless whistleblower.

There's no question that what Watkins did took guts. It is never politic to go to the top man and tell him his company is crooked. Enron executives were particularly prickly about anyone telling them their business. Before Watkins wrote her memo, Jeff McMahon, who had been Enron's treasurer, had gone to Jeff Skilling with similar complaints about Fastow's deals. McMahon was so miffed that he gave Skilling an ultimatum: Fix things, or McMahon could no longer remain treasurer of the company. McMahon laid out five steps that had to be taken.

Three days later, McMahon was no longer treasurer. Skilling made him CEO of Enron's Industrial Markets Group. It was not considered a promotion. Skilling never addressed the five steps with McMahon and did nothing about the deals he warned of. Similarly,

Cliff Baxter had complained to Skilling about LJM deals and got no reaction. He then resigned "for family reasons."

So Watkins took a chance going over everyone's head to see Lay. And the memo she wrote eventually was extremely useful to investigators. It had survived the document-shredding that went on at Andersen and Enron just prior to the bankruptcy filing.

Because she didn't actually rat out her co-workers, she may have been only a whistle-tweeter, and an indoor one at that. But at least she had the guts to tell Emporer Lay that he wasn't wearing any clothes. Or did he already know that?

9

"I Got Off the *Titanic* in Ireland . . ."

My personal belief is that Enron stock is an incredible bargain at current prices, and we will look back in a couple of years from now and see the great opportunity that we currently have.
—Kenneth Lay, Sept. 26, 2001

Lay had been spending a lot of time and energy on matters far from Houston. He was working closely with the Bush administration in shaping a national energy policy. Lay had long been a supporter and friend of Bush, who called him "Kenny Boy." There were other Enron friends in high places, including Thomas E. White, who was vice chairman of Enron Energy Services before joining the Bush administration as Secretary of the Army. Senator Phil Gramm's wife was on the Enron board of directors and served on the audit committee.

Enron supported the politicians who were friendly, mostly Republicans, though Lay also counted Bill Clinton as an ally when he was in the White House. Clinton had supported Enron in plans to build huge power plants in poor countries around the world.

Enron sewed millions into political contributions, and reaped many times that in benefits. In tax rulings alone, Enron managed to avoid paying income taxes for four of the previous five years. It had almost 1,000 subsidiary companies located in tax havens all over the globe. And it had other tax tricks. The company managed to qualify for $382 million in tax refunds. The tax department of Enron was expected to be a profit center, and it was.

But as the summer wore on, Lay's attentions were directed toward more pressing matters back in Houston. On August 21, a missile was fired at Enron by an influential Houston broker, which could have crippled Enron for good then and there.

His name was Chung Wu, and he worked for UBS Paine Webber. He e-mailed clients in the middle of the night to tell them that they should sell at least some of their Enron shares. "Financial situation is deteriorating in Enron and price drops another $7 . . . I would advise you to take some money off the table even at this point."

Some of his clients were Enron executives, and they were not amused. UBS Paine Webber still had a "strong buy" recommendation on Enron. It had good reasons to have such a positive recommendation. UBS Paine Webber handled the accounts of many big shareowners of Enron—including Ken Lay and other Enron executives. It also administered the 401(k) plans for many Enron employees and had underwritten two IPOs for Enron, the water company Azurix and New Power Co.

The reaction in Houston was exactly what one would expect from the nation's leading power company, soon to be the greatest company in the world: Shoot the messenger. Enron called for Wu's head. Enron's stock price was jittery enough as it was, and was nearing a critical point for the company. Enron stock was the collateral for the off-the-books deals. If it sank low enough, Enron's creditors would demand repayment. All hell would break loose. The stock price had to be protected at all costs. Meanwhile, Ken Lay himself was cashing out.

Chung Wu was fired within hours of reporting to his desk the morning after he sent the e-mail. He was escorted from the building and his branch manager promptly sent out another e-mail to his clients: "Mr. Wu's statements are contrary to UBS Paine Webber's current recommendation concerning Enron stock." Attached was the research report written by the company analyst who still rated Enron a "strong buy."

UBS Paine Webber said that it fired Wu because he broke company rules about sending out research to clients. Wu should have gotten the approval of his supervisor first, it said, since the message went out to more than ten people. He broke another rule by showing partiality to some customers. Brokers are supposed to communicate the same investment advice to all of its clients, not just a select few.

Wu filed a complaint with the National Association of Securities Dealers, claiming that Enron pressured UBS Paine Webber to can him. His complaint resurfaced later in the sea of lawsuits against Enron's financial backers. But for the moment, at least, Enron had disarmed Wu's missile.

Lay did follow through on Sherron Watkins's concerns, at least enough to have the lawyers question Kenneth Fastow and the Andersen accountants regarding deals she was most concerned about, nicknamed Raptors. Fastow insisted that they were great deals, and resented having to answer questions about them.

Fastow didn't like to talk to many people about Enron matters. Although he was chief financial officer, he communicated little with stock analysts and money managers. Analysts thought him arrogant and aloof; so did some of the people at Enron. But he went back a long way with Enron, and had done much behind the scenes to help Enron's balance sheet with imaginative financial instruments and deals.

Fastow was a numbers man, rescued from the loan desk at Continental Illinois, a Chicago savings and loan that had failed in the mid-1980s. Skilling hired him to engineer deals that would allow Enron to sell off some of Enron's risk, using the latest in accounting and investment devices. He was the man, along with a staff of 100 or so, who arranged all of Enron's SPEs, going back to the early nineties. They had worked brilliantly before, and he gave the impression they were working brilliantly now, in 2001. But the SPEs of the early days were straightforward, and had no trouble clearing accounting or legal muster. Many other companies used similar SPEs, and even the most conservative of lenders invested in them.

CalPERS, the California state pension fund, put $250 million into an Enron natural gas deal, for example. In four years, it received a 73 percent return on its money. Fastow insisted there was nothing wrong with the Raptor SPEs, either. He failed to mention that he was making millions from them, and so were some of his key associates.

Andrew Fastow didn't need money. He had been cashing in his options, had a fat salary, and was married to a wealthy Houston socialite, Lea Weingarten. He was from New Jersey originally, and went to Tufts, where he majored in economics and, of all things, Chinese. He received his MBA from Northwestern.

When Skilling called him about the Enron job, Fastow was thrilled at moving to his wife's hometown of Houston, and even more excited at the prospect of working at Enron. He worked closely with Skilling, knew how far-reaching his plans were, and admired him. He was not popular with subordinates, whom he would put down in public to impress his mentor and protector, Jeff Skilling.

Fastow's Raptor deals were also the topic of discussion when Lay's lawyers spoke to the Arthur Andersen partner who headed the Enron audit group, David B. Duncan. The forty-three-year-old partner in Andersen tried to reassure the lawyers. Although he admitted that the deals might look "facially questionable," they were technically fine.

That was the end of the Enron internal investigation. Although Sherron Watkins had also given the names of five key executives whom the lawyers should talk to about the deals, they never followed through. It was probably too late to fix matters, anyway, no matter what the lawyers discovered. In the wake of the Sept. 11 attack, the stock continued to slide, and the fate of the Raptor deals, which could cost Enron hundreds of millions, became more precarious.

On September 18, Enron bit the bullet. After being informed by some of his lieutenants of the gravity of the Raptor deals, Lay had no choice but to shut them down and take a massive loss—$710 million. He would have to report that loss publicly. This time, there was nowhere to hide it.

Lay's aides had some other unsettling news, too. In going over the Raptor deals, Andersen had come across a whopper of an unrelated error. Enron had overstated its net worth by $1.2 billion. The accountants didn't think that was any big deal, since the result was zero. Enron would be erasing equity that had never been there in the first place. But would the investment community read it that way?

On September 26, Lay had an internet chat with his employees, who were worried about their retirement plans. Most of them had most of their money in Enron stock, and it had dropped from $90 to $25 in a year.

Though he had cashed in some $20 million of Enron stock himself over the previous two months, Lay urged his employees to hold on.

On October 16, Lay broke the bad news about the losses in a press release that was a marvel of obfuscation. It began cheerily enough, with the announcement that earnings were up again for the quarter, by a lusty 26 percent over the previous year.

The release quoted Lay: "Our 26 percent increase in recurring earnings per diluted share shows the very strong results of our core wholesale and retail energy businesses and our natural gas pipelines. The continued excellent prospects in these businesses and Enron's leading market position make us very confident in our strong earnings outlook."

Then came the bombshell. "Non-recurring charges totaling $1.01 billion after-tax, or $1.11 loss per diluted share, were recognized for the third quarter of 2001. The total net loss for the quarter, including non-recurring items, was $618 million, or $0.84 per diluted share. After a thorough review of our businesses, we have decided to take these charges to clear away issues that have clouded the performance and earnings potential of our core energy businesses."

You could almost hear the eyeballs click in analysts' heads when they read that last paragraph. A $1.01 billion loss? Where on earth did it come from?

Much further down in the release the losses were itemized, but hardly explained: "$287 million related to asset impairments recorded by Azurix Corp.; $180 million associated with the restructuring of Broadband Services; and $544 million related to losses associated with certain investments, principally Enron's interest in The New Power Company, broadband and technology investments, and early termination during the third quarter of certain structured finance arrangements with a previously disclosed entity."

What did it all mean? What were these "structured financial arrangements with a previously disclosed entity?" The *Wall Street Journal* had been nosing around Enron for a while, and the announcement of the huge loss on October 16 began a string of articles probing Enron's mysterious deals. The paper broke the news that Enron's CEO Andrew Fastow had personally profited on partnership deals, an apparent conflict of interest.

For days, the *Journal* ran front-page stories on Enron, raising more and more questions about the company. One story focused on the $1.2 billion reduction in shareholder equity, due to an "error." The stock began dropping like a cliff diver in Acapulco. In two days it dropped from 35 to 29.

On October 22, the SEC announced that it had launched a preliminary inquiry into Fastow and his partnerships. Enron stock dropped 20 percent in a day, to $20 a share. On October 23, Lay held a conference call with analysts, which was webcast. He wanted to calm their fears, and show his support for Fastow.

But the analysts weren't in a trusting mood, and weren't satisfied with the answers they were getting from Lay. "There is an appearance that you are hiding something," said one veteran analyst who had long been an Enron fan.

"We're not trying to conceal anything," Lay answered. "We're not hiding anything."

This was going to be a long day for Lay. After the conference call, he rushed off to one of his periodic meetings with company employees. Usually, these meetings were pep talks. This time it would be different.

Enronians gathered by the thousands in a Hyatt ballroom near Enron headquarters. Other Enron employees followed the meeting on their computer screens. The mood was dark, and Lay went straight to what was most on their minds: their stock losses.

"Many of you who were a lot wealthier six to nine months ago, are now concerned about the college education for your kids, maybe your retirement, and for that I am incredibly sorry."

Then Lay made the last promise to his workers he would ever break. "We are going to get it back," he said.

To show how sincere he was being, Lay invited written questions from the floor. One question gave him pause. Enronians listened in shock as Lay read it aloud:

"I would like to know if you are on crack. If so, that would explain a lot. If not, you may want to start because it's going to be a long time before we trust you again."

Why Lay decided to read aloud that question to the entire Enron staff remains a mystery. He could easily have skipped it as soon as he scanned it. But he allowed himself to be insulted, something emperors aren't supposed to do. Employees felt worse than ever, and began fearing for their jobs.

Lay, meantime, was using his Enron stock to repay cash loans from the company, to keep the sales hidden.

One thing that could not remain hidden any longer, however, was the extent of Andrew Fastow's double-dealing. Chares A. LeMaistre, who was on the board of Enron and also head of the compensation committee, had been trying for months to get a handle on just how much money Fastow and his partners had made on the special partnerships Fastow had arranged. On October 22, LeMaistre finally got his answer from Fastow himself: The sum was $45 million.

LeMaistre was stunned.

Fastow was now history. Only one day after Lay had stood side by side with him and assured the analysts that everything was peachy, Lay announced that Fastow had taken a "leave of absence." Ironically, Jeff McMahon replaced him. It was McMahon who had complained to Skilling months earlier about Fastow's deals. For his troubles, he was removed from his job as treasurer and farmed out to run the Industrial Market's Group. Now he was being asked to clean up Fastow's mess, if it was still possible. It wasn't. After a little more digging around in the partnership deals, Enron found another "mistake" that would cost the company $405 million and cause it to restate earnings. The hull of Enron was cracking like an egg.

With financial collapse imminent, Lay called again, for the last time, on his old buddies in Washington. He told Commerce Secretary Donald L. Evans that he would "welcome any kind of support" in heading off a downgrade of Enron's stock by Moody's Investors Service. The downgrade would make it much more expensive and much more difficult for Enron to survive. Evans did nothing to help.

Lay also made several calls to Treasury Secretary Paul O'Neill, including one in which he suggested the Treasury staff study Enron's situation to assure that its problems were "not going to get translated into larger problems for the U.S. and the world capital markets." Lay's threat went ignored. No help at all came from Washington. Politicians now treated Enron like toxic waste, instead of the world's leading energy company.

Sherron Watkins, the whistle-tweeter, wrote a rather pathetic memo on October 30, proposing to Lay how Enron and Lay himself could still survive. Of course, she suggested an important role for herself in her scheme to "rebuild investor confidence." Here is what she suggested:

1. Blame subordinates, including Skilling, Fastow, Ben Glisan, and Richard A. Causey.
2. Blame the lawyers and accountants.
3. Claim Lay was duped.

"This is a problem we must all address and fix for corporate America as a whole," she wrote. "Ken Lay and his board were duped by a COO who wanted targets met no matter what the consequences, a CFO motivated by personal greed, and two of the most respected firms, Arthur Anderson & Co and Vinson and Elkins, who had both grown wealthy off Enron's yearly business and no longer performed their roles."

She thought that Lay could ride out the storm. "Nobody wants Ken Lay's head," she wrote. "He's well respected in the community." Not for long.

The board of directors of Enron had enjoyed a charmed relationship with Enron's top executives. But they now knew their own necks could be at risk. As board members, they should have known the details of the partnerships, and the extent of Fastow's involvement, but they didn't. So they launched an outside investigation to get to the bottom of things. William Powers, Jr., dean of the University of Texas Law School, directed the investigation, in which he was assisted by former SEC investigators. Since the University of Texas had been the happy recipient of Enron's philanthropy in the past, cynics thought that Powers would take it easy on the company. They were wrong.

The Powers investigation began even as Enron was gasping its last. Dynegy tried to negotiate a last-minute merger, which was an insult to Enronians. They regarded the smaller competitor with contempt. But the deal unraveled, even after Dynegy pumped $1.5 billion into Enron's leaking hull. Most of it disappeared in weeks. For all practical purposes, Enron was now dead. It would stumble around like Lee Marvin in *Cat Ballou* for a while, but Enron was mortally wounded once its stock sank into the teens. That sent the creditors clamoring for their money back, and as Enron's cash evaporated, even more creditors began demanding payment.

On December 2, the company formally filed for Chapter 11 reorganization with the U.S. Bankruptcy Court for the Southern District of New York. As part of the reorganization process, Enron also filed suit against Dynegy Inc. in the same court, alleging breach of contract in connection with Dynegy's wrongful termination of its proposed merger with Enron and seeking damages of at least $10 billion. Enron went down swinging, but it wasn't at all cool.

You have doubtless seen on the television news the streams of Enronians huddled outside Enron's Houston headquarters, jobless and in many cases near penniless. The plight of the 4,500 people who had been laid off in Houston put a human face on Enron's demise. The company that was the soul of the New Economy turned out to have the flesh and blood of the Old Economy, too. There were real people who gathered around the big Enron block at its company headquarters, consoling each other. There were real stories of hardship.

For the young, hot MBAs who came to Enron and walked away without that "first million" they'd expected to make by age thirty, the experience would be little more than a speed bump in their careers. Call it an expensive learning experience. Their dilemmas wouldn't likely be finding another job, but rather which ones to consider. Having Enron on the resume took on a reverse cachet. Anyone who hired a former Enronian could count on lots of interesting water-cooler chat, as well as a having a bright young mind that has been somewhat humbled. Bill Gates of Microsoft had even said that he preferred hiring people who had experienced failure.

For other Enronians who were not so young and not so hot as the MBA corps, being laid off from Enron was much more devastating.

Their lives would never be the same. Besides losing their generous salaries, they lost their kids' college tuition, their retirement money, and their medical and other benefits. The distribution of pain was perverse. The longer you worked at Enron, the greater the financial loss. Veteran employees held more Enron stock, now virtually worthless, and they were cheated out of more severance pay and more benefits. They also faced starting over again at middle age while trying to figure out how to make next month's mortgage.

When even the creakiest of Old Economy companies fold, workers are seldom left in such dire straits. Pension, severance, and other benefits are very seldom lost. Union protection is one of the reasons;

human decency is another. But after Enron, you could hear Joe Six-pack, muttering at the TV set:

"Yep, workers screwed by management again. Those bastards are rich, but you're out of work and your savings and your pension are gone. That's what you get for trusting management."

Joe Sixpack didn't feel any better when he took a look at his own portfolio, either. Mutual funds, major pension funds, and other institutional investors owned about 60 percent of the company's shares when Enron was at its peak, and almost all of them stayed with the stock until just before the final curtain. Among them were firms such as Janus Capital Corp., Barclays Global Investors, Fidelity Management & Research, Putnam Investment Management, American Express Financial Advisors, Smith Barney Asset Management, Vanguard Group, California Public Employees Retirement Fund, Van Kampen Asset Management, TIAA-CREF Investment Management, Dreyfus Corp., Merrill Lynch Asset Management, Goldman Sachs Asset Management, and Morgan Stanley Investment Management. Even if Joe Sixpack only owned an index fund like the Vanguard 500, he too, took an Enron hit.

Kenneth Lay was cast as the principal villain. Lay was no corporate wallflower who spent weekends curled up with printouts. He was a friend of presidents, and an important backer of a lot of powerful people in Washington. He was the Bush administration's point man on energy policy. He was a major philanthropist, and a major social figure and booster in Houston, popular enough to get elected mayor if he ever wanted to. (There had been rumors he'd run after retiring from Enron.)

Business Week had named Lay one of America's top twenty-five managers, twice. He was a rags-to-riches genius who had invented a whole new kind of company. In short, he was red meat for the press.

Not used to being called "greedy," "arrogant," and worse, Lay wanted to express his side of the Enron story. Reporters and TV crews had been hounding Lay and his wife, Linda, trying to score interviews. Finally, the Lays decided they had to do something to salvage his reputation and explain their side of the story. Ken Lay allowed Linda to go on the *Today* show to make their case.

She did not go unprepared. A. M. Shute, a Houston public relations executive who once worked on the Enron account for Hill & Knowlton, coached Linda Lay. Linda appeared calm and sincere and told *Today*'s Lisa Meyers that Ken Lay was as much a victim as any Enron wage earner whose pension had evaporated. He had done no wrong, she insisted. Evil advisors had sabotaged his company. "He didn't know what was going on," she said.

Dabbing away at tears, Linda said, "We're broke. We're selling everything we own." Lisa Meyers slumped in sympathy.

Of course, the Lays' definition of broke and that of the average Enron wage earner were different. Lay had millions in assets, including homes and real estate in Aspen and Houston, totaling at least $24 million. He had cashed in many more millions in Enron stock. And even if all of this money and property were seized, the Lays would still not go hungry.

A few years earlier, as reported in *Mother Jones*, Lay had purchased an annuity that guarantees the Lays an annual income of $900,000 for life, starting in five years. And the annuity is protected from any creditors.

Linda Lay's weepy appearance on *Today* provided fodder for columnists and jokes for Jay Leno and David Letterman. But it did nothing to sell Lay's claims of innocence.

Neither did the Powers Report, issued a few days later, on February 2. The board-commissioned inquiry into the mysterious partnership deals was devastating. It ripped apart the partnership deals on several grounds: They enriched some Enron insiders without board knowledge; they were full of accounting mistakes; and they had dubious aims, such as hiding debt.

The report stated, "Many of the most significant transactions apparently were designed to accomplish favorable financial statement results, not to achieve *bona fide* economic objectives or to transfer risk."

The report blamed the lawyers and the accountants for okaying the deals, but it held Ken Lay responsible, too. A few days after the report was issued, Powers himself testified before a House panel and said that Lay knew about so-called "hedge transactions," in which the company created an appearance that an independent third party was obligated to cover its losses in the stock market. But Enron staked that third party. There was no real hedge at all.

Ken Lay was invited to Washington to answer those charges, and at first he said he would testify before at least one of the three congressional bodies holding hearings. But he changed his mind and took the Fifth Amendment when he appeared. So did four other Enron executives, whose fortunes and freedom were now likewise at stake: CFO Andrew Fastow; Michael Kopper, who worked for Fastow; Richard Causey, who was Enron's chief accounting officer; and Richard Buy, Enron's chief risk officer. They all invoked their constitutional rights against self-incrimination.

True to form, Jeffrey Skilling, who had earned the nickname Rocky in college for never yielding on an argument, refused to take the Fifth. He didn't have to talk to the committees, and no lawyer would have suggested it. But he donned a tie and quiet business suit, slicked back his hair, and faced the television cameras and the trophy-hunting congressmen not once, but twice. First he testified before the House Energy and Commerce Committee on February 7, and then the Senate Commerce, Science and Transportation Committee on February 26.

He told House members that he was "devastated and apologetic about what Enron has come to represent," but that when he left the company in August 2001, he "fervently believed that Enron was not in any financial peril."

In other words, it didn't happen on his watch, and so he felt he was off the hook. Peppered with questions about how he could be unaware of problems brewing, he said, "Enron Corp. was an enormous corporation. Could I have known everything going on in the company?"

Skilling said he was unaware Enron's partnerships were used to hide debt. And he blamed Enron's collapse on liquidity problems.

"There are things called a run on a bank. You can have a fundamentally solvent company that has a liquidity problem," he told the House committee.

Representative James Greenwood (R-Pa.) was skeptical. "Mr. Skilling, a massive earthquake struck Enron right after your departure. People in far inferior positions to you could see cracks in the walls, feel the tremors, feel the windows rattling. And you want us to believe that you sat there in your office and had no clue that this place was about to collapse?"

Skilling didn't budge. "On the day I left . . . I believed the company was in strong financial condition."

Later in the month, he faced the Senate committee and said pretty much the same thing, and hardly flinched under some smarmy questioning.

"I am not an accountant," Skilling said.

He preferred to elaborate that a "run on the bank" had triggered the bankruptcy, and even complained that something called a "MAC clause" was the real cause of the collapse. MAC clauses allow lenders to withdraw their money right away whenever a company suffers a substantial problem. Yes, there was a run on Enron, just as blood will flow freely from a huge wound. Skilling was blaming the blood for not staying where it was before.

To more than a few observers, Skilling's arguments were lame. It appeared that he knew the company was headed for disaster, and bailed out while he still could.

Senator Byron Dorgan (D-N.D.) brought up an analogy with the *Titanic*. "Enron looks to me like the captain first gave himself a bonus, then lowered himself and the top folks down in the lifeboat and then hollered up and said, 'By the way, everything's going to be just fine.'"

Skilling bristled at the comparison. "I think it's a pretty bad analogy, Senator, because I wasn't on the *Titanic*. I got off in Ireland. . . ."

Cool.

10

The Shredding of Arthur Andersen

What we do is very different from what people think we do. We don't guarantee the financial condition of the company. But whenever a company fails, people ask, "Where were the auditors?"
—Joseph Berardino, former CEO of Andersen Worldwide

We all know accountants. Many of us hire them to do our taxes, or keep our books. We know that they love numbers, the way writers love words and painters love oils.

Watch your accountant the next time you bring in your tax return and your long face. His eyes will brighten and he'll seize your papers like a crossword puzzle fanatic, eager to come up with solutions.

We trust our accountants more than lawyers, more than bartenders, more than spouses. My long-time accountant Tony, who was a corporate accountant and did tax returns on the side, also ran a weekly football pool. It began with a few cocktail-hour acquaintances at Charley O's bar in Rockefeller Center, and soon spread all over New York City. Everyone who bet on football wanted to get into Tony's pool because he was an accountant. You could trust him to be honest and not make any mistakes. (Tony didn't take a dime for running the pool, not even a free ride.)

The profession always seemed to attract nice, honest, mild-mannered types who lived orderly, measured lives. Scan the newspapers. You would seldom see a serial killer or a drug dealer who was an accountant. It was as if the mind that finds fascination with numbers and documents could not be easily unhinged.

Arthur Andersen LLP changed that stereotype forever. It exposed another side to accountants—they can be just as greedy as the rest of us when a bunch of them get together.

In 1913, an accounting professor at Northwestern University co-founded the firm that bears his name. Arthur Andersen's timing was exquisite, as the U.S. had just passed a new law that guaranteed that accountants would never again have to worry about work. The Sixteenth Amendment to the Constitution established the personal income tax and the corporate income tax, just as Andersen hung out his shingle.

In the beginning, tax rates were low, and people with incomes of less than $4,000 were exempt from paying anything at all. Adjusted for inflation, that would be roughly $69,000 in today's dollars.

Corporate taxes ranged from 2 percent to a maximum of 6 percent. Personal taxes ranged from 1 percent up to 7 percent, if you made over $500,000 a year, which almost no one did. The average annual income in the U.S. that year was $520.

With a brand new slate to start with, Congress could have made the tax code simple. It could have established what we now call a flat tax. No deductions, no expenses, no hanky panky. If you make X dollars a year, you paid Y taxes, period.

But the accountants had already been at work behind the scenes before the Amendment was ratified, and had worked their mischief. The very first income tax forms printed in 1913 look astonishingly similar to the 1040s we use today, and were equally as baffling to the ordinary taxpayer. What did he know about depreciation? Business losses? Interest payments?

Small wonder that the very first year, the Treasury collected less than half the revenue it anticipated. Many taxpayers failed to file. (The punishment ranged from $20 to $1,000, plus taxes due.)

As the revenue stream wasn't what the government needed, it soon decided to increase the tax rates. Even though many folks were still dodging the taxman completely, the faithful filers were told to pony up even more. By 1918, the personal income tax rates jumped from 6 percent up to a maximum of 77 percent for those earning over $1 million a year. What had started as a fleabite was now an epidemic. Income tax had become very serious business for folks like Arthur Andersen.

By 1978, Andersen had become the largest professional services firm in the world, raking in over $500 million a year in revenue. It had also taken on a very profitable sideline—consulting. The business of consulting was growing rapidly as computer technology began invading the workplace. Corporations needed consultants to implement the new systems and make sure that they worked properly.

As far back as 1954, Andersen took on its first official consulting job, and it was an epic one. Working with IBM, Andersen consultants installed the first mainframe computer at General Electric Co. to handle its payroll. The new system was better and cheaper, and soon computers began replacing platoons of payroll clerks at corporations all over the country. Andersen's consultants were often on the case.

By 1984, Andersen Consulting outgrossed the auditing arm of the company, and it eventually separated from the parent and took on a new name, Accenture. The separation was a bitter one, and cost the new firm $1 billion to break free.

Meantime, like a lobster regrowing a claw that had been hacked off, Andersen again offered consulting services to its clients under the Andersen name. Consulting soon outpaced auditing in revenues once again. Industrywide, in 1976, auditing fees accounted for 70 percent of an accounting firm's revenues. By 1998, it was only 31 percent.

As the accounting firms got richer, they got even cozier with their clients, and soon their auditors became less prickly about accounting standards. A funny odor began emanating from more and more audited financial statements. By the late 1990s, the stench could knock you over. Financial statements were no longer reliable. In hundreds of cases, corporations had to restate their earnings later on. Wall Street analysts and eagle-eyed investors went cross-eyed reading footnotes or chasing down off-balance sheet obligations. In short, financial statements had lost their transparency—they obfuscated as much as they informed. Some reports, such as Enron's, were masterpieces of misinformation.

The SEC was not totally asleep at the wheel. In fact, Arthur Levitt, Jr., head of the SEC from 1993 to 2000, was fed up with what the accountants were doing, and vowed to put an end to it. If he had succeeded, Enron would never have happened, nor would a lot of the other spectacular collapses of 2002.

Levitt accomplished a lot in his tenure. He went after the NASDAQ and forced a narrowing of the price spreads quoted on over-the-counter stocks. The result shifted billions of dollars from the pockets of brokers to the pockets of investors. Levitt also brought more cases against accountants over a two-year period than had been filed in all the years going back to the SEC's inception.

In his book, *Take on the Street*, written with Paula Dwyer, Levitt recounts how his top SEC accountants warned him that they were seeing a "marked increase" in corporate numbers games. And it wasn't just a few rogue companies.

"Blue-chip companies with sterling reputations were manipulating their numbers in misleading ways," he writes. "From 1997 through 2000, 700 companies would find flaws in previous financial statements and restate their earnings. By comparison, only three companies restated in 1981. These came at a tremendous cost to investors, who would lose hundreds of billions of dollars in market value."

Levitt had already lost a battle with the accounting industry over stock options. He wanted companies to carry them as expenses on their financial statements (see Chapter Three). But it is not easy to monkey with stock options, which are corporate America's family jewels. The uproar from the business community, and from Congress itself, forced him to back down. Levitt regards not having pressed that issue as his biggest mistake as SEC chairman.

Levitt tried another approach when it came to getting the accounting firms to clean up their auditing act. He tried logic and persuasion, along with the threat of regulation.

What he asked for was simple enough: independent auditors. That would most likely mean the accounting firms would have to separate their auditing business from the consulting business. Exactly how it should be done, Levitt didn't specify. But he set up a joint SEC–industry group to hammer out what the standards should be for auditor independence.

But the group got nowhere. In fact, the accountants defiantly questioned whether there was any need for such standards in the first place. Where was the hard evidence that consulting infected auditing? The lawyer who argued that point for the accountants was Harvey Pitt, who would later become SEC commissioner himself. Levitt reports that even after becoming head of the SEC, Pitt still insisted that "the growth of consulting does not interfere with auditor independence."

Levitt was no toady for business interests, even though he was an old Wall Street hand. He had been chairman of the American Stock Exchange, and founded the brokerage firm that became Smith Barney. He believed his proposal for independent audits served everyone's best interests—except the accounting firms and their shadier clients.

In his book Levitt describes what he was up against when he called for independent auditors. He had a war on his hands, and the accounting firms had a lot more weapons than Levitt suspected.

On the public relations front, the accountants urged their satisfied clients to go to bat for them. Kenneth Lay, chairman of Enron, was happy to go on the record in support of Arthur Andersen. Especially since AA was doing both its internal and external audits, a practice Levitt's rule change would also end.

Lay wrote in a letter to Levitt that having AA as its internal and external auditor was "valuable to the investing public . . . given the risks and complexities of Enron's business . . ." Lay wrote his letter in September 2000, when Enron was sitting on top of the world, and Andersen was sitting on a powder keg.

Besides testimonials from clients, the accountants also called in chits from their allies in Congress. As major political contributors, they had many. Congress had the power to defang Levitt's proposal. They could not stop its enactment, but they could deny funds to the SEC to enforce it.

It was a crude, but effective weapon, and it soon appeared in the battle. Senator Phil Gramm called Levitt and told him that unless he cut a deal with the accountants, a rider would be attached to the funding bill that would ban the SEC from using taxpayer money to enforce its new rule.

Once again, Levitt went to the accounting firms to try to hammer out a compromise, and after months of negotiations, a watered-down version of the proposal was finally adopted on November 15, 2000. But it still allowed the accounting firms to do both auditing and consulting for the same clients. The quality of audits only got worse.

When Enron blew up in October 2001, Andersen went into a panic. What could the firm do to avoid serious collateral damage? Andersen auditors had put their stamp on financial statements that had turned out to be flights of fancy.

The first instinct of a crafty criminal is to destroy evidence. No gun, no murderer. But in the world of white-collar crime, destroying evidence is not without its risks. Getting caught destroying the smoking gun can be worse than being nailed for the shooting.

In the case of Andersen, the evidence was Enron documents and electronic files. They could be potent weapons in the hands of prosecutors and lawyers representing stockholders. Andersen could have been facing fines and settlement fees in the hundreds of millions.

The additional financial strain could break the bank. Andersen was already straining under the weight of other awards and fines. In 1998, the firm paid $75 million to shareholders of Waste Management Corp., and $7 million to the SEC, which charged Andersen with issuing false and misleading audit reports on Waste Management from 1992 to 1996.

In April 2001 Andersen agreed to pay $110 million to shareholders of Sunbeam Corp., to settle a suit over accounting misstatements. And in March 2002, in the middle of its Enron troubles, Andersen agreed to pay $217 million to settle lawsuits arising from a scandal at the Baptist Foundation of America, an Andersen client. It seems the foundation was a Ponzi scheme, and Andersen never caught it in its audits. (Andersen was unable to make that payment, however).

Andersen could barely survive any more financial punishment. The question had to have arisen in the minds of more than a few Andersen executives: What if the damning evidence were to suddenly disappear?

It may never come out who gave the order for Andersen auditors to shred Enron documents and erase electronic files. Certainly no top Andersen executives have come forward. The blame fell on the neck of one low-level individual, David B. Duncan, who was the lead man for Andersen on the Enron account. He admitted that he shredded documents that he knew would be material to an investigation. Did the buck stop there? It's doubtful.

But Duncan can take personal credit for shredding Arthur Andersen LLP into the dustbin of history. It was an ignominious end, a punishment that Pope George the Great himself would have approved if shredders had been around in his day.

Once a proud, arrogant giant in the conflicted worlds of consulting, accounting, and auditing, Andersen had been a $9.3 billion worldwide partnership, with over 85,000 employees. Andersen exists now only as a skeleton, fighting lawsuits that seek revenue that is no longer coming in.

Duncan said he started the shredding in October 2001, to adhere to the company's "document retention policy" with Enron data. In short, crank up the shredders. Madcap shredding went on at Andersen's Houston offices until the SEC announced its formal investigation weeks later, and began issuing subpoenas for those documents and e-mails that were now mountains of waste paper and blank discs.

Andersen was in a jam: It couldn't produce all the missing documents, and it dared not admit why. Andersen's outside lawyers, in searching for documents to satisfy the SEC, soon learned of the shredding. They conferred with Andersen and immediately told investigators that Enron documents had been destroyed. The press was delighted.

Readers love shredding stories. They are full of intrigue. What was so important that it had to be shredded? What was the secret they were keeping? What kind of an accounting firm was that, anyway, shredding important documents?

The shredding story gave the Enron saga new life. Jay Leno and David Letterman trotted out the old shredding jokes from the Iran Contra days when Oliver North and Fawn Hall were the shredders in the news.

The public reached a simple conclusion when it heard about the shredding: Andersen destroyed documents because it had helped Enron cook its books, and didn't want the SEC to find the proof.

Prosecutors reached the same conclusion and charged David B. Duncan and the firm of Arthur Andersen with obstruction of justice. This was not a civil case; it was now criminal, and therefore very serious. If convicted, Andersen would lose its licenses to operate.

Despite all the headlines, however, Andersen was not in mortal danger from the obstruction case. Indeed, prosecutors soon began meeting with Andersen lawyers to reach a deal that would save Andersen from going to trial. Everyone knew that a criminal conviction would have destroyed the entire firm, which no one wanted.

The Justice Department didn't want to kill Andersen because a dead Andersen could not pay any fines, or settle any stockholder lawsuits. And thousands of innocent people would be out of work. So prosecutors huddled with Andersen lawyers and a settlement was expected.

Yet Andersen had already been found guilty in the court of public opinion. More and more clients quit. The shredding had made Andersen toxic. If you had Andersen as your auditor, you were inviting the SEC to look into your books. Besides Enron, Andersen was the auditor for Sunbeam, Waste Management, WorldCom, Qwest, and Global Crossing. The collapse of these companies alone cost investors more than $300 billion. Tens of thousands of workers lost their jobs.

Andersen could survive paying fines for bad audits, and it could survive stockholder lawsuits, and it could survive the obstruction charge by plea-bargaining. But it could not survive without customers.

Prosecutors reportedly discussed a sum of $750 million for Andersen to settle claims and fines. But as customers continued fleeing the firm, it became clear that Andersen would not have that kind of money. Negotiations deteriorated.

By that point, Joseph Berardino, CEO of Andersen Worldwide, had resigned his $3-million-a-year post. He was the boss, and he should have known what was going on at Enron, though he claims he was never informed about how dicey things had become. He fell on his sword not because he was guilty, he claims, but because he was the man in charge.

Yet it is hard to believe Berardino was in the dark about Enron, especially since Andersen partners in Chicago were so skeptical of Enron's numbers that they talked about dumping the account. Enron was deemed a "maximum risk" client, but was paying Andersen about $1 million a week in auditing and consulting fees.

Carl E. Bass, a senior Andersen partner, was monitoring the audit of Enron and had a lot of serious problems with Enron's accounting. He made his views known to Enron management, which was not amused.

While the feud heated up, Joseph Berardino paid a visit to Enron's Houston headquarters to see Jeff Skilling and Richard A. Causey, Enron's chief accounting officer. Berardino told *Business*

Week that was strictly "meet-and-greet," and that he didn't even know about the conflicts over the accounting.

"If that kind of issue isn't important enough to get to Berardino's desk, then what is?" asked Allan D. Kolton, CEO of the Practice Development Institute. "He either knew and chose to look the other way or he was the most incompetent CEO in America," Kolton told *Business Week*.

Berardino quit and Paul Volcker, former head of the Federal Reserve, was invited to try to save the firm. "Andersen now is a very lame horse, a lame horse that got shot in the head," he said at the time. His efforts at working out a deal failed.

In the end, Andersen took its chances at trial, hoping that the issues would be too confusing for a jury to reach a guilty verdict. The six-week trial was boring, and some jurors supposedly nodded off from time to time. The jury of nine men and three women asked to be released after deadlocking. But they finally did reach a verdict: Guilty. The verdict drove the stake through Andersen's heart.

There are now only four major accounting firms, all now a little richer after feasting on Andersen's corpse. Have they learned a lesson? Have they at least learned that a little humility might be in order? Andersen wasn't the only firm in hot water with the SEC for its audits.

The temptation to make hay out of the Andersen/Enron follies was just too great for PwC (the result of the merger of Price Waterhouse and Coopers & Lybrand). In September 2002, PwC ran television commercials espousing its integrity. There was one great spot showing a bunch of golfers berating a fellow duffer for trying to cheat on his golf score. The ad hit home with a lot of viewers, especially since the spot ran during the Ryder Cup when golf fans were glued to the tube.

The message was the importance of trust. But should PwC be giving that lesson? Since 1994, PwC was the auditor for Tyco International which was run by L. Dennis Kozlowski. PwC is under investigation by the Manhattan District Attorney regarding its knowledge of secret bonuses paid to Kozlowski and others.

PwC might even have been put out of business completely in 1997. The SEC received a tip that the firm's audit staff in Tampa was accepting stock from its clients, a serious no-no for accountants. How can an auditor be objective if he is a stockholder?

Arthur Levitt recounts in his book that the SEC discovered that people all over the firm owned stock in companies that the firm audited, including half the firm's partners and even its CEO, James Schiro. In all, there were 8,000 violations. PwC would have been destroyed if Levitt chose to bring a case. (He chose not to, in return for PwC's support of his new audit rules.)

Moral: check your own skirts for mud before you stroll into the limelight.

The demise of Andersen did finally move regulators and legislators to do something about accounting reforms. In the wake of the corporate scandals, Congress passed the Sarbanes-Oxley Act on July 30, 2002. The act contained a slew of anti-fraud measures, including a requirement that CEOs certify their company's financial statements, under penalty of jail and fine. Another provision banned accounting firms from doing both auditing and most forms of consulting for the same client at the same time. It appeared Levitt finally got his wish.

The act established a new oversight board for the accounting industry that has sweeping powers. The Public Company Accounting Oversight Board is empowered to set industry standards for ethics and conflicts of interest. It can punish accountants and conduct annual reviews of the largest accounting firms.

After years of having its way with Congress, the accounting firms had lost a major battle. They would no longer be self-regulating. An outsider would head the new board and have all the power needed to force accounting firms to clean up their act. Provided, of course, that the head of the five-man board had the will and the inclination to impose reforms.

The accountants weren't done yet.

In September 2002, Harvey Pitt, chairman of the SEC, surprised his critics by naming John H. Biggs to head the new oversight committee. Biggs was chairman and CEO of TIAA-CREF, a huge pension fund. He was known as an advocate of investors' rights, and no big fan of the accounting firms. He was an odd choice for Pitt, who had done so much work for the accounting industry.

Sure enough, just weeks after that announcement, Pitt changed his mind. The accountants didn't want the reform-minded Biggs calling the shots. They rallied their congressmen, who called Pitt, and he backed away from endorsing Biggs.

Just what was it about Biggs that scared the accountants so much? In February 2002, Biggs testified before the Senate Banking Committee that was preparing the law that created the new oversight board. Biggs focused on "three changes we have needed for some time and that bear directly on Enron."

The changes would devastate the accounting firms, but do wonders for investors. "One, a means of dealing with the widespread overuse and abuse of fixed-price stock options. Two, the need for some basic common sense regarding auditor independence. And three, the need for a strong regulatory model to oversee the accounting profession."

The accountants found Biggs's medicine too hard to swallow. He didn't get the job after all. The SEC named instead someone who was more palatable to the accountants. Don't hold your breath waiting for Biggs-style reforms. The foxes are still in the henhouse. Congress made a big show of holding hearings and passing tough new legislation designed to help the small investor. But he is still outgunned in Washington. As Levitt told a reporter from the *New York Post:* "Right now [small investors] are the least effective political constituency in Washington, and as we speak representatives, lawyers, accountants, stock exchanges, brokers, and ratings agencies are all on Capitol Hill lobbying for things that are not necessarily in the best interests of investors.

"And nobody is representing individual investors up on the Hill. I probably could not name more than a half dozen senators and congressmen that are true friends of investors."

Hold on to your wallets; we can expect more scandals in the future.

"No one is going to wipe out all fraud," said Levitt. "Fraud is developing as we speak that may not be uncovered until three or four years from now."

11

———

The Telecom Cowboys

———

Our goal is not to capture market share or be global. Our
goal is to be the number one stock in the world.
—Bernie Ebbers, *Business Week*, July 17, 1997

On CNBC one morning in the late winter of 2002, co-anchor
Larry Kudlow was commenting on the mood of the market. After
several days of declines, the Dow Jones was starting to inch upward
again. Kudlow, ever the optimist, suggested that "the Enron thing
looks like it has finally blown over."

His co-anchor, the avuncular Mark Haines, rolled his eyes to the
ceiling as if to say, "I wouldn't go there if I were you."

Kudlow had more reasons than most to wish the Enron mess
would quickly retreat from the front pages. Kudlow had been taking
heat after it was revealed that he had accepted $50,000 from Enron
in the previous year: $20,000 for economic research; $15,000 for
attending a meeting with Enron's outside advisory board; and
another $15,000 for an Enron speech he gave in Beaver Creek,

Colo., in August. Fifty thousand dollars is about what a good young reporter makes in a year; it's pin money for Kudlow.

Kudlow explained in his column in the *National Review* on January 22, 2002, that Enron bought his economic research, just as other clients did, and there was no conflict of interest. "I did what I did with that company because that's the business I am in," he wrote. "That's how I make my living."

But Kudlow's prediction that morning, that "the Enron thing" was blowing over, proved wishful thinking. Scandals on Wall Street traditionally come in bunches, and veteran investors had been eyeing all the restatements of earnings, and were leery of the market. The thinking went that if Enron could get away with its accounting gimmickry without the auditors or regulators raising an eyebrow, other companies were cooking their books, too. The question became, "When are we going to see the next Enron?"

The wait wasn't long. On January 28, 2002, Global Crossing Inc. had filed for bankruptcy court protection, and within weeks, the SEC began an investigation into its books. Only days after that, the SEC announced it was also looking into the financial statements of Qwest, another troubled telecom.

But the biggest bomb of all dropped on March 11, 2002, when the SEC said it was probing WorldCom's accounting, including details of a baffling $408 million loan to its legendary CEO, Bernard J. Ebbers. WorldCom, like a lot of other telecommunications companies, had been struggling with overcapacity and intense competition. WorldCom was the second largest telecom in the country, with more than $100 billion in assets.

Had it been cooking its books, too? And what about the $408 million loan to Ebbers? Arthur Andersen was WorldCom's auditor, which did not bode well.

Millions of investors owned WorldCom; it was once the fifth most widely held stock in America. In March 1996, WorldCom earned a place on the S&P 500 index, which meant that tens of millions of mutual fund investors were now holders of the stock. Bernie Ebbers once told Wall Street analysts that his job was to make sure that

WorldCom stock went up, and for over ten years, that is just what he did. In a survey conducted that year, *The Wall Street Journal* reported that of the top one thousand major corporations in the U.S., WorldCom had the very best performance for the preceding ten years. It was an extraordinary run and Ebbers was a hero.

In 1997, Allan Sloan, the Wall Street editor of *Newsweek*, called WorldCom stock "a currency that's better than money." Sloan noted that "If you invested a dollar in WorldCom at the start of 1990, you had $225 worth of stock on September 30, 1997." That meant your investment doubled every twelve months. And from September 1997 to its peak in 1999, it increased another fourfold. "Money can't do that," Sloan wrote.

The man who had done such magic for his stockholders, and who was now in the crosshairs of the SEC, cast a long and familiar shadow on Wall Street. Bernie Ebbers had borrowed billions from banks and had sold billions of dollars in stock and bonds through brokers. While Bernie was lucky for stockholders, he was Santa Claus for investment bankers who made hundreds of millions on WorldCom's loans and offerings of bonds and stocks. Everyone was praying that WorldCom wouldn't prove to be another Enron. But it wound up being worse.

Bernie, as he was well known on Wall Street, didn't look the part of the dealmaker that he was—one who made over sixty major acquisitions in ten years. He looked more like a stage cowboy. He wore Western gear at the office—jeans, checked shirts, leather vests, turquoise jewelry, and cowboy boots. With his clipped gray beard and long wavy hair, he looked like he'd wandered in from the set of *Dallas*.

He wasn't cut from the same cloth as most CEOs. He wasn't particularly brainy, he had no real management experience, he didn't have a basketful of degrees, and he never pretended to know all that much about the business he was in. He seemed an unlikely finalist in the deadly game of Last Man Standing that the telecommunications industry had become in the 1990s.

Ebbers was born into a middle-class family in Edmonton,

Alberta, on August 27, 1941, had a normal childhood, and graduated without distinction from Victoria Composite High School. At six foot four, he was a pretty good basketball player, but not a diligent student. He went on to the University of Alberta, but soon flunked out.

It was the broken romance of a friend that would spring him from his hometown. Ebbers was driving a milk truck by day and working as a bar bouncer at night. He later told *Time* magazine, "Delivering milk day to day in thirty-below weather isn't a real interesting thing to do with the rest of your life."

His prospects were not great in Edmonton. But a friend who wanted to get as far away from his ex-girlfriend as possible talked him into looking into Mississippi College, in Clinton, Mississippi, deep in the Bible belt. It was long way from Edmonton.

Founded in 1826, the school is the oldest college in Mississippi and the second oldest Baptist college in the world. Religion is taken seriously. "We are a university committed to Christian higher education in the pursuit of Christian truth and in service to the world," says Dr. Lee Royce, president of the college. It was hardly a jock school, and Clinton, with a population under 15,000, was at its liveliest on Sunday mornings, when virtually everyone in town went to church or bible study at one of the town's two dozen–plus churches.

But Ebbers liked what he saw, and decided he wanted to attend the school, which offered him a basketball scholarship. He played for the Mississippi College Choctaws, but was plagued with injuries and mainly rode the pines throughout his college basketball career. But he got a lot more out of the school than splinters. He would later write in the school alumni magazine, *The Beacon*, "I came to have a fuller understanding of what my purpose was in life, what a personal relationship with Jesus Christ really meant, and how I would try to live my life from that point on."

Ebbers liked the school and the area so much he vowed to leave it only "in a box." He even established his company's world headquarters in Clinton, not a natural choice for the nation's second largest telecommunications company.

After he graduated college in 1967 with a degree in physical education, Ebbers took a job teaching science and coaching basketball at a nearby junior high school. Then he managed a garment warehouse before scraping together money from co-workers to buy a motel. By 1983, he owned nine Best Western motels.

In August of that year, Ebbers and three friends got together in a coffee shop in Hattiesburg, Mississippi, to discuss, of all things, the telephone business. The Justice Department had succeeded in breaking up the Bell system, which meant that there was soon to be competition in the long-distance telephone market. The AT&T virtual monopoly was history. The four men—Bill Fields, David Singleton, Murray Waldron, and Ebbers—concocted a scheme to buy long-distance capacity wholesale, and then sell it retail to business customers. They reckoned that AT&T and other carriers would be glad to sell blocks of long-distance capacity at a discount, and they were right.

Legend has it that the original name of the company came from the waitress in the coffee shop. It was like a mouthful of grits: Long Distance Discount Service. But people got the message. LDDS's first customer was the University of Southern Mississippi, and others quickly followed.

By 1985, the new company was stumbling, however. Ebbers and his pals weren't the only ones to come up with the idea of discounting long distance telephone service. And the cost of starting up such a business was minimal. Competition meant narrowing margins.

Ebbers managed to turn a small profit within a year, but he saw that the quickest way to grow was to make acquisitions. Once he started, it was like eating pistachio nuts. He kept on going until the bowl was empty. Murray Waldron, one of Ebbers's partners in LDDS, told the *Washington Post*, "He wanted to be the biggest and just do whatever it took to get there. Bernie was going to be king of the mountain."

After a half-dozen acquisitions, his company was no longer a small regional reseller. It was operating in most areas of the country. In 1992, Ebbers bought Advanced Telecommunications Corp., making LDDS the fourth largest long-distance provider in the U.S. It was still a long way behind AT&T, Sprint, and MCI, but Ebbers had only been at the wheel a few years.

As he added to the company, the stock began to take off. That made it possible for Ebbers to acquire even larger competitors, which would, in turn, immediately add value to the company and move the stock even higher. It was like paying for something with a $10 bill and getting back $18 in change. Alan Sloan was right: the stock was better than money.

In 1993, the company merged with two other telecoms, Resurgens Communications Group and Metromedia-ITT Corp., owned by John Kluge. The next year, LDDS Communications, as the company had become known, went global with the addition of IDB WorldCom and its international long-distance business. Next came WilTel, a spanking new, fiber-optic network that the Williams Co., an energy company, had built inside decommissioned gas pipelines.

Renamed WorldCom in 1995, the company kept up the buying spree, and the stock kept on rising. At the end of 1996, WorldCom added two more trophies, MFS Communications, owner of many small fiber-optic networks, and UUNET, the big internet service provider.

WorldCom had become, in the words of the *New York Times,* "the nation's first fully integrated local and long-distance phone company since the breakup of Ma Bell." Bernie Ebbers was standing in tall cotton.

Throughout this period of geometric expansion, Ebbers never considered moving WorldCom's headquarters to, say, New York where it did so much of its business, or even a major city that is a transportation hub. The airport in Jackson, Mississippi, would have to do as WorldCom's gateway.

The transplanted Canadian was revered by workers who watched their 401(k) plans blossom from three, to four, to five, then six, and even seven figures. Paper millionaires walked the streets of Jackson and Clinton singing the praises of Bernie Ebbers and planning their early retirements. He brought thousands of jobs to rural Hinds

County, Mississippi, for blacks as well as whites. Ebbers was no red-neck. He hired basketball legend Michael Jordan as WorldCom's spokesman on TV. In 1998, Jesse Jackson came to town to speak at Tougaloo College, near Clinton, and started to blast Ebbers for ignoring local black students. But Jackson had failed to do his home-work. Ebbers had supported programs for disadvantaged black youth and had donated $1 million to Tougaloo College. He also helped local black businessmen, including LeRoy Walker, Jr., a board member of Tougaloo. According to *Time* magazine, Walker pulled Jackson aside to set him straight: "Bernie Ebbers is my men-tor," he said.

Ebbers gave money to local charities, churches, the museum, and especially his alma mater, Mississippi College, the shadow of which he hadn't left since walking on campus as a gawky basketball player in 1963. When Ebbers moved his corporate headquarters from Jackson to Clinton, he located it on land that WorldCom bought from the college for $50 million. He also helped raise $100 million for the Baptist school, and served as board trustee for twelve years. None of the new buildings built with those funds bears the name Ebbers; none of them have to.

His social life in Clinton was ordinary. He mowed his own lawn, and went to Hudgey's Family restaurant with his family after teach-ing Sunday school at the Easthaven Baptist Church. He played ten-nis at the Brookhaven Country Club and attended Mississippi College basketball games. He was a good ole boy. And a very rich one.

In 1998, Ebbers's net worth had risen to such a level—thanks to WorldCom stock and stock options—that *Forbes*'s researchers took notice. Ebbers made the *Forbes* Rich List for the first time in 1998, and in 1999 made the elite Billionaire List, with an estimated per-sonal net worth of $1.4 billion.

But Ebbers hadn't put all his eggs in one basket. He invested heavily in land, purchasing a huge tract of 265,000 acres of farmland in his hometown of Brookhaven, Mississippi, worth an estimated

$318 million. He also became a timber baron when he bought 480,000 acres of pineland in Alabama for $400 million.

In a curious move for someone who was so rooted in Mississippi, Ebbers also bought the Douglas Ranch in British Columbia—64,000 acres with 20,000 head of cattle. The cost was estimated at $67 million. Ebbers's heart may have been in Clinton but he had at least a big toe back in Canada. Ebbers took out bank loans and mortgages to pay for the real estate binge, rather than part with his WorldCom shares.

He also built a mansion deep in the woods and well away from prying eyes. But he shot pool, drank beer, and liked to listen to Willie Nelson. He didn't live lavishly and didn't expect others to, either, especially his own employees. Cost-cutting was an obsession. He drove salesmen crazy by insisting on coach-only flights (discount if possible), taxis instead of limos, $89 motels instead of $200 hotels. When in Jackson, visiting executives were wise to stay at the $59-a-night Hampton Inn, owned by Ebbers. When the company bought MCI, it sold three of its corporate jets.

He even removed water coolers in the company headquarters. Employees were expected to drink from the tap or bring their own bottled water. Ebbers was sending a message to employees, as well as burnishing his own image as a brilliant cost-cutter. Wall Street loves to hear stories about penny-pinching CEOs who deny their employees potable drinking water so a few more cents can dribble to the bottom line. It shows how tough they are.

Ebbers's fixation on cost-cutting stayed with him right to the end. In the spring of 2002, with the company already well on its slide into bankruptcy and the SEC sniffing through the books, Ebbers called an important strategy meeting at company headquarters in Clinton. According to *Business Week*, top company executives flew in from all over the world to attend the critical meeting.

But instead of hearing his grand plans for WorldCom's future, the baffled executives heard their esteemed CEO go into a tirade about the theft of coffee in the company break room. Ebbers had suspected that someone was nicking coffee bags, so he matched the filters and bags. At the end of the month, the filters outnumbered the bags, meaning coffee bags were indeed being stolen. Ebbers advised his executives to make sure to count the filters and bags in their own divisions and reminded them to push up thermostats to keep air-conditioning bills down.

"Bernie is running a $40 billion company as if it were still his own mom-and-pop business," one WorldCom executive told *Business Week*. "He doesn't know how to grow the company, just shave pennies."

WorldCom's top official bean counter was Scott D. Sullivan, chief financial officer. Behind every megalomaniac CEO is a very sharp CFO who has to do the financial dirty work. Sullivan was kept busy making deals from the moment he arrived at WorldCom in 1992 when the company acquired Advanced Telecommuncations Corp., where the thirty-year-old Sullivan was vice president and treasurer. Despite his youth, and even more youthful appearance, Sullivan was made CFO of WorldCom in 1994. He worked on so many acquisitions—seventeen in five years—that his alma mater, Oswego State University in upstate New York, hailed the *summa cum laude* grad from the class of 1983 as the "Master of the Mega Merger."

But Sullivan and Ebbers were an odd couple. They shared adjoining offices in Clinton, but not much else. Theirs was a pairing of convenience, like Oscar Madison and Felix Unger sharing a Manhattan apartment. Ebbers and Sullivan shared the same vision for WorldCom, but personally got along like chalk and cheese.

Ebbers was Oscar—brash and mercurial, with no patience for details. Sullivan was controlled and polite, with a love of numbers. Sullivan didn't like his boss, and he didn't like Clinton. He never moved there, commuting instead each week from his modest house in Boca Raton, Fla., where he lived with his wife, Carla, who was in chronic poor health. He bought a simple condo in Clinton as a crash pad, and rarely socialized with co-workers or other locals. Sullivan was a Yankee, and would never feel comfortable in Mississippi. Still, Sullivan wasn't looking to go anywhere. WorldCom offered an opportunity like no other company in the world. He was a key part of a team bent on building the largest telecommunications company in the universe, and that was well worth the discomforts of Clinton.

He had become a multimillionaire on paper thanks to stock options, but he still lived in a modest ranch house in Boca Raton, bought in 1990 for $170,000. He loved deep-sea fishing, but never bought anything bigger than an eight-foot-long Sea-Doo. (Ebbers, in a rare public display of his wealth, owned a sixty-foot, custom-built yacht that he named the *Aquasition*.)

But as any prudent numbers man would, Sullivan turned some of those paper millions into hard cash. According to *USA Today*, from 1995 to 2000, Sullivan sold 1.46 million shares, about 45 percent of his holdings, which netted him $45.3 million. The stock sales did not endear him to other company executives, however, least of all Ebbers, who seldom sold any shares because it would appear disloyal.

One evening, at a local steak house named Tico's, the normally cool Sullivan almost came to blows with another executive because of his stock sales. According to *USA Today*, Ebbers looked on in amusement as Sullivan tried to defend his sales while he'd been criticizing others for doing the same.

In 1997, Sullivan engineered the biggest merger in the history of corporate America. WorldCom made a bid to buy MCI, the third largest telecom in the world, which was triple the size of WorldCom. The deal was valued at $37.4 billion. MCI had been conducting merger talks with British Telecom, but Sullivan figured WorldCom could make a sweeter offer.

"I was convinced that we could unseat BT as the incumbent acquiring company to a position where they would not be able to bid against us," he told his college alumni magazine.

WorldCom made the unsolicited bid directly to MCI's shareholders, who jumped at the higher offer—especially since it was payable in WorldCom stock, which was still better than money.

The deal took months to pass muster with regulators, and there were plenty of critics, from Ralph Nader on up. They claimed it would be anti-competitive and would give the new company too much control over the internet. To get final approval, MCI had to sell off its internet business, but the merger was finally approved on September 15, 1998. WorldCom became the second largest tele-communications company in the U.S.

While regulators fussed over the proposed merger for most of 1998, Sullivan decided it was time to live a little. He bought a choice piece of lakefront property in Boca Raton, in the exclusive commu-nity of Le Lac, and started building a dream house for Carla and their adopted baby daughter. The five-building estate, complete with its own movie theater, boathouse, and pool, cost $15 million. Sulli-van still had about $30 million in cash, and still owned over 3.3 mil-lion shares of WorldCom, which ended the year at about $47, giving his shares a value then of over $155 million. He could have walked away from the company, sold his shares, and lived happily ever after.

But he continued making his depressing commute to Clinton each week, leaving his baby and sick wife, to toil long hours with the boss he couldn't stand. There were still deals to be made—including WorldCom's boldest move yet.

In 1999, when WorldCom stock hit its all-time high of $64.50, the company offered $129 billion for Sprint, its arch competitor. While the resulting company would still be smaller than AT&T, it would dominate many markets, especially in Europe.

The governments in the U.S. and Europe fought the deal. The U.S. Department of Justice opposed it on grounds that WorldCom sought to dominate the telecommunications market. The deal fell apart due to all the delays and uncertainty.

The music was now coming to a stop for WorldCom. There were no more big mergers in the offing; no targets were even in view. If WorldCom was going to make its stockholders happy now, it would have to make money the hard way—by earning it from its businesses, not just by acquisitions and nimble accounting. It had been a wild ride for WorldCom, but the party was starting to end.

12

The Biggest Bankruptcy in History

I still rate it a buy.
—Jack Grubman, stock analyst, Salomon Smith Barney

The first clue should have been all that telemarketing. There was a message behind those unsolicited telephone calls that began driving us crazy about a decade ago.

Outraged like everyone at the rude intrusions, which usually occurred at my cocktail time, I wrote an article about the telemarketing menace in *Forbes*, entitled "Whose Phone Is It Anyway?"

You buy the phone and pay dearly for the monthly service, then the phone company lets tele-hustlers pester you. The phone companies themselves pester you with their sales pitches, too. The old Ma Bell would never have tolerated such practices. The old Bell system was short on innovation, but long on customer relations.

Deregulation has its price. As telephone rates came down, telemarketers popped up like mushrooms over a cesspool. The phone

143

companies gave the telemarketers big discounts on their phone bills—which could only mean one thing. They had lots of idle capacity.

The second big tip-off was the advertising. Telecoms poured hundreds of millions of dollars into television, radio, and print advertising. The ads were great career enhancers for folks like Michael Jordan, James Earl Jones, and Jamie Lee Curtis, but the messages only confused and irritated customers. If you wanted the best deal on long distance, it seemed you had to change your phone company as often as your socks.

The mad scramble among telecoms for customers, and for each other, proved a bonanza for equipment suppliers. The telecoms all raced to add more high-tech capacity. They borrowed heavily, betting that future revenues would pay off the debts for adding new, highly efficient broadband and fiber-optic networks. Build the networks, it was assumed, and the traffic and profits would come. Fail to build them, and you will lose your customers to rivals who can offer cheaper rates.

Suppliers of telecommunications equipment like Lucent, Cisco Systems, Nortel, and others could barely keep up with equipment orders, and their stocks soared. In a single year, 2000, telecoms spent $275 billion on new equipment.

Where was all this money coming from? A lot of it came from a guy named Jack.

Jack Grubman, a security analyst at Salomon Smith Barney, was the unlikely godfather of the telecommunications industry. If he liked you, he would invite you into his club where billions could be borrowed or raised for the asking. If he *really* liked you, he helped put you in business from scratch, told you how the telecom game really worked, advised you on mergers and acquisitions, and even helped you hire people. Some of Grubman's clients were double dippers—they founded telecom networks, took them public, sold them, and started all over again.

With all those billions flying around, there were inevitably many millions that would stick to the fingers of the people closest to the money. That included the Wall Street firms that were doling out the cash—like Salomon Smith Barney—as well as the CEOs whose companies were borrowing it. In Grubman's playbook, your company did not have to succeed for you to become rich. All you had to do was be a customer of Salomon Smith Barney, and watch your timing.

With Grubman's help, SSB helped eighty-one telecoms raise $190 billion from 1996 to 2001, according to Thomson Financial Securities Data. All the swinging telecoms did business with Grubman—WorldCom, Qwest, Global Crossing, Winstar, Teligent, Rhythm Net Connections, Williams Communications, Focal, and many more.

The firm raked in hundreds of millions in banking and underwriting fees and tens of millions more for helping with mergers and acquisitions. Grubman was paid $20 million a year, unheard of for an analyst.

Why did the emerging telecoms give Grubman so much business? If you did business with SSB you could expect two things. The first was essential to your company's health and the value of your stock options: a glowing stock recommendation from Grubman. He was the most influential analyst in the telecom field and a "buy" rating from him propelled many a telecom stock into the stratosphere. A high stock price meant that it was a lot easier to raise more money and to buy out more of the competition—as Bernie Ebbers had been demonstrating since the early 1990s. The soaring stock prices also made many CEOs, directors, and other insiders multimillionaires.

The smart, or lucky, ones cashed out just as the telecom party was about to end. No one had more at stake than Philip F. Anschutz, the billionaire founder and chairman of Qwest Communications. He had made fortunes before, in oil and railroads, but his chunk of Qwest was the crown jewel. He owned 38 percent of the company, worth at one time over $10 billion. In the year 2000, *Forbes* pegged Anschutz as the sixth wealthiest person in America, worth a total of $18 billion.

Anschutz, who also owns the L.A. Kings hockey team, watched most of that wealth evaporate when the telecom bubble burst in 2000 and 2001. But not before he'd whisked a substantial pile of chips off the table. Just as WorldCom's Scott Sullivan thought it prudent to turn some of his WorldCom shares into hard cash in 1998, Anschutz began dumping his stock, and managed to pocket $1.9 billion from Qwest shares before they sank from a high of $63 in early 2000 to under $3 in late 2002.

To be sure, he left a lot more on the table. And as Qwest stock sank, those paper billions vanished. His fortune dropped from $18 billion in 1999 to $4.3 billion in 2002 because of Qwest's dive, costing him 76 percent of his nestegg. Anschutz enjoys the dubious honor of being both the biggest winner and loser in the telecom bubble. But shed no tears: Anschutz still ranks among the richest Americans, now ranking thirty-sixth instead of sixth. After all, $4.3 billion is still very serious money. (To put that in terms more familiar to the rest of us, that sum invested at only 5 percent would throw off $215 million a year, or $4.13 million a week.)

Anschutz wasn't the only one selling Qwest shares. So was his CEO—said to have been handpicked by Jack Grubman—Joseph P. Nacchio. He sold $227 million in stock before he was forced to resign.

Another big Grubman client, Gary Winnick, who founded Global Crossing, also managed to cash in before his company collapsed in bankruptcy. His stock sales netted him $734 million.

Below is a list of executives in the telecom world who netted at least $100 million from stock sales since 1999. Their companies include both telecoms and telecom equipment providers. Investors will recognize some of the companies as among the hottest stocks of the late 1990s. Now all of them have lost at least 75 percent of their value from their peaks. Nonetheless, their top people often made out very nicely indeed.

Allegiance Telecom: Former director Paul D. Carbery cleared $111 million from his stock sales.

Ariba: Former executive vice president Rob DeSantis walked off with $222 million from stock sales. Chairman Keith Krach netted $191 million, while the former top executives Paul Hegarty and Edward Kinsey raked in $127 million and $114 million respectively. They were hardly long-term investors; they began selling within five months of the company having gone public.

AT&T: Former director John C. Malone netted $340 million on his stock sales.

Broadcom: Co-chairman Henry Samueli netted $810 million while co-founder and CEO Henry Nicholas took home $799 million.

Cisco Systems: President and CEO John Chambers netted $223 million and Judith Lenore Estrin, former chief technical officer, took home $106.5 million. Seven other insiders netted from $29 million to $86 million.

Comverse Technology: Former chairman and CEO Kobi Alexander netted $122 million.

Exodus Communications: Former CEO and co-founder K. B. Chandrasekhar netted $131 million.

Foundry Networks: Bobby Johnson, CEO, netted $308 million.

Global Crossing: In addition to Gary Winnick (see above) seven other officers cashed in from $9 million to $118 million (including David Lee, the company's president).

JDS Uniphase: Fourteen company officials netted at least $10 million from stock sales. Joining the nine-figure club were former CEO Kevin N. Kalkhoven ($246 million), former CFO David E. Pettit ($199 million), and CEO Josef Strauss ($150 million).

McLeod USA: Richard A. Lumpkin netted $117 million, topping a list of 11 officers and former officers who cashed in at least $10 million each.

Metromedia Fiber Network: Former vice chairman Howard Finkelstein netted $104.5 million; five other officers netted at least $10 million.

Nextel: Part owner Craig McCaw netted $115 million and former CEO Daniel F. Akerson took in $113 million.

Qwest: Besides Anschutz ($1.9 billion) and Nacchio ($227 million), 11 other company officials netted at least $10 million.

It's nice to know that not every stockholder was wiped out in what *Fortune* called "the biggest wreck in corporate history."

We now enter into a gray area on Wall Street. When does a favor become a kickback? When is a lagniappe a bribe? In the wicked ways of Wall Street, such questions are never asked.

For years, investment bankers leaned on their stock analysts to award good ratings to the companies they did business with. Sophisticated investors and money managers knew that the analysts from the brokerage houses could become as giddy as schoolchildren when they wrote about their own clients in their research reports. Investors read the reports and peered at the numbers, but took the "buy" or "accumulate" recommendations with a grain of salt.

As long as no one seemed to be hurt by the practice, no one did anything to stop it. As a result it was rare to hear an analyst from a brokerage house issue a "sell" recommendation, least of all on one of its clients. In fact, a "sell" recommendation often meant the end of an analyst's career. Donald Trump reportedly had an analyst fired for trashing his casino stock, for example. There are many other examples of clients pressuring their bankers to chastise analysts who are even lukewarm about their stock.

Enter here CNBC, and its audience of unsophisticated investors who are not in on the joke. As the market kept rising in the nineties, so did CNBC's ratings. More Americans than ever were invested in stocks and funds and they tuned in for market news.

To pep things up, CNBC came up with a format that makes each trading day seem like the Kentucky Derby. Each morning begins with a pre-race show, where viewers are told where the action is likely to be in the market that day and what are the stocks to watch. Experts and CEOs are hauled onscreen to give their views, like jockeys and trainers and owners being interviewed before the big race. When the market opens at 9:30 a.m., the horses sprint out of the starting gate and all day long viewers are given running accounts of what stocks are doing well and which are lagging. Experts appear to explain why.

If the viewer wants in on the action, he can make bets with his own broker, or just click on to the station's website and open an account with a discount broker. It's simpler than Off-Track Betting.

It's fun to watch the market shows on CNBC, CNN, Fox, and elsewhere—as long as the market is rising. Dave Pullman, a retired security executive living in Cocoa Beach, Florida, started investing seriously in 1995 and listened closely to the stock tips offered on the market shows. He insisted that he always followed up with his own research, too, but I doubt it. He told me that he first heard of Cisco on TV, and it was one of his biggest gainers. So, too, JDS Uniphase, Amazon, and a slew of other high-tech stocks, which all skyrocketed. In 1999, he was closing in on seven figures in his portfolio and was thinking of buying another home.

Dave knew well, as every viewer did, the names of Abby Cohen of Goldman Sachs, Henry Blodget of Merrill Lynch, and Jack Grubman of SBS. They were the superstar analysts. What Dave did not know, as professional investors did, was that analysts could speak with forked tongues when it came to their own clients. But no one had bothered to clue in Dave or the millions of other newbie investors.

While CNBC's anchors constantly reminded viewers that analysts from the brokerage firms often had notoriously bad track records with their recommendations, viewers seemed to ignore that ugly fact. It was too much fun getting in on the latest dish, straight from the horse's mouth. CNBC showcased the hot analysts and a lot of viewers bet on their stock tips. Like Dave Pullman, those who bought and held on to the stocks got hammered. They are still waiting for the analysts to tell them when to sell.

Investment banks gave CEOs more than rave reviews in return for their business. As underwriters of new stock issues, or initial public offerings, the investment bankers had other goodies to dole out. They rewarded favored clients with hot IPO shares that usually took off as soon as they were issued to the public. Everyone wanted to buy those IPO shares, of course, but only a lucky few could. If you were a CEO shopping for investment banking business, you were one of the lucky ones.

The practice was called spinning and it was widespread. CEOs had come to expect hot IPO shares in return for their business. They bought the shares at offering prices, then quickly sold them to ravenous buyers on the open market, pocketing millions in profits.

If this sounds unfair or even illegal to you, it seemed at least newsworthy to the *Wall Street Journal,* which first reported the practice back in the mid-nineties. But despite several stories, nothing happened. The investment banking industry even defended itself, claiming that since the shares have to go to someone, why shouldn't they go to valued customers?

But at least one reader of the *Wall Street Journal* didn't think spinning was fair, and maybe not even legal. His name was Eliot Spitzer, who would later become attorney general of the state of New York. And he wouldn't forget about the practice of spinning, or the touting of client stocks by analysts. His day would come.

The collapse of the telecom business was brief and ugly. The seemingly insatiable demand for more telecommunications capacity slacked off into single digits. The need for more capacity by internet startups disappeared along with many of the new dot.coms that were once big customers. Telecoms that that had been blithely predicting 20 percent annual growth for a decade straight were stunned. Soon, they were very worried. Not nearly enough cash was coming in to cover expenses and debt service. Earnings disappeared. Stock prices plunged. They had the networks, but nobody came. Usage of the new fiber-optic networks averaged 3 percent in 2001, while price wars drove down rates. Business customers bargained hard for discounts, and got them. Residential users watched their rates drop from an average of about 35 cents per minute to as little as 10 cents.

There was no escaping the damage. All the telecoms were wobbly with debt, and their stocks plunged as their earnings dried up. In

Kenneth L. Lay, co-founder and former CEO and chairman of Enron, went down with his ship. But he kept unloading stock while urging employees to buy.

Photo © Ron Sachs/Corbis Sygma

Jeffrey K. Skilling, former CEO of Enron, suddenly quit in August 2001, just months before the bankruptcy. He blamed the collapse on a "a run at the bank."

Photo © Douglas Graham/Roll Call/Corbis Sygma

Home of Jeffrey Skilling in River Oaks, an exclusive suburb of Houston. The 9,000-square-foot spread is valued at $4 million.

Photo © F. Carter Smith/ Corbis Sygma

Sherron Watkins, an Enron VP, testifies at Senate hearing about her whistle-blowing memo to Kenneth Lay.

Photo © Martin Simon/Corbis SABA

Andrew Fastow, former Enron CFO, took the Fifth after being sworn in at a Senate hearing in early 2002. His special partnership deals spelled doom for Enron and himself.

Photo © Douglas Graham/RollCall/Corbis Sygma

Playboy's "Women of Enron" pose at "the crooked E" outside headquarters in Houston. The ex-Enronians are as bare as Enron's offices in the magazine's August 2002 issue.

Photo © Frank Casimiro/ Corbis Sygma

Bernard J. Ebbers, co-founder and former CEO of WorldCom, was no hayseed at making deals—more than sixty over a decade. Then the music stopped.

Photo © Philip Gould/Corbis

Scott D. Sullivan, former CFO of WorldCom, leaves a New York courthouse after posting bail on securities fraud charges.

Photo © Steven Hirsch/Corbis Sygma

Scott Sullivan's lakefront estate. The $15 million spread in Boca Raton, Florida, includes a small theater.

Photo © Carl Seibert/South Florida *Sun-Sentinel*/Corbis Sygma

Bernard J. Ebbers, Scott D. Sullivan, and telecommunications analyst Jack Grubman (*left to right*) are sworn in before a House committee probing WorldCom's accounting fraud in August 2002.

Photo © Ron Sachs/Corbis Sygma

Philip Anschutz, co-chairman of Qwest Communications, pocketed $1.6 billion from sales before the stock crashed.

Photo © Axel Koester/Corbis Sygma

Joseph P. Nacchio, former chairman and CEO of Qwest, cashed in stock worth $230 million before resigning due to stock slide and SEC probes.

Photo © James Leynse/Corbis SABA

Gary Winnick (*right*) former CEO and founder of Global Crossing Ltd., managed to unload $735 million of his stock before his company went bankrupt.
Photo © James Leynse/Corbis SABA

John J. Rigas, founder and chairman of Adelphia Communications, was charged with using the company as a "personal piggy bank" to the tune of $3 billion. Adelphia went bankrupt.
Photo © Kim Kulish/Corbis SABA

L. Dennis Kozlowski, ex-CEO and chairman of Tyco International Ltd., is shown here reaching into his own pocket for a change. He was charged with looting multimillions from Tyco.

Photo © Jason Grow/Corbis SABA

L. Dennis Kozlowski's oceanside mansion in Nantucket, valued at $15 million.

Photo © Steven Hirsch/Corbis Sygma

ImClone Systems founder and former CEO Sam Waksal outside Manhattan Federal Court after pleading guilty to thirteen counts of securities fraud.

Photo © Michael Appleton/Corbis Sygma

Martha Stewart, a friend of Sam Waksal, labeled insider-trading case against her as "ridiculousness" until the Feds hit her with securities fraud charges.

Photo © John Hryniuk/Corbis Sygma

Sanford Weill, chairman and CEO of Citigroup, agreed to keep analysts and bankers apart at its Salomon Smith Barney unit.

Photo © Noboru Hashimoto/
Corbis Sygma

Eliot Spitzer, New York State attorney general, announces that Merrill Lynch will pay a $100 million penalty for misleading investors with "tainted" stock research.

Photo © Steven Hirsch/Corbis Sygma

Stan O'Neal (*left*) president and COO of Merrill Lynch, and David H. Komansky, chairman and CEO, took Spitzer's medicine without a fight.

Photo © Steven Hirsh/Corbis Sygma

Stephen M. Case, CEO of AOL (*left*), Gerald Levin, CEO of Time Warner, and Ted Turner at the press conference announcing the big merger. All three are now history at the company.

Photo © Les Stone/Corbis Sygma

three years, they lost 95 percent of their stockholder value, a total of about $2 trillion. Half a million jobs were lost. Virtually every investor felt the pain, as the giant telecoms were all listed on the S&P 500. So even holders of index funds were whacked.

Global Crossing went bankrupt. Winstar and XO Communications and others went bankrupt. All the telecoms were reeling. All eyes now turned to mighty WorldCom. Yet during 2000 and 2001 the company seemed to be defying gravity. Its bottom line was still strong. Still strong, too, was the voice of Jack Grubman, who remained an avid cheerleader. While the industry was swooning in March of 2001, Grubman wrote in his "State of the Union" report: "We believe that the underlying demand for network-based services remains strong. In fact, we believe that telecom services as a percentage of GDP will double within the next seven or eight years."

Grubman remained bullish on WorldCom, too, and still rated it a "strong buy" all through 2001. He maintained that it had the best assets in the industry. Maybe so. But investors thought otherwise and started to hammer the stock as hard as the other telecoms, despite a rosier balance sheet.

Grubman did not change his recommendation on WorldCom until April 22, 2002, when the company cut its revenue goals for 2002. The stock had dropped to $4 from a high of $64.50. Grubman felt moved to reconsider his recommendation, and now rated World-Com a "neutral." Eight days later, on April 30, Grubman's good pal Bernie Ebbers resigned under pressure from his board. He still owed the company about $400 million, borrowed to meet margin calls on his stock. Everyone from the SEC on down to stockholders wanted to know how he had ever been able to swing such a loan.

The door to Jack Grubman's telecom club was crowded no longer. The last thing the telecoms needed was to add more capacity. Suppliers were equally devastated. The demand for new equipment dropped from $275 billion in 2000 to $190 billion in 2002, and wasn't expected to change much until at least 2006.

Telecom suppliers—which included developers of the newest technology—were hurt so badly that the chairman of the Federal

Communications Commission even came to their aid. In a speech in October 2002, Michael K. Powell urged telecoms to spend more money on new equipment in order to ensure the survival of companies like Lucent, Nortel Networks, and Cisco Systems. The telecoms, shy of cash but not new equipment, were not moved.

WorldCom was in worse shape than its suppliers. After the SEC began snooping around the books in April, and Bernie Ebbers departed under a cloud, the new CEO of the company, John Sidgmore, ordered his own internal audit. Sidgmore, who had earlier feuded with Ebbers and stepped aside from the company's daily operations, wanted to assure customers and investors that while the whole industry was suffering, WorldCom was still healthy. He could never have dreamed of what the auditors would find. WorldCom had not only been cooking its books, it had been roasting them.

On June 25, 2002, the company announced that it would have to restate its financial statements for the entire year of 2001 and the first quarter of 2002. On Wall Street "restating earnings" means, "My numbers were all wrong last time. Sorry about that." WorldCom had to admit that its statements for the previous five quarters were bogus.

It turned out that certain line costs were charged to capital accounts. Expenses were counted as income. The accountants found improper transfers of $3.055 billion for 2001 and $797 million for first quarter 2002. The swap from income to expenses meant that WorldCom actually lost money in 2001 and the first quarter of 2002.

Scott Sullivan, the chief financial officer, who had been promoted to executive vice president after Ebbers's departure, was immediately hauled on the carpet and fired. David Myers, senior vice president and controller, resigned. Things didn't look good for either of them.

They looked even worse a few weeks later after auditors found another $3.8 billion on the wrong side of the ledger sheet, making the fraud total over $7 billion. WorldCom earnings would have to be restated for the entire year 2000, as well as 2001 and the first quarter of 2002. The fraud had been going on since 1999, yet the company auditor, Arthur Andersen, had found nothing amiss.

Mississippi hadn't seen anything like it since the Yazoo Land Fraud in 1795. In that year land developers paid off crooked politicians in the Georgia legislature to buy most of what is now Louisiana and Mississippi for $500,000. Those culprits got away with it; the WorldCom crew would not. In August 2002, Scott Sullivan was charged with securities fraud, conspiracy to commit securities fraud, and five counts of filing false financial statements.

The revelation about the accounting fraud destroyed WorldCom and on July 21, the company filed the largest bankruptcy case in U.S. history. WorldCom, Ebbers's baby from the beginning, was broke. It listed its assets as $107 billion and its debts as $41 billion, but had a mere $200 million on hand as of Friday, July 19. The company listed bond debts at more than $52 billion, including $17.2 billion to J.P. Morgan Trust Company, $6.6 billion to Mellon Bank, and $3.3 billion to Citigroup. Other WorldCom lenders included J.P. Morgan Chase, Bear Stearns, Goldman Sachs, Deutsche Bank, Icahn & Co., and Morgan Stanley. It takes a lot of blue-chip players to pony up $52 billion of debt. But now WorldCom couldn't even pay the interest. The stock dropped to pennies a share.

Back in Mississippi, Bernie Ebbers refused to take any blame for the accounting fiasco. He told the congregation at the Easthaven Baptist Church that "no one will find me to have knowingly committed fraud."

Like Kenneth Lay at Enron, Ebbers has insisted on his innocence, but clammed up when hauled before Congressional committees. Both took the Fifth.

Reid Weingarten, Ebbers's attorney, indicated that Ebbers would be taking a dumb-dumb defense if charged. "When the investigation is done, there will not be a shred of credible evidence that Bernie Ebbers had a thing to do with those accounting decisions. Accounting decisions are arcane. They're mysterious for people who are not trained in the science. Bernie Ebbers certainly was not."

13

Gerald Levin:
When in Doubt, Merge

This is the worst acquisition in media history.
—Jessica Reif Cohen, media analyst with Merrill Lynch

On January 10, 2000, radio man Don Imus was kibitzing on the air as his sidekick, Charles McCord, delivered the morning news. McCord had just announced the news of the merger of AOL and Time Warner.

"What?" Imus huffed. It was as if he'd just heard that a dear friend had lost his marbles and run off with a crafty young golddigger. "You mean some little dot.com bought Time Inc.?"

Imus didn't even say Time Warner, just Time Inc., even though Time and Warner had merged a decade earlier. To people in the media, there never really was a Time Warner. The Warner part sold music and movies and television shows and books and had Bugs Bunny and a film library and was a very successful entertainment company.

Warner's merger with Time in 1990 created the largest media

company in the world, owning assets in excess of $20 billion. But so what? Critics claimed that Warner had no more business being grafted on to Time Inc. than an iron foundry. There was a lot of talk about synergy, but Warner people continued to run their show and Time people ran their show, and the two only really met at the bottom line.

The deal seemed to have made sense for only two people— Steven J. Ross, the head of Warner, who pocketed $75 million on the deal; and Jerry Levin, vice chairman of Time Inc., who had grand visions for himself and the new company. That perception was strengthened when Paramount made a hostile bid for Time after the Warner merger plan was announced. The Paramount deal was a better one for Time shareholders and employees, who would have received $200 a share for their stock, a total of $12 billion.

But thanks to Levin, the deal with Warner eventually happened anyway, but at a steep price. To ward off Paramount's bid, Time had to buy Warner, instead of merging. The new deal was great for Warner shareholders, including its top executives, but not for holders of Time shares. Instead of $200 a share, they got stock in the new company, which was $16 billion in debt after the merger. Many Time shareholders and employees never forgave Levin for denying them the chance to vote on the Paramount offer.

Steve Ross ran the new company, but not for long. Diagnosed with prostate cancer, Ross died in 1992, leaving the CEO chair up for grabs. A master at corporate politics, Levin outmaneuvered his chief rival, Nicholas Nicholas, and emerged as the chief executive.

Levin, who had been an early and enthusiastic supporter of the merger, saw cable TV as the common denominator of the two companies. By owning the pipes into people's homes, you could pump all kinds of content from Time and Warner into the homes of millions of captive customers.

But while Levin spent billions expanding cable TV operations, Wall Street yawned. Cable TV had lost its sizzle with investors, as costs per customer soared and complaints about pricing mounted. Competition was looming from phone companies and satellite TV.

Meanwhile, Time Warner was groaning under a heavy debt load from the merger and from further investments in cable.

For years after the merger, Time Warner stock went nowhere while the rest of the industry was feasting on the greatest bull run of the century. Pressure was mounting on Jerry Levin to get the stock moving. The pressure only intensified after an expensive experiment with interactive TV in Orlando, Florida, flopped badly. Orlando was an important trial run of Levin's vision for the future. The highly touted Full Service Network was unveiled in October 1993. Levin reported that the company planned to wire 4,000 homes with interactive access to 500 cable stations, via broadband cable. Customers could order up video games and movies on demand, browse multiple interactive shopping channels, do their banking, and glean the latest news and reference information from Time Warner sources at will. The hope was that Time Warner would eventually be able to bring the same five-hundred-channel access and interactivity to 100 million customers in the U.S., and perhaps hundreds of millions more around the world.

Levin believed strongly in the project and the company earmarked $5 billion for its development. "I've staked my career on it," Levin said.

But the project hit technical snags, and a year after its debut fewer than four hundred homes had been wired. Even by then it was obvious that the Full Service Network would be a very expensive alternative to something that was already taking over America—the internet. The internet provided users with a lot more information, games, shopping, and entertainment than the Full Service Network. And it was cheap. What about videos on demand? They would just have to wait.

Levin had to do something to keep his stockholders happy, and Ted Turner served up a golden opportunity. Levin sat on the board of Turner Broadcasting, since Time Warner owned 18 percent of the company. Levin often voted against some of Turner's more ambitious proposals for his cable network.

Levin, who had been a thorn in Turner's side on the TBS board, offered Turner a solution: sell out to Time Warner. Turner would still be able to run his show, but he would also have the vast resources of Time Warner behind him. He would become the largest single shareholder in the new company, with 3 percent of the company's stock. "I'm tired of being small," he said at the press conference announcing the merger in 1995. "I want to be big." There were anti-trust problems, but in the end the $6.5 billion deal was approved, on September 12, 1996.

Disney had purchased ABC; Rupert Murdoch was cobbling together the Fox network to expand his media empire; it appeared that Time Warner had pulled a coup. Time Warner was once again the largest media conglomerate in the world. But no huge purse went with the title—just more debt.

For a while, the stock got a good bump as the pundits buzzed once again about all those synergies. But the debt load soon pulled the stock back down again. It was clear that no matter how well the combined companies performed, the debt would be a drag on earnings for years to come and keep the stock price in the doldrums. There were other problems, too. Edgar Bronfman had bought a chunk of stock and his intentions were unclear. There were management problems at Warner. Some equity sales to strategic partners were causing headaches.

Then, in the year 2000, along came AOL, the sassy young beauty with the bedroom eyes. Time Warner, even with its debt problems, still looked awfully good to AOL, which was looking for some hard assets to buy with its bloated stock. It was selling at a preposterous multiple over its earnings; a result of the "irrational exuberance" investors felt about internet companies whose growth seemed boundless. AOL had 20 million internet customers and was by far the leading internet service provider in the world. It still had a lot of momentum. In fact, that was the reason for the astronomical price of the stock—the future. Its growth seemed boundless. All those customers—and all that advertising revenue. That was the dowry AOL promised.

Time Warner wasn't the only Daddy Warbucks that AOL pursued, however. Sumner Redstone, chairman and CEO of Viacom, told *USA Today* that he had been approached by AOL, too.

"What I said to them was that I didn't see the alleged synergistic advantages of marrying our brands to an internet company. And I don't trust their currency, either."

Time Warner, however, was blinded by the light. Steve Case met with Jerry Levin and a merger was discussed. With great fanfare on January 10, 2000, AOL and Time Warner announced "a strategic merger of equals to create the world's first fully integrated media and communications company for the Internet Century." Whatever that meant. The price of the merger—in AOL stock—was $165 billion. AOL shareholders wound up with one and a half shares of the new company for each AOL share they owned, while Time Warner shareholders received one share for each Time Warner share.

The new company certainly had an impressive bag of products and services to offer, including AOL, *Time,* CNN, CompuServe, Warner Bros., Netscape, *Sports Illustrated, People,* HBO, ICQ, AOL Instant Messenger, AOL MovieFone, TBS, TNT, Cartoon Network, Digital City, Warner Music Group, Spinner, Winamp, *Fortune,* AOL.com, *Entertainment Weekly,* Warner Book Group and Looney Tunes.

The new company predicted boldly that in its first year after the merger was approved, it would see a 30 percent jump in operating profit, to a total of $11 billion—$1 billion more than the two companies' previous projections. A lot of that new profit was going to come from internet advertising.

Still, to a lot of laymen, including Don Imus, the whole deal was strictly Looney Tunes. To help get a better understanding of what it all meant that morning in January, 2000, Imus called in one of the market experts from CNBC to help decipher it all. But try as Ron Insana did to explain why AOL was the major player in the deal, and what the new company hoped to accomplish, Imus remained unconvinced. Wall Street loved the deal, and the press was generally favorable, but it turned out Imus was on to something. "I still don't get it," he said.

The proposed merger was barely announced when the air began

whooshing out of the internet bubble in March 2000. The collapse of the dot.coms meant a steep drop in internet advertising.

But AOL seemed immune. In October 2000, AOL reported a 91 percent increase in quarterly earnings. Chairman Steve Case described AOL's vulnerability to the dot.com collapse as "only a few percentage points." Indeed, AOL somehow realized gains of over 80 percent in internet advertising revenue in each quarter of the year 2000. AOL, it seemed, was bulletproof.

On January 12, 2001, the marriage took place in Manhattan, and again company executives boasted of a $1 billion jump in earnings, to $11 billion the first year of the merger.

After only a few months, however, at least some executives wanted to back off the rosy projections. Advertising revenues, no matter how much massaging was done, were not going to come in anywhere near what had been projected. In July 2001, Chief Financial Officer J. Michael Kelly wanted to lower cash flow projections but was overruled.

About the same time, Jerry Levin told an advertising conference in Cannes, France, that advertising was stabilizing generally, and even growing at AOL. "There's no question there's an advertising slowdown that's very much affecting broadcast television and newspapers," he said. "But for us, we have several high-growth areas such as AOL, which we expect to grow at a healthy pace."

Either Levin remained in the dark about AOL's problems with ad revenue, or he was fibbing in the hopes of a quick rebound. In either case he was dead wrong.

AOL was getting gored just as badly as the rest of the industry and had been employing questionable accounting methods to make the numbers look better than they were. There is always leeway in accounting for advertising income, but AOL had stretched it to the limit.

In January 2002, AOL Time Warner reported that it had failed to realize its promised $1 billion gain in profit after the first year of the merger. In fact, profits had dropped from $10 billion to $9.65 billion. Six months later, the company owned up that advertising revenue at AOL had dropped 40 percent from the previous year. Shareholders were up in arms as the stock nose-dived. By January 2002, the price of the stock had dropped 80 percent from the date the deal was first announced two years earlier.

No one was more put out than the largest shareholder in the company, Ted Turner. Turner had been virtually fired from the new company by Levin, and was hurt and angry that he had lost control of his own network. In an article by Ken Auletta in *The New Yorker*, Turner recalls the words Levin used to fire him. After telling Turner that TBS would no longer report to him, Levin added, "Sorry Ted, but you lose your vice-chairman title as well."

Turner was stunned. He was the largest shareholder, yet had no say in the company?

"The way it was handled was really shocking," Jane Fonda told Auletta. "It makes me mad. How dare they give him a phone call!"

But Turner did not go off and count his buffalo. As the stock fell like an anvil, he began to bellow louder and louder. He was down billions of dollars and he wanted Levin's scalp.

On December 5, 2001, Jerry Levin had suddenly announced his resignation, effective the following May. Levin was sixty-three and said he wanted to step down and put some poetry in his life. He alluded to the grisly murder of his son Jonathan, a teacher killed by one of his students four years earlier. Levin still needed to reflect on that, he said, and on the events of September 11, 2001, and many other things.

Was Levin asked to resign by the board? Did Turner succeed in getting him fired, the way he had been fired?

According to Nina Munk's account in *Vanity Fair*, Turner banged on the boardroom table and screamed for Levin's head at the fall board meeting. Anyone who has dealt with Turner knows how likely it is that he did throw a fit and blame Levin for the stock's collapse. The question remains: Did the board agree with him?

But whether the board pushed him out or he jumped by himself, Levin was gone and few mourned his departure. He did not depart a poor man, despite the fact that the stock had tanked. According to

Forbes, Levin's total compensation for the preceding five years was $209 million. Plus, he had a cushy retirement package and picked up another $1 million a year as a consultant.

At the annual meeting on May 12, 2002, Levin was onstage at the Apollo Theater in Harlem for his final day of employment at the company for which he'd worked thirty years.

Levin was not standard Time issue. He wasn't a WASP who once edited an Ivy league newspaper. His father didn't belong to any clubs. He was the son of an immigrant grocer from suburban Philadelphia, who studied biblical literature at Haverford before going to law school at the University of Pennsylvania. He became a Wall Street lawyer, then worked abroad in Iran and Colombia as a consultant on agricultural projects.

He became involved in cable TV as an investor, and helped create Home Box Office. It was his idea to use satellites to tie stations into HBO, instead of expensive microwave transmission. When Time bought the company, Levin wound up in charge of HBO. It was then a backwater operation and Time executives ignored Levin. The CEO of the company, Andrew Heiskell, reportedly said he was "a snake oil salesman."

Yet Levin had outfoxed them all, and survived to put together the world's largest media and entertainment company. And as his last hurrah he had just hammered together "the world's first fully integrated media and communications company for the Internet Century." Whatever that was.

Stockholders were not impressed, and they spoke up at the annual meeting. "These are our hard-earned dollars that we trusted to you, and you have decimated us," said one. (He'd done worse than that. "Decimate" means reducing something by one tenth. The stock was off much more than that.) Another shareowner complained about the money being spent on a new corporate headquarters in Manhattan that he called "the Taj Mahal on Columbus Circle."

Levin did not take questions, leaving the new CEO, Ralph Parsons, and Chairman Steve Case to face the music, and left the podium after delivering his farewell remarks. Ever the diplomat, Levin thanked his family, his wife of thirty-two years, Barbara, the board, present and former executives, and the company's employees. He asked shareholders for "faith, hope, and above all, patience."

As Levin walked offstage, the audience fell into an embarrassing silence until Jesse Jackson and a few others stood and applauded. But some shareholders never left their seats. They were too weighted down with their losses.

"It's a sad ending," said Jessica Reif Cohen, a media analyst with Merrill Lynch. "But this is the worst acquisition in media history, given the decline in market value of AOL," she told the *Los Angeles Times.*

It appears AOL Time Warner stockholders will have to be very patient, indeed. In the months that followed Levin's resignation, more ugly details about AOL's accounting surfaced. SEC probes were launched about advertising revenues. Earnings had to be restated. Massive write-downs were taken. The stock slipped even more.

There were other damaging disclosures. It turned out that during the year 2001, Chairman Steve Case sold $475 million worth of his stock. Chief Operating Officer Bob Pittman had sold stock worth $225 million and Jim Barksdale, a director, sold $217 million in stock. The rice had barely been swept from the church steps before they were dumping shares.

Since these sales occurred in the months immediately following the merger, they did little to cheer shareholders and analysts. Especially since the company had maintained that it would have a 30 percent gain in earnings that first year, which never materialized. Even *Fortune* magazine, which is owned by the new company, had to rate Case, Pitttman, and Barksdale high among the year's "Greedy Bunch."

Did the AOL crowd know something the rest of the investing world didn't—that the AOL bubble was about to pop? According to a research report published by Merrill Lynch in September 2002, the value of the world's leading internet service, AOL, had dropped

92 percent since the announcement of the merger. Yet the value of the Time Warner assets—the cable TV, the music, and movie studio, the magazines, etc.—had remained relatively stable. AOL Time Warner has too many good parts to fail, but whether those parts will ever mesh together to satisfy some grand vision remains to be seen.

But Jerry Levin's legacy is spelled out in three letters—AOL.

"In retrospect, I wish the AOL deal had never happened," John Malone told *USA Today*. Malone, a major shareholder, had seen the value of his stake in the company drop $10 billion from the date of the announcement through mid-year 2002. "He [Levin] got caught up a little bit in the hype, as we all did."

Other critics were much less forgiving. Michael Fuchs, former chief of HBO and Warner Music, who was fired by Levin in 1995, blamed the fiasco on Levin's ego.

"He's been a great actor on the corporate stage," Fuchs told *USA Today*. "He was a genius at survival and manipulation. He was hell-bent on being the visionary in the new age. He went completely solo on this deal so it would be the capstone of his career and reputation. Unfortunately, it was the opposite. He rolled the dice with everyone's equity, savings, and net worth and lost."

Few corporations in the U.S. get more press coverage than AOL Time Warner. It's partly because the media finds itself so fascinating it can't stop covering itself. It's also because of the volatility and widespread ownership of the stock.

But there is another reason, too. Tens of millions of Americans buy and trust Time, Inc. publications. They relate personally to the company. They don't want anyone messing around with their magazines.

At its peak, in the 1950s, 1960s and 1970s, no other magazine publishing company in the world equaled Time in revenues, readers, advertisers, or influence. It was successful, powerful, admired, and on the side of the gods.

Like most young journalists in New York City, I envied the writ-

ers and editors I knew at *Time, Fortune, Life,* and *Sports Illustrated.*
They were brighter, more talented, better educated, better paid, and
usually better looking than the ink-stained wretches commonly
found at most newspapers and magazines. What's more, the company was run by former and current writers and editors, not people
from the advertising side, as is common with most publishing companies.

You could trust what you read in a Time Inc. publication. Sometimes the facts might be stacked in odd ways, but you knew that the
facts were right. Fact checkers verified every detail in every story.
Writers and editors labored over wording that was precise as well as
colorful. There was a premium on accuracy and a respect for language that set standards in journalism.

Hurley's saloon, on the corner of Sixth Avenue and Forty-ninth
Street, was a short sprint from the Time-Life building, and it was
there I met a *Time* book reviewer named Alwyn (Harry) Lee in the
late sixties.

He was an Australian journalist, author, and poet who had earned
awards as a correspondent during World War II when he went
ashore with the U.S. Marines at Iwo Jima and lived to be the first to
write about it.

But Harry came to *Time* to review books and write stories about
literary trends and authors, and his skills were up to it. He quoted
poetry as part of his normal speech. When in his cups, which was
often, he would speak for hours at a time in rhyming couplets. He
was infused with James Joyce, "taking to tavern and to brothel/the
mind of witty Aristotle."

Standing erect at the bar, wearing his fedora at a rakish angle, he
would tell stories about John Updike and Ernest Hemingway and
William Faulkner and Anthony Burgess, all of whom he knew.

Harry had the *Time* swagger, but paid for it dearly. He would
come into Hurley's on closing nights, where he waited for his editors
to work on his reviews. A half-dozen scotches and a pack of Camels
later he would get a call to go back to the office to review the final
version.

After I got to know Harry he would show me the flimsies of his original copy. The reviews were usually brilliant, but the length and style were totally inappropriate for *Time*. *Time*'s book reviews filled a few column inches at best. Harry wrote six or seven double-spaced sides of copy, more suited to the *New York Review of Books*. He would return to Hurley's clutching copy that had been cut and rewritten into something unrecognizable and have a few more scotches.

One night I asked him why he wrote such long, well-crafted reviews when he knew there was only a few inches of space available for it.

"Because that's the way I write," he said. "That's what they pay me for."

Yet Harry was determined to have one of his reviews run just as he had written it. He was assigned to review a book called *The Naked Ape*, by Desmond Morris. Harry wrote his review in the form of a sonnet.

He was giddy that night in Hurley's after he'd submitted his copy. It consisted of fourteen lines of iambic pentameter, in the appropriate rhyme scheme of the Shakespearean sonnet, *ababcdcdefefgg*. It was a masterpiece—concise, funny, apt.

For hours Harry reveled in the agony his editors must have been going through. They could barely change a word of his text without ruining the rhythm or the rhyme scheme of the sonnet. Hours went by and finally Harry was summoned to see the final version.

It was the world's only twelve-line Shakespearean sonnet. Harry's editors had managed to lop two lines from the poem, just to show who was boss. Harry was delighted. He had created a new form of the sonnet, and the language was all his, every word, and it appeared in *Time* magazine.

Fast forward to 1998, and it was a good thing Harry was no longer around to see what had happened to *Time* under the leadership of Jerry Levin. Synergy now counted more than accuracy.

In June 1998, the company launched a new weekly TV magazine show called *NewsStand: CNN Time*. The new show was intended to promote *Time* and to rebuild CNN's sagging viewership, which had dropped an alarming 12 percent since 1993. The new weekly TV show would be yoked to magazines like *Time, Fortune,* and *Entertainment Weekly.* The magazines would steer readers to CNN, while CNN would steer viewers to *Time* and the other company publications. Synergy in action.

Rick Kaplan, the president of CNN and the driving force behind the new magazine program, wanted a blockbuster story to kick off the series. Kaplan, formerly a producer at ABC who had run afoul of the facts before while producing TV news shows, decided to make his debut with a Vietnam War story. The story was very old, very nasty, and very, very wrong.

Jeff Greenfield, one of the show's anchors, stated its premise simply: "CNN and *Time,* after an eight-month investigation, report that the United States military used lethal nerve gas during the Vietnam War."

In tandem with the TV report, *Time* published a 2,000-word article entitled "Did the U.S. Drop Nerve Gas?" One of the bylined writers was Pulitzer winner Peter Arnett of Gulf War fame, though he later claimed he had very little to do with the reporting.

The story claimed that U.S. forces operating in Laos during Operation Tailwind in 1970 had used a lethal nerve gas called sarin to kill not only enemy solders, but also to kill American GIs who had defected from the battlefield. This was explosive stuff. The use of nerve gas is a war crime under international law. And here the U.S. military was using it on our own troops.

The show had immediate repercussions. The Pentagon denied the use of the nerve gas at any time, and veterans of Operation Tailwind were up in arms at the allegation. CNN's own military analyst, Perry Smith, a former major general who had served in Vietnam, called the report "sleazy journalism" and quit the network in protest.

Investigations were called for. (In ordinary journalism, investigating is done *before* a story is made public. It's called reporting. But this was the new CNN/*Time* journalism, where you don't let the facts get in the way of a good story. You run with it and worry about the consequences later.)

At first, the suits in charge circled the wagons and defended the story. But as doubts of its accuracy grew, CNN hired the noted lawyer Floyd Abrams to conduct an investigation. Again, why in the name of Henry Luce did they wait until after the story was published and telecast to find out the facts? Abrams's findings were devastating. In his sixty-page report he concluded there was insufficient evidence to support the accusation that nerve gas was ever used, or that American defectors were targeted, or that Americans were even in the Laotian camp. In short, the story was sleaze, just as Perry Smith said.

Time and CNN then retracted the story, which is the ultimate disgrace in journalism. It's worse than restating earnings. "CNN alone bears responsibility for both the television reports and for the printed article in the June 15 issue of *Time* magazine," said Tom Johnson, head of CNN. "We apologize to our viewers and to our colleagues at *Time* for this mistake." *Mistake?* It was a bloody outrage.

There was no apology offered to the U.S. forces involved in Operation Tailwind, who had been accused of using killer gas to snuff out their own comrades.

I thought then about Harry, and how much *Time* had changed. As a correspondent who had trudged through the real horrors of war, and as a lifelong *Time* writer who treasured its respect for the printed word, Harry would have tossed his scotch into the faces of Johnson, Kaplan, and Levin.

Thus it was that this great experiment in journalistic synergy shamed a great magazine and a highly respected news network. Heads rolled, starting at the bottom. The TV show was eventually cancelled; CNN has yet to recapture its audience or its credibility. *Time* still wears a black eye from the fiasco.

Ted Turner, who founded and built CNN into the world's best news network, was horrified.

"I couldn't hurt any more if I were bleeding," he said. "If committing suicide would help, I've even given that some consideration."

AOL Time Warner is not about to crumble, however. The reshuffling of management gave control of its future to people from the old Time Inc. part of the company. Let's hope they never forget Tailwind, or the likes of Harry Lee.

14

Dennis Kozlowski:
Takeout from Tyco

The point is that you can't be too greedy.
—Donald Trump

At some point between graduating from school and becoming CEO of a vast conglomerate, L. Dennis Kozlowski did something to his name.

He was Dennis Leo Kozlowski at West Side High School in Newark, New Jersey, from which he graduated in 1964. He was still Dennis L. when he got his accounting degree from Seton Hall University in South Orange, New Jersey, in 1968.

But by the time he became CEO of Tyco International Corp. in 1992, it was L. Dennis Kozlowski on his business card. Perhaps he thought it sounded better, but he needn't have bothered. Now his name is mud, no matter what the order of his first and middle names. He will always be remembered as that guy Kozlowski with the $6,000 shower curtain, who was charged with stealing $600 million from his company.

The man whose name became synonymous with corporate greed—and whose picture ran on the front page of the *New York Post* with the headline "Oink, Oink"—started off humbly enough. Though he would one day throw around Tyco's money like confetti, money was scarce in his youth.

He grew up in Central Newark, New Jersey, where his family had a home on South Nineteenth Street. It was a working-class neighborhood in transition, as the population of Italian, German, and Polish families was supplanted by Hispanics and blacks. Kozlowski's father, Leo, had been a minor-league baseball player with the old Newark Bears, a Yankee farm team. He never made it to the majors and gave up baseball to become a cop and eventually a detective in Newark.

Dennis's mother, Agnes, was a school crossing guard when her three children, Dennis, Joyce, and Joan, were youngsters, and later worked as a claims investigator with the New Jersey Dept of Consumer Affairs.

Dennis was tall, reaching 6'3", and was a good athlete at West Side High, where he starred in basketball. But he was hardly up to the near-pro caliber of the players on the Seton Hall roster and he never played college ball. In fact, he was something of a ghost at the school. In his four years, his name never appeared in the school paper. That would change.

He lived at home and commuted to college each day, working nights, weekends, and summers to pay his tuition. Besides playing in a band, he worked as a waiter.

In later years, Kozlowski liked to tell the story about his days waiting on tables and the lesson it taught him. At one of the restaurants where he worked the custom was to pool tips. But Kozlowski balked at sharing what he'd made. He hustled harder than all the others did and wanted to keep his own tips, so he quit. A man had to have an incentive, he insisted, in order to work harder. He would later use that story to illustrate why he rewarded Tyco managers with big incentive bonuses for meeting or exceeding goals. You have to reward the best people, he insisted.

The photo in his college yearbook shows an intense young man with a thin, oval face, hooded eyes, and stringy blond hair. Instead of the traditional suit jacket, he's wearing a loud plaid sport coat, one he likely wore for his weekend job playing guitar in a wedding band. You can almost see him strumming the "Hokey Pokey."

After college, Kozlowski toyed with becoming an airline pilot. He had taken flying lessons and become licensed, but the airlines weren't hiring. So he shopped his new accounting degree across the Hudson River in Manhattan. He became an auditor with SCM Corp., working on mergers and acquisitions. SCM was one of the last of the old-style conglomerates—corporations that owned everything from pizza parlors to communications networks. He didn't like working for a large corporation, but he did learn a thing or two about how to evaluate a company, and how best to account for mergers and acquisitions. That knowledge would serve him well after a headhunter recruited him in 1976 to work for a small holding company called Tyco, up in Exeter, New Hampshire. It was a fledgling conglomerate of sorts, and the young accountant was given a lot more to do than pore over ledgers. Pretty soon he would be asked to help run some of the businesses that Tyco purchased.

Kozlowski hadn't studied much about management, and so he enrolled in nearby Rivier College, in Nashua, New Hampshire. His entry in *Who's Who* claims Kozlowski earned a master's degree in business administration in 1976. But Rivier's director of college relations informed me that he took only three courses in 1977, and he was never enrolled in a degree program.

MBA degree or not, Kozlowski enjoyed being the man in charge, instead of just looking at numbers. He told *Barron's*: "There's nothing like running a business unit and having the daily pressures of building sales and market share, developing new products, controlling costs, collecting receivables, reading inventories, and managing working capital. I highly recommend such a grounding in the real world for anyone who aspires to run a company one day." Very puffy stuff. He was really after the money.

Kozlowski moved up the ranks as the corporation continued to be a small but clever player in the merger and acquisitions game. Tyco's CEO at the time was Joe Gaziano, who was always on the prowl to find companies that fit his mix of properties. But if he happened upon vulnerable prey that was out of the mix, he wasn't above greenmailing the company. "Greenmail" is a legal form of blackmail in which company "A" buys a sizable chunk of stock in company "B," then threatens to make a hostile bid for the rest of the company unless "B" coughs up a fat premium to buy back its stock.

Gaziano didn't shy away from hostile takeovers, even though they can be nasty as well as risky. In 1981, Gaziano tapped Kozlowski to fix one company he had acquired in a hostile takeover, Ludlow Plastics Corp. Kozlowski never forgot what it was like.

"It turned out to be a terribly difficult experience because the ill will and rancor of the takeover battle drove many of the good people we wanted and needed out of the company and it took much longer than it should have to put the pieces together again at Ludlow," he told *Barron's*.

Kozlowski decided then and there that hostile takeovers were not worth the trouble or expense. When he became CEO himself in 1992 and became known as Deal-a-Month Dennis, he avoided hostile takeovers. He was fond of repeating the old saw that most acquisitions fail, and most of the time it's because of a lack of due diligence. That means really knowing what you are buying.

In a hostile takeover, the target company will conceal its financial secrets, which can lead to very nasty surprises later. However, if the target agrees to being taken over, he will gladly open his books and auditors can do a much more thorough job of due diligence. Kozlowski's handpicked team of auditors and investigators not only pored over the books, they visited plant sites, interviewed employees, and checked inventories. Kozlowski never bought a pig in a poke.

There was another practical reason he preferred friendly takeovers: management. In a friendly takeover, managers will usually stick around, even if they are a bit shell-shocked, to see what will happen to them. Kozlowski would pick their brains for ideas while he kept a sharp eye out for talent lower in the ranks. When the pink slips were handed out, it was usually the senior executives who got them. In their stead, Kozlowski elevated younger, hungrier managers and promised them fat bonuses for meeting tough goals. Older managers were bought off. In most cases the young Turks proved their mettle. Kozlowski especially liked to elevate men with his own working-class background—the kind of guys who don't like to pool tips.

He always disliked paperwork, and would stage a little demonstration every once in a while at the offices of a new acquisition. He would line up trash carts outside all executive offices and have the staff toss out every unread proposal and memo. The carts would soon be full. The point was made. Even when he headed Tyco at its peak, he rarely read or sent a memo, and he kept his staff lean. Fewer than one hundred people made up the corporate staff, which ran businesses that ultimately operated in some eighty countries with some 250,000 employees.

When Tyco completed an acquisition, heads would roll. Lowering costs by lopping off heads may have seemed cruel, but, hey, that was the way to look good in a hurry. When Tyco acquired ADT, the giant security company, Kozlowski cut 1,000 of 8,000 jobs. After another big acquisition, AMP, he chopped 8,000 of 48,000 workers. The bloodshed came quickly; most firings were carried out within a month of the deal, which gave an immediate jolt to Tyco's earnings. Kozlowski claimed that laying off employees was the "crummiest" part of being a CEO, but "if you don't do it your competition is going to."

It's an old argument, but it has its flaws. It presumes the target company is overstaffed to begin with. Maybe so, but eventually you will need to hire new talent in order for the company to grow. It's expensive to attract and train bright people who might otherwise shy away from a company with a reputation for laying off so many people. But those costs don't appear until long after an acquisition is made.

Back in 1984, Kozlowski ran the automatic sprinkler system division of the Grinnell Corp., which was owned by Tyco, and he turned it around. In two years, the company's profits rose from zero to $15 million, and revenues rose from $185 to $255 million. Top management took notice.

His CEO at Tyco in the late 1980s was John Fort, and when he set out on a buying binge Kozlowski was at his elbow as chief operating officer. It may have appeared that Fort's acquisitions had little in common, except that they were all pretty boring companies. There were no high-tech or internet or entertainment companies on Tyco's shopping list. (Tyco Toys, by the way, has nothing to do with Tyco International.)

Tyco stuck to a basic four-part menu: flow control products (water, gas, etc.); electrical and electronic components; fire alarms and security systems; and disposable and specialty products. Tyco wasn't so much a conglomerate as it was a loose linkage of four different businesses. The aim was to become the most profitable in each of those businesses, around the world.

The four-part harmony meant that Tyco could be a lot more aggressive in making acquisitions than old-style conglomerates like ITT and LTV. No matter how large an acquisition, only one part of the company would be affected at a time. Each of the four pythons had time to digest its pig before another meal came along.

In 1992, Kozlowski got the call he had been waiting for, to come to New York and meet with the board of directors. It must have been a grand moment for the forty-six-year-old, once again walking those Manhattan streets he'd walked twenty years before when he was an auditor at SCM. Perhaps he strolled over to the West Side and peered across the Hudson toward Newark, a grimy smudge on the horizon where planes buzzed over Newark Airport like flies over a carcass.

Whatever was on his mind distracted him so much that as he crossed Lexington Avenue he tripped on the sidewalk and crashed to the gutter. Perhaps reflecting his mood, he'd been walking along merrily with his hands in his pockets, so he couldn't break his fall to the pavement. Passersby helped him to his feet and called a cab to take him to the hospital, where he was diagnosed with a separated shoulder.

After the doctors popped the shoulder back in place, Kozlowski continued on to the boardroom, hours late for the meeting. "Do I still get the job?" he asked when he finally arrived. Indeed he did, and Tyco was about to embark on its wildest ride.

By this time he was known as L. Dennis Kozlowski, instead of Dennis L., and he was no longer struggling to make tuition bills. He was getting rich, and would become a lot richer, and began to indulge himself. He flew his own plane and company helicopter, and had a garage full of Harley Davidson motorcycles, which he liked to ride without wearing a helmet.

An avid sailor who used to skipper boats in the Bermuda Cup races, Kozlowski bought the legendary yacht *Endeavor*, a 130-foot J class boat built in the 1930s. The yacht, a restored antique, cost about $20 million, or $154,000 a foot. Kozlowski delighted in inviting friends aboard for sailing parties out of Nantucket, where he had vacation homes. Nantucket had become the favored playground of a number of Yankee CEOs, including GE's Jack Welch, whom Kozlowski greatly admired and hoped to surpass. (Author's note: I tried to get Welch to comment on Kozlowski and some of the other disgraced CEOs in this book, but he declined.)

He became active in island fund-raising and charity events and was a generous donor. He also bought a winter palace in Boca Raton, and became part of the social set there, always ready with a checkbook for a worthy cause, always willing to show up at an event. Wherever he went, he was selling. Or, more often, offering to buy.

Kozlowski didn't need a nest of investment bankers hovering about to come up with acquisition targets. His own staff was pretty good at that. His in-house team of six merger specialists combed over 1,000 possible acquisitions a year, and prided themselves on their due diligence and ability to close deals faster than investment bankers, and at a lot lower cost.

Kozlowski was a walking dealmaker who wouldn't hesitate to let a CEO know if Tyco was interested in buying his company. He liked to approach CEOs directly himself to make deals whenever he could. He put a bee in the bonnet of the management of U.S. Surgical in the mid nineties, and a few years later, management decided to call Tyco and a deal was done.

One merger evolved from his daughter's friendship with a Middlebury College classmate. The father of the classmate worked for a leveraged buyout firm that owned a company Kozlowski wanted. So he made a call to the partner and within a few months the deal was done.

As he reached the rarefied air of top corporate management, Kozlowski took a renewed interest in his old alma mater, Seton Hall. He joined the Board of Regents in 1991, and became a big booster of the school's athletic program as well as a contributor to the alumni scholarship fund building project. His donation of $5 million for a new classroom building was hefty enough to warrant a nameplate. In 1997, the university opened Kozlowski Hall with a dedication ceremony that must have brought tears to his eyes—and maybe a splinter of glass, too.

As part of the ceremony, Kozlowski and his family were to have been presented a large, framed picture of the new building that, in the words of the chancellor, "will bear his family name, and so for many decades, and perhaps centuries to come, his dedication will be known." But as another dignitary was making remarks during the ceremony, a gust of wind blew the picture from the stand, shattering the glass frame.

The chancellor, Rev. Thomas R. Peterson, tried to make the best of the incident, but it proved an ill omen nonetheless. It turned out that Dennis Kozlowski had no more right to have his name on that building in the photo than did anyone else who worked at Tyco International Corp. The donation came from the pockets of Tyco shareholders, not Dennis Kozlowski. But that, and other ugly details of Kozlowski's casual use of the company checkbook, would only surface later.

Kozlowski was also inducted into the school's Athletic Hall of Fame, although he had never donned a Pirate uniform. He shared the honors that year with former Seton Hall basketball coach P. J. Carlesimo, who led the Pirates to within one point of winning the national championship in 1989.

Sadly, Kozlowski was not the first infamous Seton Hall alumnus and benefactor to bring embarrassment to the university. Robert J. Brennan (see Chapter One) was likewise a member of the board of regents and a major fund-raiser and donor. In his prime, Brennan had a very high profile, thanks to all the TV ads he made for his First Jersey Securities Corp, a glorified bucket shop. In the TV ads that he starred in, Brennan urged investors to "come grow with us." First Jersey became notorious for pumping penny stocks and was the subject of several major articles in *Forbes* magazine, which led to federal investigations. In 2001 Brennan was ultimately convicted of money laundering and bankruptcy fraud and was sentenced to nine years in prison. Afterwards, the Robert E. Brennan Recreation Center at Seton Hall was quietly renamed, but Kozlowski Hall remains. When you're a struggling school in the shadow of Newark, you can't be too choosy about your benefactors.

The shattering of the picture frame at the dedication foretold bad luck for Kozlowski, but it would be a while in coming. For the next few years, he was riding high. Wall Street had caught on to Tyco, and liked the growth thing. As long as Tyco was making all those acquisitions, its earnings and revenues were growing by upwards of 30 percent a year, and the stock reflected it. Wall Street gave the stock a little extra sheen because Tyco was no longer domiciled in the U.S.

When the company acquired ADT in a reverse merger in 1997, Tyco wound up being headquartered in Bermuda. As an offshore corporation, it didn't have to pay taxes on business operations outside the U.S. The change of address cut its tax from 36 percent to 25 percent. By 2000, the company was saving about $500 million a year in taxes by being based on the island, which has a zero tax rate. It's also a nice spot for annual meetings.

Late in 1999, Tyco announced its biggest acquisition to date— AMP Corp., the world's biggest maker of electronic connectors. The price was $11.3 billion in stock, topping a rival bid by AlliedSignal, which had offered $9.8 billion. But Kozlowski made it clear the party wasn't over. He made dozens of additional acquisitions in 2000 and 2001, culminating in the $9.2 billion purchase of CIT Group, Inc., the largest independent commercial finance company in the nation.

Though most people still thought Tyco was a toy maker, it had become one of the largest corporations in the world, worth more than $90 billion. It was bigger than Ford, General Motors, and Daimler Chrysler combined. *Business Week* ranked Tyco at the very top of its list of the fifty best performing companies.

Kozlowski was feeling his oats, and was exhibiting visions of grandeur. In early 2001, he spoke of a five-year plan to spend another $50 billion on acquisitions, while still showing 25 percent annual growth in earnings. That kind of growth is scary—the company would double in size every thirty-two months. Tyco would have become the biggest corporation in America in just a few years.

"Hopefully, we can become the next General Electric," Kozlowski bragged to *Business Week*. He said that he wanted to be remembered as "some combination of what Jack Welch put together at GE . . . and Warren Buffett's very practical ideas on how you go about creating return for shareholders."

Putting himself in the same league with Welch and Buffett was quite a stretch. Tyco's stock had risen to $53 a share in May 2001, from about $12 at the start of 1997. But Wall Street valued the company at only 18 times expected earnings, while it awarded General Electric a multiple of 38, more than double that of Tyco. One reason for the huge difference was Jack Welch, who had an astounding twenty-year record at GE. He had put together the largest corporation in the country, and the most admired. The stock had risen from about $2 a share to a high of about $60 under Welch. And GE's products and assets were a lot more glamorous than Tyco's pipes and valves and surgical products and electrical connectors and garbage bags and security systems. GE owned NBC; it made jet turbines and huge generators; it had a huge finance company; its logo was in everyone's kitchen.

There was another reason Wall Street valued Tyco at less than half the multiple of GE. There was a cloud over the company's accounting. In late 1999, an accounting analyst named David W. Tice alleged that the company was using accounting legerdemain to goose Tyco's earnings.

Kozlowski was furious at the allegation, and pointed out in a conference call with analysts that Tice's company was a short-seller, meaning it made money on falling stocks, not rising ones. But Tice's allegations were noted by SEC Commissioner Arthur Levitt, who was a severe critic of shady accounting practices. He sent in his own bloodhounds.

Tice's allegations and the SEC probe hammered Tyco's stock even more. It lost more than a third of its value in a matter of months. The SEC concluded its investigation the following July and took no action, in effect giving Tyco a clean bill of health. The stock resumed its climb, but Wall Street was still wary.

When Enron's accounting scandal erupted in the fall of 2001, Tyco got tarred with the same brush. Investors feared Tyco might be up to similar accounting tricks because its financials were so complicated. In a matter of a few months, Tyco's stock had lost over 60 percent of its value.

In an effort to reassure shareholders, Kozlowski appeared on CNBC one morning in February 2002. Luck was not with him that day, for the person who interviewed him wasn't one of the regulars, but a guest interviewer, Jack Welch. Welch, who had recently retired, was on the show to promote his bestselling book, *Jack: Straight from the Gut*, which he wrote with John Byrne, a writer at *Business Week*. Welch doubtless recalled Kozlowski's boasts about Tyco being another GE. He put Kozlowski's feet to the fire about the $9.2 billion acquisition of CIT Financial. CIT was intended to serve as the company's financing arm. But CIT had proven to be a dumb deal and Tyco was now saddled with a company worth far less than what it had spent.

"CIT was not something I would have done had we known a year ago what we know now," Kozlowski admitted to Welch. The former GE chairman also grilled him about some unusual dips into the corporate treasury, including a $10 million finder's fee paid to a Tyco director named Frank Walsh for his role in the CIT merger. Welch also brought up Tyco's $10 million contribution to a charity in which Walsh was a trustee. If Welch ever takes it into his head to anchor a financial show on TV, it would be a ratings winner.

A chastened Kozlowski said that it would never happen again. He sounded like a schoolboy caught cheating on his homework. To prevent the stock from plunging any further, Kozlowski then proposed a stunning plan to break apart the conglomerate he had built. Deal-a-Month Dennis was now saying that Tyco was worth more in pieces than as a whole. It was a complete about-face from his acquisition strategy. He proposed dividing Tyco into four publicly traded companies: security and electronics; health care; fire protection and flow control; and financial services. The plastics division was to be sold outright, for an expected $4 billion.

But stockholders questioned the scheme and punished the stock even more. A few weeks later Kozlowski was forced to reverse himself and said that it would be a mistake to break up the company. Only the CIT financial unit would be sold off; Tyco would remain intact after all. To help sagging earnings, the company announced the closing of twenty-four factories and the elimination of 7,100 jobs, primarily in its electronics and telecommunications businesses. The layoffs represented about 3 percent of the company's worldwide work force of 250,000 people.

What was Tyco's board of directors doing while Kozlowski was shifting gears so often? They might as well have been making sand castles at Elbow Beach. They were mainly pals and insiders led by former CEO John Fort, and anything he did was okay with them.

But to a lot of observers, it looked like Kozlowski was riding his Harley without a helmet.

"When a company reverses itself in this manner, it puts investors ill at ease," said Alan Ackerman, a market strategist with Fahnestock & Co.

The stock continued its skid. As accounting scandals spread from Enron to Xerox to Global Crossing to WorldCom, investors began treating Tyco like kielbasa left out in the sun too long. Yet while Tyco was tanking, Kozlowski was shopping. He needed a few hangings on the wall to dress up his thirteen-room, $17 million duplex on Fifth Avenue, one of his four multi-million-dollar residences. The Koz was living large.

Between December 2001 and June 2002, he bought six second-rate but expensive French impressionist paintings, including "Fleurs et Fruits" by Pierre Auguste Renoir and "Pres Monte Carlo" by Claude Monet. The cost of the paintings was $13.2 million, which Kozlowski could well afford. His income had soared with Tyco's stock. In just three years, his total compensation had amounted to $332 million. So much for pooling tips.

Nonetheless, as usual, he reached first for the company checkbook, rather than his own, vowing to settle up later. Tyco's money was used to pay for the name-brand art, and the duplex, and the other residences in Boca Raton, and Nantucket, and a whole lot more. Apparently, the board was not informed of the extent of these interest-free loans, which were often later forgiven, anyway.

Kozlowski was now a billionaire, but it still irked him to pay taxes. When he bought the $13.2 million worth of art, he allegedly tried to escape the city's sales tax on the purchases, which would have amounted to about $1.1 million. What a dumb move. Tax cops are always on the prowl for rich, high profile tax cheats, from Al Capone to Leona Helmsley. They serve as object lessons for the rest of us.

One of the easiest taxes to dodge is New York City's sales tax, which can only be levied on local residents. If you live outside New York and send your purchases there, no local tax is due. According to the Manhattan district attorney, Kozlowski used a number of different ruses to evade the tax. In some cases he had the paintings sent out of state to the company's U.S. headquarters in Exeter, New

Hampshire, then had them returned to his apartment in the city. In other cases, the prosecutors charged, he had the art dealer send empty boxes to New Hampshire, while the paintings never left Manhattan.

At the press conference announcing Kozlowski's indictment on June 5, 2002, Manhattan District Attorney Robert Morgenthau referred to a memo from the art gallery consultant to the trucker which read, "Here is the list of the four paintings that are going to New Hampshire (wink, wink)." The memo also instructed the shipper to make boxes that matched the size of the paintings.

"The city needs the money," Morgenthau said. "Nobody's going to wink. If you don't pay your taxes, you're going to be prosecuted." The newspapers ate it all up.

Although Kozlowski pleaded innocent to the charges, his career was over. The day before the indictment, he resigned as CEO of Tyco International. But his troubles were just beginning.

Immediately after he resigned, Tyco board members launched an investigation of Kozlowski's use of the company funds. The SEC and the state attorney general in New York also launched investigations. The details of what emerged from those probes made Kozlowski a household name, forever linked with a $6,000 shower curtain.

To furnish his Manhattan duplex, Kozlowski had pulled out the Tyco checkbook to buy some sundries and knickknacks. In addition to the gold and burgundy floral-patterned shower curtain, they included: $15,000 for a three-foot-high umbrella stand in the shape of a poodle; $6,300 for a sewing basket; $17,100 for a toilette box; $2,200 for a gilt metal wastebasket; $2,900 for coat hangers; $6,000 for two sets of sheets; $1,660 for a leather notebook, and $445 for a turtle-shaped pincushion.

Wendy Valliere, the interior designer, said that the total bill for decorating his apartment came to $5.7 million, paid by Tyco.

Yet the decorating bill, and even the $17 million spent for the duplex, were peanuts compared to what Kozlowski and some of his lieutenants were accused of looting from the company.

On September 12, 2002, the Manhattan district attorney's office filed criminal fraud charges against Kozlowski, former CFO Mark Swartz, and former general counsel Mark Belnick, alleging that the trio stole $170 million directly from the company, and another $430 million through the fraudulent sale of securities. The prosecutors charged that Kozlowski had diverted $242 million from an employee loan program to buy yachts, fine art, and luxury homes.

The SEC also filed civil charges against the three men, as did the new management of Tyco, which also accused Kozlowski of "taking personal credit for more than $43 million in charitable donations that were actually made by Tyco." That included a $10 million pledge to the California International Sailing Association, as well as gifts to Seton Hall and other schools, colleges, and hospitals. The donations were paid by Tyco but made in Kozlowski's name. Tyco also accused Kozlowski of using $700,000 of its money to invest in a movie on the life of Ernest Shackleton, the South Pole explorer.

Another relatively small expense got particular attention: the fortieth birthday party that Kozlowski threw for his new wife, Karen, in the summer of 2001. Tyco picked up half the tab for the $2.1 million junket to sunny Sardinia, where guests were flown in for a bash that included a performance by Jimmy Buffett. The birthday party had a Roman theme, and Caligula himself would have applauded Kozlowski's libidinous tastes. The giant birthday cake had exploding breasts, and dominating the room was an ice sculpture of Michelangelo's *David—sans* fig leaf—with Stolichnaya vodka dribbling out of his penis. Cheers, Dennis.

While facing charges that could put him in prison for the rest of his life, Kozlowski nonethless put on a happy face and spent the July Fourth weekend throwing another party for his thirsty friends at his Nantucket spread—a 3.7-acre complex on Squam Road. Hiding in the bushes were reporters for the *New York Post,* and they didn't miss a sip. They reported that Kozlowski spent the weekend "entertaining pals like the corporate king he once was: sport fishing, quaffing vintage wine, buying drinks for bars full of people, and sailing the high seas on his historic 130-foot sloop."

They quickly found witnesses who thought Kozlowski should

have been breaking rocks instead of pouring drinks over them. "It's preposterous that this guy could walk the street," said one. "He's a symbol of the whole culture of greed that has become embedded in our economy over the past five years."

But some island residents were willing to cut him some slack. Kozlowski was, after all, employing quite a number of them. He needed a sizable staff to tend his properties, which included his main home, Sea Rose Farm, and its guest house, as well as a pair of wharf-side cottages (valued at $2 million and up). Other locals found work tending to his antique yacht, *Endeavor*, which had once competed in the 1934 America's Cup yacht race. The vessel, which sleeps eight, had a regular crew of nine, including a gourmet chef. According to *Forbes*, the tab for maintaining the boat ran to $700,000 a year. Kozlowski often skippered it himself. Tyco also sponsored a high-tech yacht to compete in the round-the-world Volvo Ocean Race.

Besides employing a good number of islanders, Kozlowski supported a number of local charities, as was also his custom at his winter retreat in Boca Raton, Florida, where he had a $30-million spread.

"Karen and Dennis have given an enormous amount of money to this island," said a friend to the *Post*. "If that stops, it's going to be a great loss to many of the institutions on this island."

Later on in the summer of 2002, the partying, the spending, and the giving came to an abrupt halt when the courts froze all his assets.

Tyco, which had a new, no-nonsense CEO in Edward Breen, seized most of Kozlowski's physical assets, including the $17 million Fifth Avenue apartment, a $7-million Park Avenue apartment he had signed over to his ex-wife, as well as the compounds in Nantucket and Boca Raton.

With his assets seized, one of the greediest CEOs in American corporate history was virtually penniless. "He can't even go to an ATM machine because all of his assets are blocked," Kozlowski's lawyer told a reporter. In order to make bail and stay out of Riker's

Island prison pending trial on the criminal fraud charges, he had to borrow $10 million from his ex-wife, Angie.

Deal-a-Month Dennis now faced a new set of priorities: trying to work a deal with prosecutors to avoid spending the rest of his natural life in prison. He pleaded not guilty to all the charges against him.

15

Adelphia: The Rigas Family Piggy Bank

Nepotism is fine, as long as you keep it in the family.
—Malcolm Forbes

Coudersport (pop. 2,650) is an old, polished heirloom of a town in north central Pennsylvania that dates back to the early nineteenth century when loggers were working their way west through the state to harvest hemlock and white pine. Recalling those early days, a lumber museum stands on the east side of town, complete with the old steam engines that once hauled the lumber to market.

The town has a New England feel, with a Gothic style courthouse and a gazebo in the square where seasonal concerts are still held. The commercial buildings are mainly one- and two-story red brick structures, most at least a century old. A covered bridge marks the western end of the borough, spanning the Allegheny River, which is just a stream at this point.

On North Main Street is the fifty-seat Coudersport Theater,

housed in one of those old red brick buildings. The art-deco marquee and lobby are unchanged from the days of the opening of the movie house, back in the 1930s.

The theater, which even today charges only $3.50 to see a movie, is still owned by John Rigas, the seventy-seven-year-old former chairman of Adelphia Communications, who did more good for Coudersport than any resident in its 195-year history.

John Rigas came to town in 1951 from nearby Wellsville, New York, to seek his fame and fortune. It was an odd place to start, but with money borrowed from family and friends, Rigas purchased the movie theater and embarked on an extraordinary business career. Over the next fifty years, he built the nation's sixth largest cable TV empire with 5.6 million customers in thirty-one states and $3.6 billion in annual revenues.

The company, which he called Adelphia Communications, started life and is still headquartered in tiny Coudersport. About 25 percent of its residents work for Rigas's company, and all of them are beholden to him for his generosity to the community.

Adelphia made Rigas and his family wealthy, but the patriarch was never an in-your-face spender. Essentials came first. He built a big comfortable home and sent his kids to the best schools. Eventually, he started other businesses, and formed partnerships that bought cable systems (operated by Adelphia) and Pennsylvania timberland.

As Adelphia made him very rich, Rigas bought vacation homes in Cancun, Mexico, Beaver Creek, Colorado, and Hilton Head, South Carolina. He didn't collect art or own a big yacht or furnish his home with $6,000 shower curtains. His biggest indulgence was the purchase of the Buffalo Sabers hockey team, which he bought in 1998 for $150 million. When he went to games the local cable station, owned by Rigas, made sure that he was shown on camera.

By 2002, Rigas should have been enjoying a comfortable semi-retirement in a town that revered him as a deity. But the son of immigrant Greek parents wound up spending his time sequestered in his home, afraid to show his face. John Rigas had become known far beyond Coudersport as one of the biggest corporate crooks in American history.

On July 24, 2002, Rigas and two of his sons were visiting his daughter in Manhattan when federal agents rapped on the door at 6 a.m., slapped them in handcuffs, and dragged them off to the U.S. District Courthouse. The men were stripped of their neckties, belts, and shoelaces and hauled before Judge Gabriel W. Gorenstein, who needed six minutes to read the charges against them. They included conspiracy, securities fraud, and wire and bank fraud. The complaint alleged that the family members "stole hundreds of millions of dollars and through their fraud caused losses for investors in excess of $60 billion."

If convicted on all counts, the men faced a maximum of one hundred years in prison and millions of dollars in fines. In addition to those charges, the SEC and Adelphia Communications filed separate suits against the Rigases and several corporate executives, alleging "violations of the RICO laws, breach of fiduciary duties, waste of corporate assets, abuse of control, breach of contract, unjust enrichment, fraudulent conveyance, and conversion of corporate assets."

After the criminal charges were read, John Rigas and the two sons, Michael and Tim, were paraded in handcuffs before the press and national TV cameras. The old man looked bewildered and frightened, and appeared to have been weeping.

Coudersport residents were flabbergasted. In just a few short months, they'd seen Adelphia, their lifeblood, topple into bankruptcy. Now they sat glued to their TV sets watching the founder and his sons herded out of court like murderers. Residents couldn't recall anything as shocking since a local doctor, J. Irving Bentley, suddenly burst into flames in his bathroom one day in 1966. All that remained of Dr. Bentley after his spontaneous combustion was a pile of ashes and a small portion of his leg. Townsfolk wondered what would remain of Adelphia and the Rigases once the smoke cleared. Many of them prayed for John Rigas and his sons. They couldn't believe the Rigases were world-class crooks.

In Buffalo, New York, however, about two hours' drive north of Coudersport, there were a lot more curses than prayers for John Rigas. Rigas not only owned the Sabres, which had come within one game of winning the Stanley Cup in 1999, but had also pledged to build an office tower and bring a lot more jobs to a city on life support.

As they sipped their beer and watched the evening news, a lot of fans in Buffalo feared that Rigas would now have to sell their beloved Sabres. A new owner might not want to keep the team in Buffalo, when richer markets beckoned.

The new office tower that would have employed 2,000 was also supposed to anchor a new waterfront development project that would now be stopped in its tracks, meaning the loss of even more jobs.

While residents of Coudersport prayed, and Buffalonians cursed, Adelphia stockholders could only cry. They were completely wiped out. Adelphia's stock had fallen from $87 a share in 1999 to $30 at the start of 2002 to mere pennies when the company filed for bankruptcy in June of the same year.

What had gone so wrong so quickly with the seemingly sound cable giant? What on earth had John Rigas and his troops been doing?

In the words of prosecutors, they were using the company as their own piggy bank, which was now stuffed with billions of dollars in IOUs. John Rigas ran Adelphia as if it belonged to him and his family—period.

That Rigas put family first was hardly surprising. He came from a Greek culture where ties to family and friends were as strong as uozo. Parents, sons, and daughters came first. Then came your friends and neighbors, and then the church. All others were a distant third. In ancient Greece, the word for strangers was *barbaroi,* meaning barbarians.

Rigas was proud of his Greek heritage and his family's achievements in the New World. His father, James, was born in a small mountain village in central Greece called Arahova, where there were more sheep and goats than people. He emigrated to the U.S. at age eighteen, eventually settling in Wellsville, New York, in 1920. James and a Greek friend opened a restaurant called Texas Hot, which specialized in hot dogs and sandwiches doused with chili sauce. The food was cheap, hot, and hearty and the place thrived.

The partners shared an apartment above Texas Hot while James started a search for a bride. He wrote to his brother back in Greece, who suggested he marry a girl from Arahova named Eleni. The families back home approved of the arrangement, and within a few months the eighteen-year-old girl boarded a boat and embarked for the U.S. to marry a man she knew only by reputation. James had seen only a photo of her.

James and Eleni were married above the restaurant in 1922, and two years later, on November 14, 1924, John Rigas was born in that same apartment. Eighty years later, Texas Hot is still open, still thriving, and still run by a Rigas, John's nephew.

John himself worked at the grill after graduating Rensselaer Polytechnic Institute in nearby Troy, New York, in 1949 with a degree in engineering management. He later told an interviewer from The Cable Center that it was due to the urging of his Greek friends and the existence of the GI Bill that he attended R.P.I., not any particular love of engineering.

Rigas had served with the Twentieth Armored Infantry Division for three years during the Second World War, and had seen combat in Belgium and Germany. Despite his small size and frame, he impressed his officers with his stamina. When bigger, stronger men fell out on long marches during training, little John Rigas never faltered, even under a full pack. He was held up as an example.

He was a capable soldier but never made it beyond the rank of Pfc. He was busted back to buck private three times for failing to clean his rifle and other minor transgressions, and only made Pfc again just before his discharge.

After returning home and graduating college, he took up the spatula at Texas Hot, but he wasn't much of a short-order cook, either. "I worked in the restaurant for approximately nine months, but I really began to feel that the restaurant wasn't going to be my niche because believe it or not there's a knack to cooking and I really didn't perform the best," Rigas said.

A Greek friend suggested that he consider buying the movie theater in nearby Coudersport, Pennsylvania, which was on the market for a hefty $72,000. The banks turned him down for financing, so he turned to his family. "My dad had $5,000 to contribute," Rigas recalled. "I didn't have anything. Then we went to some of our Greek friends for another $25,000 dollars, which they were willing to essentially lend my dad, and then the seller took a mortgage on the rest of it."

It was not the great investment he'd hoped for. Television was sweeping the country, and a lot of families made the monthly payments on their TV sets with money they would otherwise have spent at the movies. The movies on TV were old and grainy, but they were free. And, you got Milton Berle.

Rigas cut sharp deals with distributors, and sold tickets and popcorn himself, but the movie house didn't generate much profit. To keep it alive, and keep up with the loan payments, he worked as an engineer for Sylvania Electric in Emporium, New York, by day, then drove to Coudersport to work in the movie house at night. Sometimes he slept on a cot when too exhausted to drive back to Wellsville.

Then along came cable TV, then in its infancy. A salesman friend persuaded Rigas that in order to protect his investment in the movie house, he should buy the local cable TV franchise. John was broke, as he was essentially subsidizing the movie house with his day job. He couldn't let his father and the other backers down. But his friend was so persuasive that John overdrew his checking account and ponied up $100 for the license to wire Coudersport.

With his brother Gus as a partner, Rigas started the company that he named Adelphia—Greek for brothers. Together they would go door to door in Coudersport selling cable hookups. The logistics of the business were simple: You put a big antenna high on a hill, and run wires into customers' houses. Cable delivered only a few channels, depending on which way the wind was blowing, but the reception was still a lot better than you could get with your own rooftop antenna. To convince customers to buy the service, John and his brother offered to buy and remove customers' existing TV antennas.

The business succeeded. After Coudersport, Rigas wired Wellsville and other rural towns where over-the-air TV transmission signals were weak. The business grew quickly throughout the region.

By now, Rigas was a married man and a father. On February 1, 1953, he married Doris Nielsen, a popular student at R.P.I. who later taught high school English in Wellsville. Doris wasn't Greek, but she was the daughter of immigrants, which counted for something. And there was at least one Greco-Danish connection. "The Greek king was Constantine and he married a Danish princess and we always thought that was a pretty good follow-up," Rigas said.

They had four children. Michael J. was born in 1954, Timothy in 1956, James P. in 1958, and Ellen in 1960. Doris and John were demanding parents, always pushing the kids to excel. They were all straight arrows who didn't drink or smoke and three of the four graduated high school as class valedictorians.

Gus Rigas eventually sold his interest in the company, and John planned on having his sons at his side to replace the family connection. They were certainly bright enough.

Michael went to Harvard and Harvard Law. Tim earned an economics degree from Wharton. James graduated Harvard and then Stanford Law School. Ellen, the youngest, also went to Harvard, then moved to Manhattan to become a film producer, and later married an investment banker named Peter Venetis, who was likewise of Greek ancestry.

One by one the sons joined the company, and Adelphia continued to expand, buying larger and larger cable systems, always leveraged to the hilt.

By 1986, Adelphia needed a lot more capital if it was going to survive. The industry put a high premium on the economies of scale. The bigger you were, the better deals you could make for equipment and programming and other services. It was grow or sell out, and so Rigas took Adelphia public.

From the very beginning, the shareholders were treated worse than poor relatives. Adelphia issued two kinds of shares—A and B. Every B share of stock had the voting power of ten A shares. Rigas and his family kept enough B shares, so there would never be a problem with *barbaroi*. As Adelphia acquired larger cable systems around the country, Rigas sold more stock and issued more bonds, but the family still retained voting power with their B shares.

As John had hoped and planned, all the boys had returned home to join the business. As is common when Dad is the boss, they rose rapidly in the organization. Michael became executive vice president of operations; Tim was finance chief; and James executive vice president of strategic planning. James married a pediatrician and moved into a restored Victorian home that was once owned by federal agent Eliot Ness, who had died of a heart attack in the kitchen. He and his wife, Mary Ann, had four sons, but his brothers remained bachelors and moved into separate wings of John Rigas's sprawling ranch home, complete with pond and swans.

The senior Rigas ran the company pretty much the way his father had run Texas Hot in Wellsville. There were always a lot of relatives in the kitchen. Since the Rigases controlled the voting shares in Adelphia, they could name anyone they wanted to the board without having to worry about stockholder votes or challenges. So Adelphia's nine-member board of directors had five Rigas family members— John, his three sons, and his son in law, Peter Venetis. The other four board members were friends and business contacts. There were no *barbaroi* on the scene.

Public or not, Adelphia belonged to John Rigas, and he saw nothing wrong with that. It was all in the family, by the family, and for the family.

Adelphia continued adding systems and subscribers, and was quick to employ new technology like fiber-optics and the latest set-top devices. In 1999 Adelphia bought three large cable systems in a span of four months, making it the sixth largest cable company in the U.S.

But those deals alone cost the company $8.5 billion, bringing its total debt to $14 billion. Rigas was sailing closer to the wind than ever, but the rising stock price kept the ship afloat as giddy investors bid up all the cable stocks. By the end of the year, Adelphia hit an all-time high of $87 a share.

Rigas now took on Herculean proportions. The financial press discovered him, and Coudersport residents got used to giving interviews to reporters and TV crews looking for color in their profiles of Rigas. In 2000 he was elected to the Cable Hall of Fame, and made the *Forbes* 500 list of best-paid CEOs. The *Buffalo News* named him Buffalo's (Most Powerful and Effective Business Leader.) Decker Anstrom, CEO of the Weather Channel, said, "If there's one person I'd like my son to grow up to be, it would be John Rigas."

He became known as much for his philanthropy and community service as his business acumen. He had served as a trustee on several college boards including St. Bonaventure University and Mansfield University. He served on the boards of the local bank, the chamber of commerce, the local hospital, and the rotary club, among other civic and business organizations.

He made the company Gulfstream jet available for locals who needed medical treatment at faraway hospitals and treatment centers. He gave away hockey tickets to kids, and bussed them to Buffalo for Sabre games. At the HSBC Arena, the Sabres' home ice, he noticed an elevator operator who had very bad teeth, and paid for his new dentures.

He was always quick to open his wallet for locals in need, and people who knew him would hang around his favorite restaurants like Kaye's Hometown Restaurant on Main Street to hit him up for handouts or loans for their businesses.

Rigas never lost his appreciation for simple restaurants like Texas Hot. "I probably do my best business in restaurants where I can hear the dishes clanging and the orders barking in the background. Sometimes I get in an office and it's much too peaceful and too quiet for me to concentrate," he said.

Each year, Rigas threw a big Christmas party for the whole town at the local Masonic temple, with lavish decorations arranged by his wife, Doris. He even imported the Buffalo Philharmonic Orchestra to perform the *Nutcracker Suite.*

In business, however, Rigas threw nickels around like manhole covers. Even old friends sometimes had to wait a long time for payment. A local lawyer once confronted John over an outstanding bill and settled for leaving Rigas's house with several gallons of pool paint. It took two years for the purchase of the Sabres to become final.

Rigas had a somewhat cavalier air toward debt, which by the late 1990s had ballooned to 11 times the company's capitalization, enough to cause some stock analysts to shy away. "It has caused the stock to trade at the steepest discount to estimate net asset value of any cable operator," wrote one.

Steep discount or not, the value of Adelphia shares kept rising, though none of the Rigases cashed in shares. In fact, as the company issued more stock, they kept buying more shares, often on margin, to maintain control. No one seemed to know where they got the money for these huge purchases, however, or to support their lifestyles. The company paid no dividends, and the Rigases paid themselves rather modest salaries. John Rigas made $1.4 million in salary in 2000, while the sons Michael, Tim, and James took home only $237,000 each.

Yet the stock purchases continued. One bond analyst for Merrill Lynch, Oren Cohen, suspected funny business. According to *Fortune*, in February 2001, Cohen noticed that the Rigases were buying $1.8 billion worth of Adelphia stock and convertible bonds. He wondered where in the name of Zeus that cash was coming from.

Shortly after those purchases, Adelphia's stock began to slip badly, dropping from $40 to $20. Cohen estimated that the Rigases were in the hole for $900 million to $1 billion. Cohen called Adelphia's head of investor relations. "How is this stuff being funded?" he asked. But he didn't get a straight answer.

On March 27, 2002, the bomb dropped. On the last page of a

company press release announcing quarterly earnings was a startling admission: Adelphia showed a liability of $2.3 billion in loans to the Rigas family that were off the balance sheet. Huh? The Rigases had borrowed $2.3 *billion*?

Off the books?

With the horrors of Enron's loopy accounting still fresh in their minds, investors began dumping the stock, which dropped 35 percent in a few days. Red flags went up at the SEC, which decided to take a closer look at Adelphia's books. A few weeks later the company said that it would be restating earnings—not just for the past quarter, but for the years 2000, 1999, and 1998. In short, its earnings for the last three years were wrong. The company also announced that its annual report for 2001 would be delayed.

The more details that came out, the worse it was for the Rigas family. Auditors disclosed that the Rigases had been dipping into what was known as the "cash management account," which commingled Adelphia's funds and those of the Rigas family partnerships. The stocks sank even lower.

Finally, on May 15, 2002, John Rigas resigned as chairman and CEO from the company he had started half a century earlier. His sons resigned shortly thereafter, and the family was asked to relinquish its voting control of the company. Erland Kailburne, one of the board members, was made CEO.

John Rigas couldn't quite believe what was happening, and even after his resignation showed up at a director's meeting still hoping to patch things together. He was told to leave the kitchen. The four remaining board members were not amused at having been duped, and faced their own problems with stockholders. They had become *barbaroi*.

Though he was an old friend of the family from Wellsville, Kailburne was no longer in the Rigas camp and hired hotshot lawyer David Boies to examine Adelphia's finances. The probes resulted in the criminal indictments and civil fraud charges against the Rigas family, including Ellen Rigas and Doris Rigas and two company executives, James Brown and Michael Mulcahey.

Here are some of the juicier charges that emerged from the various probes:

- That the Rigases took $241 million from Adelphia since January 2001 to pay margin calls on their stock. About $175 million of that was taken after March 27, when Adelphia disclosed it had guaranteed loans now estimated at $3.1 billion to Rigas-owned partnerships.
- That Adelphia guaranteed much of the $150 million that John Rigas borrowed to recapitalize his private investment in the Buffalo Sabres hockey team. It was unknown whether the board knew about the loans.
- That Adelphia put up $65 million in 2001 for a 99.5 percent stake in an investment fund, Praxis Capital, run by John Rigas's son-in-law Peter Venetis. He owns the remaining 0.5 percent, collects 16 percent of the profits, and received a $1.96 million management fee. To that point, Praxis had made one investment amounting to $1 million.
- That Adelphia paid $13 million to build a golf club on Rigas-owned property.
- That Adelphia paid for condos in Beaver Creek, Colorado, and Cancun, Mexico, that were used only by the Rigas family.
- That Adelphia owned two New York City apartments used solely and rent-free by Peter and Ellen Rigas Venetis. (They have since paid back rent.)
- That Adelphia advanced more than $3.7 million to documentary film companies in which the Rigases own equity. (Ellen Rigas Venetis had produced a film called *Songcatcher*, which won critical acclaim, but which John Rigas walked out of when it was screened in Coudersport because of a same-sex love scene.)
- That the Rigases never reimbursed the company for private use of corporate aircraft.
- That Adelphia routinely bought furniture, automobiles, and services from Rigas-run firms.

- The total amount of money that the Rigases borrowed for their own partnerships, but secured by Adelphia assets, was $3.1 billion, not the $2.3 billion that was stated in the release of March 27.

There were other charges, too, alleging inflation of the number of Adelphia's cable TV subscribers to help boost the stock price. Also, that the Rigases told security analysts that Adelphia could provide two-way communications to 50 percent of its customers, while the real number was 35 percent.

The mystery of where the Rigases were getting their money without selling any stock was now brutally clear: They borrowed it, by the billions. But the party was over. The handcuffs awaited.

The Rigases insisted on their innocence, naturally. And they vowed to fight the charges that could put some of them in jail for the rest of their lives, besides huge fines and the confiscation of their property. To the end, they were family.

"Regardless of what comes out of this, the family unit will be stronger than ever," James Rigas told the *Buffalo News*. "We've always had a close family, and hard times draw you closer together."

John Rigas was philosophical. "It's a Greek tragedy," he said. "It's very ironic."

16

Joseph Nacchio:
In Qwest of Riches

I should be allowed to make more than a second baseman.
I create more economic value than they do.
—Joseph P. Nacchio, ex-CEO, Qwest Communications, Inc., who
made more than $300 million while CEO

You probably remember the television commercial a few years back. A weary traveler enters a rundown motel and asks the clerk if there is cable TV in the rooms. "Every movie, ever made, any time," the clerks drawls in response. It was a clever ad for Qwest Communications, boasting of its vast fiber-optic network, which could carry broadband signals almost anywhere.

With an infinite movie library like that to choose from, you could pick out quite a few titles to describe the stages of the career of Joseph Nacchio, the ex-CEO of Qwest. *The Loneliness of the Long Distance Runner* would be the first. The Brooklyn-born Nacchio, who was never very fast when he was captain of his track team in high school, became a long distance man in more ways than one. He competed in the New York Marathon and he competed in the long distance phone business. He gave both his all, and when that wasn't enough, still managed to come out a winner, one way or another. Never mind if some rules were bent.

While racing in the New York Marathon one year, he needed to beat a certain time in order to qualify for the Boston Marathon. Seven miles from the finish, his right foot was so badly blistered and bleeding that he could barely go on. "I had already hit the wall," he told *USA Today*. He still made it to the finish line, but was a minute over the qualifying time. Nonetheless, he sent Boston race officials a picture of his bloody running shoe and they let him run anyway.

He was no less tenacious in his twenty-six-year career at AT&T, where he started at the back of the pack, slowly elbowing past an endless line of executives ahead of him. By the early 1990s, he was closing in on the leaders and was hard to ignore. As president of AT&T's consumer long-distance operation, he'd launched the True USA and True World discount calling programs, which won 25 million accounts in their first nine months. The brash executive vice president even featured himself in a Super Bowl spot for AT&T's long distance service. He offered new long-distance customers $100 checks—signed by him—to switch to AT&T. (Nacchio had calculated that it cost AT&T $300 in sales and marketing costs to sign up a new long distance customer, so the company saved $200 for every new customer who cashed his check.)

Under his leadership, the consumer long distance business won the Malcolm Baldridge National Quality Award for excellence. By 1996, Nacchio was finally closing in on the top position at AT&T. Or so he thought. Chairman Robert Allen was under pressure from the board to groom a successor before stepping down himself. Nacchio, who was president of consumer services, expected he'd be named, and that he would then become CEO when Allen retired. But Allen surprised everyone when he picked John Walter, an outsider from R.R. Donnelley & Sons, the Chicago-based printing giant. Walter was a likeable salesman but had little experience in the telecommunications industry. Nacchio was incensed at being passed over for the job, clashed with Walter, and soon started looking around for a new track to run on. It turned out to be a very fast one indeed, at tiny upstart Qwest Communications, then just a flyspeck on AT&T's radar screen.

Walter never did get the top rung at AT&T, and left only nine months later. He never got along with Allen or the board, though he was well liked by other top executives, while Allen was hated. His departure triggered even more defections from the troubled company. But he didn't walk away broke. Walter had received a $5 million bonus when he left his job as chairman of R.R. Donnelley & Sons to join AT&T. He received another $3.8 million in severance from AT&T, plus $22.8 million to cover what he would have potentially earned at Donnelley. In effect, Walter earned over $3 million a month while at AT&T.

You couldn't fault Nacchio for being bitter, but he never did fit the mold of a typical Bellhead. He was not the polished Ivy type that AT&T favored. He was a fast-talking, in-your-face New Yorker, who was born in Brooklyn, grew up in Staten Island, and at one time or another lived in all of the city's five boroughs.

His college campus was literally the streets of Manhattan. He earned a bachelor's degree in electrical engineering and an MBA at New York University, in the heart of Greenwich Village, doing much of his studying on the ferry from Staten Island and on the subway while commuting from home. "I had to get the math done by South Ferry," he said. He also earned a master's in management at Massachusetts Institute of Technology.

The grandson of immigrants and the son of a longshoreman turned bartender, Nacchio had few outside interests other than AT&T and his family. To relax, he ran, or cycled with his family. He read books on history, and not just bestsellers. One of his favorites was *The Year 1000: What Life Was Like at the Turn of the First Millennium*, by Robert Lacey and Danny Danziger. When he reached the upper ranks of AT&T, Nacchio moved to the executive enclave of Mendham, New Jersey, near Morristown, to raise his family of two boys with his wife, Anne. His Colonial-style mansion sits on six fenced-in acres near a park that marks the site where George Washington once had his headquarters.

It's a picture-postcard spot, and Nacchio never left it, even after taking on the top position at Qwest, which is headquartered in Denver, Colorado. He chose to commute on weekends rather than part with the estate and uproot his family. His sons were then students at Delbarton, an exclusive Catholic school where Nacchio chaired fund drives.

Nacchio was both proud and touchy about his Italian heritage. In 2000, he received the National Italian American Foundation's Special Achievement Award in Communications. When *The Economist*, which can be surprisingly churlish at times, poked fun at him as a Mafioso type, the magazine soon got a bristling letter. The New Yorker in Nacchio never let him ignore a jibe.

Nacchio would later say that he only arrived at AT&T by accident, having strolled into its recruiting booth by chance. Maybe so, but he started out as an engineer and stayed twenty-seven years. It's not easy to walk away from a place where you've spent your entire career. He later told an interviewer from *Brandweek*, "A lot of people might say, 'You're crazy, man. You're in the top five or so of people at AT&T, you make all this money. Why don't you stay there and live a comfortable life?' I think at the end of the day, it's more than comfort. It's passion and excitement."

After he took over at Qwest, he seldom missed a chance to take a dig at the communications behemoth, and even joked about taking it over one day. He also delighted in hiring talented AT&T executives away who likewise had been stymied at the company for failure to fit its golf-and-politics culture.

Nacchio's selection as CEO of tiny Qwest came about through his friendship with Jack Grubman, the telecom analyst at Salomon Smith Barney who would later become a laughingstock but who at the time wielded extraordinary influence in the industry. Grubman knew everyone who counted, and was a talent broker, among other things. Nacchio had been all set to take a top position with a technology company after Walter's appointment when Grubman suggested that Nacchio talk to Philip Anschutz, a billionaire who owned a small telecom business that was a spin-off from his railroad, Southern Pacific Rail. The subsidiary, Southern Pacific Telecommunications Co. (SPT), had put down fiber-optic cable along the railroad's right of way. It was Anschutz's notion to create a high-speed, national network and sell the capacity to long-distance carriers. He needed someone to piece together the national network and take the company public. A deal was soon made. It was a major comedown for Nacchio, who once had the power and vast resources of AT&T at his fingertips. The country's largest telecom had an advertising budget of $1 billion, for example.

But the entrepreneurial Anschutz could offer Nacchio something AT&T could never match—the chance to become a centimillionaire, maybe even a billionaire, and kick some AT&T butt at the same time. It was an offer he couldn't refuse.

He didn't waste any time in firing off his first salvo after joining Qwest. "They're not worried about tomorrow's revenue stream," he told *Brandweek* in early 1997. "Somebody's going to make a couple million phone calls today using AT&T and they'll go out for the day and play golf. Little companies don't behave that way. Over time, you take all that cultural overhead and even with ambitious, aggressive, customer-oriented, energetic people, it kind of wears you down because the system doesn't support it."

AT&T ignored Qwest the way an elephant ignores a flea crawling up its leg with rape on its mind. When Nacchio took the helm, Qwest had 700 employees and $225 million in annual sales. But not for long. The manic world of telecom was now entering its giddiest stage.

Dot.com madness was turning everyone's thinking mushy, and the need for telecom capacity seemed infinite. Every month, an average of two new telecom upstarts went public to raise billions to build new, high-capacity networks. Investors who had the right connections at brokerage houses were allotted precious shares in the initial public offerings, and the stocks took off. Formerly tiny companies like WorldCom were now threatening the established giants. The long distance business was now a free-for-all in which only the Baby Bells, restricted by government regulations, couldn't play. In 1997, there were 1,400 companies in the long distance business, with 140 in California alone.

In June 1997, Qwest joined the party and went public at $5.50 a share (adjusted for later splits). The stock took off, as did all the telecom IPOs in those days, and it wasn't by accident. A $10,000 investment in Qwest stock in June 1997 would have been worth $74,300 by the end of 2000. Nacchio used the cash from the IPO to continue expanding the fiber-optic network, which would eventually stretch over 140,000 miles.

To add more traffic to the network, Nacchio began buying small internet service providers like Phoenix Network, EUnet International, and SuperNet, in addition to supplying capacity to long-distance carriers like WorldCom and Frontier.

In December 1998, annual sales had risen to $696 million, but in the grow-or-die atmosphere of the time, a big acquisition was needed. Using its lofty stock as currency, Qwest bought LCI International, then the fourth largest long-distance carrier in the country, which had annual revenues of $1.6 billion.

A few months later, Nacchio made a shrewd move that not only added even more capacity to its network, but also gave it a pot of cash to make even more buys. It sold 10 percent of itself to Bell South, the Baby Bell that served Alabama, Georgia, and the Carolinas. The price: $3.5 billion. Nacchio clearly had designs on making Qwest a lot more than a pipeline for long-distance companies.

After the Bell South deal, US West's CEO, Solomon D. Trujillo, approached Qwest about a merger. Unlike the high-flying telecoms like Qwest and WorldCom and Global Crossing and a dozen other new telecoms, the Baby Bells were ugly ducklings on Wall Street. While they still enjoyed huge revenues from their local customers, deregulation kept them out of the consumer long distance business and the boom in wireless phone use posed a serious threat to their existing business. Hidebound Bellheads were not as aggressive as they might have been in growing their businesses.

US West was one of the uglier ducklings. Consisting of the old Pacific Northwest Bell, Mountain Bell, and Northwestern Bell, its service area covered fourteen thinly populated states, with few major cities and relatively few huge commercial customers. It made nice profits, but promised no great future growth, which was the only thing that Wall Street cared about at the time. The stock was going nowhere and the enemy was closing in, which was why Trujillo went looking for a suitor, rather than waiting for a stranger to appear at the door.

Qwest turned down Trujillo's merger offer, so he went elsewhere. He found a willing partner in Global Crossing, another hot telecom with a snazzy new fiber-optic network and a high multiple on its stock. Global Crossing liked the idea and signed a merger agreement. But before it was finalized, Qwest came back into the picture. Maybe US West wasn't so ugly after all, Nacchio decided. He made a hostile bid for US West's shares, and a bidding war was on. Qwest wound up paying $69 a share to acquire the company for a total of $36.5 billion in July 1999.

It was not an easy takeover and took more than a year to complete. Even before it was finalized, Trujillo had serious misgivings when he got a close-up look at the way Qwest did things. According to the *Wall Street Journal,* Trujillo blew his top when he found out that Qwest suggested doing some fancy bookkeeping to account for a $60 million outlay US West was making for new computer equipment. Qwest would buy the computers and sell them to US West. That way Qwest would get credit for a capital expense of $60 million, while it booked the payment from US West as revenue. It's like buying dinner for a friend who pockets your cash then pays the bill with his corporate credit card.

This kind of aggressive accounting was not to Trujillo's liking. He explored backing out of the deal, but it was too late in the game. Nonetheless, he announced in February 2000 that he would not be joining the new company. It was a very expensive resignation, as Trujillo surrendered $16.3 million in compensation by leaving when he did.

But once the deal was done, Nacchio wasted no time in letting US West know who was boss. As soon as the ink dried on the contract, he ordered the signs on US West's headquarters in downtown Denver to be covered with Qwest logos.

To cut costs, he eliminated charity at US West. For years, the company had donated $25 million annually to worthy charities, and also matched employees' gifts to non-profit institutions. He cancelled a $1-million remodeling of US West's headquarters, and put up a sign on the fifty-second floor: "Excuse our appearance. We're entrepreneurs. This building was built in a different era and we save cash by not remodeling."

He even turned off the air conditioning at 6 p.m., a move reminiscent of Bernie Ebbers's removing the water coolers at WorldCom. It doesn't save much money, but it's the kind of thing analysts and investors loved to hear because it shows how cost-conscious the CEO is.

Executives at US West were also being sent a message: pack your bags. Nacchio perceived the same sort of corporate culture that he detested at AT&T. He called the company "US Worst" for its sloppy service, and called its executives "clowns." Several states had sued the company for failure to make repairs or perform new installations within reasonable time limits. The company needed shaking up, and Nacchio grabbed it by the throat. Right from the start, employees took a strong dislike to the New Yorker who didn't even live in the area. Nacchio stayed in a Denver hotel during the week and returned to his New Jersey mansion on weekends on the new $20-million Falcon jet that the company bought for him.

They liked him a lot less a few weeks later when Nacchio cut 16 percent of the company's workforce of 71,000. Most of those chopped were white-collar workers. Only a handful of the original top managers survived. In December of 2001 he would cut another 7,000 jobs.

No one was more unhappy with Nacchio that US West retirees and other stockholders looking for income, however. Before Qwest took over, US West was paying a very nice dividend of $2.12 a share.

Nacchio slashed it to a nickel. Investors who had relied on that income now found themselves holding a volatile stock that paid peanuts, instead of the traditional Baby Bell stock that supported "widows and orphans." But atomizing the dividend gave Nacchio about $5 billion more a year to finance his next moves.

Qwest was no longer a tiny upstart, but number 12 among the world's top twenty-five telecommunications companies. The flea had metamorphosed into a yapping dog. Qwest now had annual revenues of $20 billion a year, versus $64 billion for AT&T. Nacchio began to talk about building a telecommunications supercarrier. "I want to build a company that basically sets rules to how this industry works in the twenty-first century in the United States and has a strong influence globally," he told *Red Herring*.

The *Loneliness of the Long Distance Runner* phase of Nacchio's career was over, and the next had begun. Another movie title fits it: *Field of Dreams*. In the movie, a farmer in Iowa builds a baseball diamond in his cornfield. "Build it, and they will come." In that happy fantasy they did come.

Nacchio had built his fiber-optic network, but the customers didn't come. Not enough of them, anyway. It wasn't the only game in town. There were other new fiber-optic networks around now, including Global Crossing, 360Networks, Level 3 Communications, Metromedia Fiber Network, and William Communications. They were all struggling to survive. Prices for using fiber-optic cable use plummeted.

As the economy continued to sour and the internet fallout worsened, the telecom stocks were getting pounded. But Qwest didn't seem ruffled, despite its alarming debt levels and softening demand for its service. In January 2001 Qwest reported record revenues and earnings for 2000, including a 44 percent jump in profits. Nacchio himself wound up having a spectacular year, with total compensation of just under $100 million, which ranked him the seventh highest paid CEO in the U.S., according to *Forbes*. Most of this came from exercising stock options.

But despite rosy forecasts from Nacchio, the year 2001 would be

a very rocky one for the company, its employees, and its shareholders. The first sign of trouble came from, of all places, a pair of security analysts. On January 25, two analysts from Morgan Stanley—
Simon Flannery and Jeffrey Camp—downgraded Qwest from a
"strong buy" to "outperform." In their report, the analysts explained
that the slight downgrade was due to Qwest's stock price, which
remained very high relative to the other telecoms. At the time,
Qwest's stock was at $44 a share.

The new rating raised a few eyebrows because analysts were
notorious for sucking up to big borrowers like Qwest and the other
telecoms. An evaluation that displeased a company could mean the
loss of lucrative investment banking business. Morgan Stanley had
been the major underwriter in the IPO of KPNQwest, a joint ven-
ture between Qwest and KPN, Holland's national telephone company.

They were not the only ones who thought the stock was too high,
and investors began backing off the stock in the months that followed, despite first and second quarter results from Qwest that indicated the company was doing better than its peers were.

The chief financial officer, Robert S. Woodruff, resigned "to
spend more time with his family." It's never a good sign when the
CFO up and quits. Other top executives from the original Qwest
had left in the preceding months, too. Did they know something
about the company no one else did?

Nacchio tried to downplay their departures, claiming they had
made so much money on their options that they lost their edge.
"Look, it's hard to keep guys and gals who work in the normal corporate structure and then all of a sudden, over a period of two or three
years, make fifty to seventy million," he told the *Rocky Mountain
News*. "I mean, they never believed it would happen. It did happen.
That is a life-changing experience."

Nacchio, Anschutz, and other top officials continued to sell
shares by the barrelful. According to Thomson Finance/First Call,
Nacchio unloaded more than four million shares in the twelve

months between June 2000 and June 2001, for a total of $183 million. He said he did it to diversify his holdings.

The analysts got curiouser and curiouser, and started probing Qwest's financial statements. How in the name of Alexander Graham Bell was Qwest making money when other telecoms were bleeding? According to *Business Week,* they discovered a few things that looked fishy. The company carried its investment in KPNQwest at more than $7 billion, although the value of KPNQwest shares had dropped so low that the market value of the investment was less than $2 billion. They also noted that the company was reporting $405 million in income from its pension plan, which seemed hard to justify. It assumed an annual return of 9.4 percent at a time when the market was reeling. There were some other items they questioned, too.

On June 19, the analysts downgraded the stock again, to a "neutral." In the analyst-speak of the pre-Enron era, "neutral" meant dump the stock. Nacchio reacted like a pit bull whose master had just been attacked. In a conference call the next day he said, "There are no accounting issues or improprieties in Qwest's financial reports. Let me repeat that. There are no accounting issues or improprieties in our reports."

Nacchio, who had held a conference call only a day earlier, explained in tortured syntax that he felt obliged to call another one because "innuendoes on our integrity are not going to be tolerated, irregardless of who makes them, including what I used to believe was a reputable branded firm, Morgan Stanley." He told the *Rocky Mountain News* that the Morgan Stanley analysts were hardly "the sharpest knives in the drawer." On the conference call, Qwest's new CFO, Robin Szeliga, rebutted the analysts' report point by point. The stock dropped only slightly that day, and even rallied a bit in the next few days as other analysts rallied to Qwest's defense and slammed the pair from Morgan Stanley. Among the loudest cheerleaders was Jack Grubman of Salomon Smith Barney, the man who never saw a telecom he didn't like, as long as it did a lot of investment banking business with his firm.

By the end of June, Qwest stock was at $30 a share. Nacchio reiterated that the company was on track to meet its increased revenue goals for the year, while he continued to sell his own shares. But the Morgan Stanley boys weren't finished causing fits for Nacchio. On August 22, they raised pesky questions about how Qwest managed to meet its revenue targets for the second quarter, when most other telecoms were in the tank. (WorldCom was an exception, but its financial team had its own scam going.) The analysts noted that over a third of Qwest's 12.2 percent revenue growth of the second quarter was due to a big jump in sales of something called IRUs, or indefeasible rights of use. These were slices of the fiber-optic network. What was Qwest doing, selling the family jewels to pay the rent?

Nacchio went on CNBC this time to rebut the analysts and insisted that the company would never run out of fiber optic capacity. But Nacchio's credibility was now in question and the stock slipped to $22. On September 10, Qwest finally bit the bullet and lowered its double-digit projections for the year.

More bad news followed. It involved a telecom startup called Calpoint LLC. The ploy seemed like a variation of the credit card trick. Qwest would buy telecom gear from Ciena Corp., then resell it to Calpoint. The company planned to book as much as $300 million in revenues from the deal, according to *Business Week*. When world of the Calpoint deal got out, Qwest stock dropped to $17. Nacchio again called a conference call to explain that Qwest was buying the equipment for Calpoint because it could get bigger discounts than the upstart could. Hmm.

Nacchio was clearly exasperated when he addressed a group of institutional investors on October 3. "Anything I tell you, you're not going to believe anyhow," he said. "We're obviously under a cloud. You all think we lie, cheat, and steal."

No one had suggested any such thing—yet. The Morgan analysts had merely pointed out that Qwest's accounting was very aggressive and its dealmaking highly unusual. The stronger accusations would come later, from the SEC, the Justice Department, stockholders, and other investigators.

Typical of Nacchio, when the *Business Week* story about the Morgan Stanley analysts appeared, he fired off a stinging letter to the editor defending himself and Qwest and attacking the analysts for "impugning my character and Qwest's integrity." He took a swipe at the magazine, which had called Qwest's bid for US West "a colossal mistake" two years earlier. He also explained why the company had to modify its growth projections on September 10. "It's the economy, stupid. How could your reporter have forgotten it?"

We now enter the final phase of Joseph Nacchio's career. Call it, *Look Back in Anger.*

With the economy still soft, the credibility of the CEO questioned, and the company's accounting under a cloud (Arthur Andersen was the auditor), the stock of Qwest continued its descent. Qwest's ability to keep up payments on its huge debts weakened and its credit rating dropped. More layoffs would be announced. Stockholder lawsuits had been launched over Nacchio's stock sales in the first part of 2001, while the promised double-digit growth was never realized. The telecom capacity glut worsened, and prices slumped even lower. Qwest's future looked dim, as other telecoms washed up on the shoals of bankruptcy.

In early November 2001, Qwest announced an unexpected third quarter loss of $142 million, which sent the stock under $12 a share, its lowest point in four years. Yet the board of directors, under chairman Anschutz, signed Nacchio to a new, four-year contract, a 40 percent raise in salary and bonus, and another 7.25 million new stock options. Nacchio had already made nearly $250 million from exercising options, and still had millions more. For the year 2001 alone, a horrible year for the company, Nacchio's total compensation was $102 million, making him the eighth highest paid executive in America, according to *Forbes.*

In the months that followed, Enron collapsed, Global Crossing and other telecoms went into bankruptcy, and Qwest came under SEC scrutiny itself. On March 11, 2002, the company disclosed that the SEC had opened an informal inquiry into the company's accounting practices. It also came to light that Philip Anschutz, the behind-the-scenes founder and chairman of Qwest, had sold 10 million shares of stock in May 2001, for $408 million. The sale of the stock was reportedly done through a Cayman Islands subsidiary of Donaldson, Lufkin & Jenrette. In all, Anschutz had cashed in about $2 billion worth of Qwest stock before it hit the skids.

Qwest employees now joined angered shareholders in launching lawsuits. They claimed that they had been encouraged to hold on to the stock in their retirement plans, even as top officials were big sellers. It was a sad but familiar story to people who had followed the Enron debacle. Shades of Kenneth Lay.

"Senior management had a fiduciary duty to employee stock plans, and here they are urging employees to invest while selling off their own stock," John Whatley, one of the attorneys who brought suit against senior managers, told *Business Week*.

Qwest employees who had come from the old US West were especially bitter. They were the ones who had been disparaged and insulted; they were the ones who had endured the pay freezes and job cuts. Yet it was the old US West, the ugly Baby Bell, that was keeping the company alive. Qwest's debt-laden fiber-optic business was hemorrhaging money. Without US West, it would have gone belly up months before.

A lot of employees and outraged stockholders were screaming for Nacchio's scalp. The annual stockholders' meeting in June promised to be a nasty affair. But it would not be as nasty as it might have been if it were held in Denver, Qwest's headquarters, where many more employees and retirees could have attended. Instead, it was staged in Dublin, Ohio, where the company had a smaller facility. About 300 shareholders showed up for the June 3 meeting, two hundred less than a year before when the meeting was held in Denver.

After being advised to adhere to the "rules of conduct" printed on the back of the agenda, and passing through tight security, the shareholders crowded into a small room and faced Joseph Nacchio and other Qwest officials. Only two directors were present, not including Anschutz.

No one ever accused Nacchio of lacking chutzpah, and he took the heat from angry stockholders, including a couple of dozen employees who had trekked in from Denver. The stock price had dropped from $40 to $5 since the last meeting.

In his prepared remarks, the embattled CEO insisted the company was still viable. "Despite what you may have heard or read, the company is financially strong." He said that the telecom industry was in the worst shape he'd ever seen in his thirty years in the industry. "It's truly a depression in the telecom sector," he said, adding that two thirds of the new telecom companies had failed, costing 500,000 jobs.

The stockholders were not assuaged. They criticized Nacchio for his extraordinary compensation package. They raised the issue of the heavy stock sales by Anschutz and other company officials and the SEC investigation of Qwest's capacity swaps. Nacchio answered by saying that in the U.S., one is innocent until proven guilty.

US West veterans did a slow burn as he outlined how he planned to keep the company viable—by selling off some of US West's parts, including the highly profitable Yellow Pages business and some of the rural telephone lines.

More than a few stockholders called for Nacchio's ouster. "It's a shame what you've done to US West," said one angry employee, who added that he was quitting the company in disgust after twenty-two years. "You shouldn't have a job."

Two weeks later, Nacchio didn't. The stockholders' meeting was his last hurrah. Anschutz flew to New York and delivered the news himself. On June 16, 2002, Nacchio publicly resigned "to spend more time with my family." Richard C. Notebaert, an industry veteran who once ran Ameritech, replaced him. Employees cheered when they heard the news.

Anschutz resigned his non-executive chairman post, though he remained on the board and still owned 18 percent of the company he founded. The news of the resignations gave a 20 percent bump to the stock, but that was short-lived after more accounting details began to emerge after the new CEO took over.

Notebaert had a new auditor pore over Qwest's books for the previous few years, and announced on July 28 that he expected to restate the firm's financial results for 1999, 2000, and 2001, saying that the company had incorrectly accounted for $1.1 billion in transactions. More restatements could be in the offing. The stock closed at $1.50 that day, a decline of over 96 percent from the previous year. Four months later, the stock was still trading at under $4 a share.

Nacchio did not stroll quietly into the sunset to enjoy his megamillions, however. He had to spend a lot of time with lawyers at his New Jersey mansion. Besides the stockholder and employee lawsuits, there were investigations by the SEC and the Justice Department to worry about. And on October 1 he was summoned to testify before the House Energy & Commerce Committee. Congressional investigators were investigating swaps of network capacity between Global Crossing and Qwest, and whether such exchanges artificially pumped up revenues.

To add to his troubles, just the day before New York State Attorney General Eliot Spitzer had weighed in with personal lawsuits against Nacchio and Anschutz, as well as WorldCom's Bernie Ebbers and some other telecom executives. Spitzer wanted them to return $1.5 billion that they obtained from the sale of stock in their companies, including the exercise of options. The suit also sought the return of $28 million in profits made from selling shares of IPO stocks that were doled out to them by Salomon.

When he testified before the Commerce Committee, Nacchio had to follow a tough act. Gary Winnick, the chairman of Global Crossing, had just disarmed the committee by promising to write a check for $25 million to Global Crossing employees' 401(k) plans. The committee had earlier listened to the stories of a Global Crossing employee who lost $86,000 in her retirement plan, and a laid-off Qwest worker who had lost $230,000 due to the drop in Qwest stock.

Winnick could easily afford such generosity. He'd sold $734 million in Global Crossing stock before the company went bankrupt in January. After denying he'd done anything wrong by dumping his shares, Winnick said he'd nonetheless write out the $25 million check to help reimburse employees for some of the money they'd lost. Winnick challenged other executives to open up their wallets, too.

Then Nacchio took the stand, sounding unusually subdued. Representative Diana De Gette, a Colorado Democrat whose district includes Denver, tried to score some points with voters back home at his expense. She invited Nacchio to follow Winnick's lead and cough up some of his stock gains for Qwest employees.

Nacchio didn't hesitate to turn her down.

"I guess your answer is . . . tough luck," she said.

Nacchio didn't reply.

17

Investors Finally Get Fed Up

The safest way to double your money is to fold it over
and put it in your pocket.
—Kin Hubbard

July is usually a quiet month on Wall Street. It's hot. The bankers and brokers want to take it easy. Investors normally lighten up and read novels instead of financial statements. But July 2002 was not a typical July. It was hot, but it wasn't quiet.

In the last couple of weeks of that month a number of market records were set. All of them were related to the corporate scandals that had been hanging over the market for months like black clouds. In late July, the heavens opened up.

The market had tried to break out earlier in the year after the Enron debacle, but more bad news kept surfacing. Enron wasn't the only corporation caught committing fraud on a massive scale. Every week there was another company caught steaming its books, from Adelphia and AOL Time Warner to WorldCom to Xerox.

Small investors had been patiently holding on to their stocks and mutual funds, hoping that this crisis, too, would pass. They had been through three major market crises in as many years and still held on. When the dot.com bubble popped, they hung in there. When the general market went into a funk led by the blowout in high tech stocks and a softening economy, they were patient. When the terrorist attacks on New York and Washington closed the markets for a week, they thought it their patriotic duty not to sell at the first opportunity. They had faith in the system; they stayed the course. The bull market of the eighties and nineties had brought millions of new investors into the market, and they proved to be remarkably committed to the "buy and hold" philosophy.

In many cases, they became investors whether they liked it or not. The IRA and 401(k) retirement plans that their employers provided *made* them get into the market, most commonly through mutual funds. For a lot of reasons, employers were dumping their conventional retirement plans and replacing them with the 401(k)s. That meant that a lot of folks who would not have gone near the stock market on a bet were now wagering their financial futures on it. What's more, they had to call their own shots.

The typical plan offered a menu of four to ten funds, but it was up to the employee to decide how to allocate his money into stock, bond, or money market funds. Some plans also gave employees a big incentive to buy shares in the companies they worked for, usually by adding additional shares gratis, as long as the stock was held until they left the company. In some cases, employers gave employees one share of stock for every one they purchased with their 401(k) money. This is why so many Enronians lost everything when the Crooked E collapsed. All their money was in that stock and they weren't allowed to sell it.

For most of the nineties, almost everyone was happy with his 401(k) except those who had stayed on the sidelines and left their cash in risk-free money market funds. They didn't lose any money; but their low single-digit returns paled against those of the major market indexes—the Dow Jones Industrials, the S&P 500, and the

NASDAQ 100—as well as a majority of the stock funds. And there were plenty of funds around. By the end of the decade, there were over 7,000 and still counting. In fact, there were more mutual funds than there were stocks traded on the New York Stock Exchange.

This was a brave new world, in which the market would accelerate your retirement, allow you to buy a house sooner, and make it possible to send your kids through college without going into permanent hock. The market was a rising tide that floated all boats. It almost didn't matter what you invested in. Most investors had success beyond their dreams, but not beyond their appetites for even more.

Emboldened by what was happening to their retirement portfolios—which are virtually untouchable until retirement without severe tax penalties—many small investors also opened other investment accounts, outside their retirement plans. As interest rates dropped, some of them took out home equity loans to finance their forays into the market. Some began buying on margin—borrowing from the broker to buy more shares than their investment cash would otherwise allow. A few of them even felt cocky enough to quit their jobs and day trade on their home computers. "The market" replaced football and O.J.'s trial as the universal topic of conversation. Everyone had a hot stock tip and a great story to tell. A bartender pal of mine wouldn't shut up talking about priceline.com. I guess he was a fan of Star Trek and liked William Shatner's commercials.

In the 1920s, the legendary investor Bernard Baruch said that when your shoeshine boy starts giving you stock tips, it's time to sell. He might have well said bartender.

As long as the market kept on heading for the moon, ignorance was bliss. When Alan Greenspan warned of "irrational exuberance" a few years earlier, he was hooted down. Greenspan disclosed that he had all of his own money in Treasury bonds. It seemed silly at the time, but he had the last laugh when stocks tanked in the year 2000.

No one wanted the party to end, and everyone and his brother seemed to have shown up—except Greenspan. Forty-nine percent of U.S. households owned mutual funds in 2000, versus only 5.7 percent in 1980. As recently as 1992, only 27 percent of American households owned funds, according to the Investment Company Institute. It wasn't just high-income earners who owned shares. Fifty-eight percent had incomes of $25,000 to $75,000, and another 9 percent earned less than $25,000 a year. The market's rise even prompted legislative proposals to allow taxpayers to buy securities with their Social Security contributions. Think tanks like the American Enterprise Institute produced papers proving how it would not only enrich taxpayers but also solve the government's chronic problem of funding the program.

No one wanted to throw a damper on that party. The few financial journalists who consistently shouted that the end was near were ignored or mocked. Chris Byron, who then wrote for the *New York Observer* and the MSNBC website, delighted in ripping apart new IPOs that had spectacular jumps in price, yet had little or no earnings, and sometimes laughable business plans. For his prescience, Byron was bitterly attacked by the new breed of cybertouts who took advantage of the internet to rip into anyone who knocked the stocks they owned. Some of these cyberpunks even accused Byron of short-selling the companies he dissected. Their flaming e-mails and posts in chat rooms were downright libelous.

How could anyone not believe in the New Economy and its high-tech ways? It was supposed to be changing everything. *Business Week* ran a cover story on January 11, 2000, with the headline, "The New Economy—It Works in America. Will It Go Global?"

In the New Economy, the boom-bust business cycle was dead. The graph of market performance from 1982 to 2000 looked like an escalator ramp. This market didn't pause to digest gains; it just went up.

In the financial chat rooms, newbie investors whose research consisted of watching TV and gleaning tips from friends, bragged about their investment savvy. They threw terms around they dimly understood. Large cap growth stocks were okay for sissies, but if you really wanted to score, you went to the NASDAQ, where the real action was, in high tech and internet stocks. If you didn't know which ones to buy, you needn't have worried. There was now a nifty NASDAQ index that you could buy with just a few keystrokes on your computer. It tracked the one hundred largest stocks on the NASDAQ. Never mind what they were. The QQQ, nicknamed "Cube" was where the smart money was going.

Like many small investors, I used to browse those chat rooms on financial websites. (Full disclosure: For a year, I worked for one such site, Microsoft's moneycentral.com.) I remember a posting on one of those sites in late 1999 that made a permanent impression. It typified the euphoria of the times. An investor was confidently predicting his retirement in two years, based on his faith in the QQQ, which had been doing extremely well. "One more double," he wrote, "that's all I need. I don't want to be greedy. Just one more double and I'll be out of here." He was already shopping for a retirement home in Florida. He figured the QQQ would double in two years, and no one called him nuts. The index had only been trading since March of 1999, and closed out the year up an astonishing 79 percent. What could be easier? No research, no due diligence, no muss, no fuss. Just buy the QQQ and go shopping for a retirement home.

But there is an old saw in the investment business: Past performance is no guarantee of future performance. Smart investors have memorized it. Yet as Warren Buffett has noted, most investors make investment decisions by looking into a rear-view mirror.

In the spring of 2000, I was sitting in for Bob Brinker on his financial call-in program, "MoneyTalk," when a woman in her seventies called in. She had recently been talking to a broker, she said, who urged her to put her entire nest egg—several hundred thousand dollars, everything she had in the world—into Cisco Systems. When I asked her what the company made, she said she didn't know, but her broker said everyone was buying it, so it didn't matter. It didn't matter? She didn't know Cisco from Crisco, and she was putting every penny in the world into it? When I told her that her broker should have his license taken away from him for even suggesting something so absurd, she became defensive. "All it does is go up." Cisco was then trading at about $70 a share and had enjoyed a spectacular run, up from about $25 a share since January 1999. I pleaded with her not to buy it and told her never to speak to that broker again. I begged her not to put any money into anything she didn't understand, especially one stock. I go along with Bob Brinker that you should not invest any more than 4 percent of your investment money in any single company, even the one you work for. If you have stock options, you should diversify your portfolio whenever you exercise your options.

Finally, the caller relented and promised me that she would not put her money into "Crisco." I hope she meant it. Otherwise, she would have lost almost 80 percent of her nest egg. As of November 2002, Cisco was trading at $14. For the record, Cisco makes networking and communications products and services. Its biggest customers are telecommunications companies, major corporations, and public institutions. Its business hit a wall as soon as the telecoms stopped expanding. It would not have taken a lot of homework to predict it.

I don't hold myself out as a market guru, and don't pretend to know where the market is headed at any given time. Nor do I make evaluations on individual stocks. I prefer to invest in index mutual funds and their cousins, like SPYders and Diamonds, as well as bond funds like GNMAEs and bond index funds. Not very sexy, but there you have it. There are two reasons for this. If you are a financial journalist and have a portfolio of stocks there is always the possibility of a conflict of interest. You might have to write or edit a story about a company that you own. Or you might know of an upcoming story that could move a stock. The best financial publications put all kinds of rules and restrictions on trading by employees. At *Forbes*, for example, you were never allowed to short a stock, and all short-term trading was discouraged. As a result, most financial writers I know invest in mutual funds.

There's another reason I like funds, especially index funds. Historically, they outperform portfolios of individual stocks yet have a lower risk rating because of all the diversification they offer. A no-load fund is also cheaper to own than a portfolio of stocks.

Bob Brinker is also a believer in index funds, and for the ten-plus years that I substituted for him on "MoneyTalk," was a long-term bull. But Brinker, who is indeed a market guru who also publishes an investment newsletter called *Marketimer*, made an extraordinary call on his national radio program and in his newsletter in January of 2000. After ten years of recommending that investors put 100 percent of their investment cash into stocks, he suddenly advised investors to yank most of their chips off the table. His suggestion: Put 60 percent of your money into cash and only 40 percent in equities. (He later upped that to 65 percent in cash.)

Bob had become a bear, and predicted it would be a long winter. At the time, the Dow Jones was very close to its all time high of 11,722, which it hit on January 14, within days of Brinker's call.

His prediction did not go over well. He was telling the crowd at the party that the cops had just pulled up outside the door. No one wanted to believe him. But listeners and readers who heeded his counsel largely avoided the market's long slide over the next several years. The slide started quickly and dramatically. On March 7, 2000, the DJIA stood at 9,796, a drop of 16.5 percent in just seven weeks. The longest economic boom in history was over, after 107 months of expansion. Bob was right on the money. He would be one of only a few investment newsletter writers to beat the market over the decade according to the *Hulbert Financial Digest*.

In November 2002, thirty-three months after Brinker gave his sell recommendation, the DJIA was at 8,513, and he had still not issued a buy signal, meaning he thought that the bear was still in control. His long-awaited MOABO ("Mother Of All Buying Opportunities") was not yet at hand.

Few investors bailed out of the market when he suggested. They stayed the course through the lean years 2000, 2001, and into 2002.

But the corporate scandals that kept on unfolding that year finally sparked a significant number of them to leave the market in disgust.

Most investors don't know a balance sheet from a balance wheel, but they had assumed that corporations' numbers were legitimate, and that the people who ran those companies could be trusted. They were wrong on both counts, and they were made acutely aware of it all in the summer of 2002.

In late June, WorldCom disclosed that it wrongly took $3.8 billion worth of expenses, and charged it as income. The $3.8 billion should have been charged as losses, not profits. Sorry about that. Somehow, it took years for anyone to spot the fraud. That extraordinary flip-flop was later revised upward. In fact, the misstatement was really $7 billion, making it far and away the biggest act of fraud in corporate history.

That little disclosure led to the first important record that was set in July: the largest bankruptcy in American corporate history. WorldCom's bankruptcy far surpassed Enron's, and its cause was the same—massive fraud and blind accountants. Its auditor was—guess who—Arthur Andersen.

The moment of shame came for WorldCom on a sultry Sunday afternoon, July 21, in a crowded courtroom at the U.S. Bankruptcy Court in downtown Manhattan. WorldCom's lawyers filed for protection under Chapter 11 as a handful of executives and reporters observed and sweated in the steamy courtroom. The replacement CEO, John Sidgmore, showed up himself, as if to say, "Hey, this mess isn't my fault."

Everyone knew this was Bernie Ebbers's mess; he was at the controls until being booted out as CEO a few months earlier, even before the $3.8 billion (later $7 billion) error was reported.

WorldCom, Ebbers's baby from the beginning, had become the second largest telecommunications company in the country but it no longer had enough money to stay in business. The company's list of creditors was long, from unpaid individuals and corporations to the company's own 401(k) plan. WorldCom had even welched on its own employees.

It had been obvious for days that WorldCom's bankruptcy was soon to come, and the market didn't like that news at all. Anticipation of the bankruptcy, and of the spreading scandals, had already put the market into a swoon.

On the Friday before the filing, the New York Stock Exchange experienced its busiest day ever, with stocks plunging 4.6 percent in a single session. The already sour market was off a total of 15 percent in a matter of only two weeks. No one was calling it a panic, because no one wanted to get killed running for the exits. But if there is such a thing as a controlled panic, this was it. From German banks to pension funds to mutual fund holders, the word was "sell." More shares changed hands that day at the New York Stock Exchange— over 2.6 billion shares—than on any other day in stock market history.

The weekend only suspended the exodus. On Monday, July 22, after a quiet morning, huge blocks of stock began trading at rapidly falling prices all afternoon. Curbs had to be put in to slow the selling.

The collapse of WorldCom wasn't the only bad news driving the market down that Monday. There was word that Citigroup and J.P. Morgan Chase were also in trouble with the feds. The corporate scandals were now reaching into the *sanctum sanctorum* of American capitalism. Citigroup was the largest bank in the world and J.P. Morgan Chase second. Were the largest financial institutions in the world crooked, too?

Investigators had been looking at the banks' books in connection with the Enron collapse, as both banks were big lenders to Enron. They found that some very peculiar financial transactions had taken place. With its insatiable need for cash, and reluctance to show loans on the balance sheet, Enron had concocted ways to borrow billions from the banks without calling them loans.

The loans were disguised as commodity trades, known as prepayments. Of course, no commodities ever changed hands. What would a bank want with a trillion cubic feet of natural gas? The transactions went through some evasive loops—including the use of offshore vehicles controlled by the banks—to make the loans look like trades.

In testimony before a Senate committee that Monday in July, investigators put it bluntly: "The evidence indicates that Enron would not have been able to engage in the extent of the accounting deception it did, involving billions of dollars, were it not for the active participation of major financial institutions." The investigators claimed that banks including Citigroup and J.P Morgan Chase were "willing to go along with and even expand upon Enron's activities."

The banks were already facing lawsuits from pension finds and other institutions that had taken pieces of the Enron loans. It was bad enough to lose money on the loans; now investigators were alleging that the banks helped Enron perpetrate its fraud.

The old saying about bad news coming in threes was borne out yet again for Citigroup. As a matter of fact, it came in fours. First was the WorldCom bankruptcy, then the Enron business. On the very same day that federal investigators accused the banks of enabling Enron's kooky deals, Sandy Weill, Citigroup's CEO, got a third shock. The National Association of Securities Dealers announced that it was prepared to take regulatory action against Salomon Smith Barney—a division of Citigroup—and its infamous security analyst, Jack Grubman.

The NASD is not a lobbying group for the financial community, nor a trade association, but it is hardly an enemy. It does police its members, but it is like the friendly cop on the beat who gives a kid a smack on his rear with his nightstick instead of hauling him in front of a judge. But here it was claiming more foul play at mighty Citigroup.

Jack Grubman, the never-say-die WorldCom tout, was being charged this time for making deliberately misleading calls on yet another telecom stock, Winstar. Winstar was also a big customer of Salomon Smith Barney, and Grubman was bullish on Winstar right up until its end in the spring of 2001. He had remained a cheerleader just as he had for Global Crossing and WorldCom, two other telecoms that went bankrupt. Jack Grubman was turning out to be the best contrary indicator in history. If you shorted the telecoms that he touted, you would have made a fortune.

In addition to the NASD, New York State Attorney General Eliot Spitzer was also considering charges against Grubman and Salomon Smith Barney for misleading small investors with overly optimistic research reports on companies that gave Salomon investment banking business.

Before Weill could clear his throat, the fourth torpedo hit. There was yet another probe to deal with, involving the allocation of shares of IPOs, or initial public offerings. On July 22, House Financial Services Committee Chairman Michael Oxley ordered WorldCom and Arthur Andersen to submit records showing which of their executives received allocations of IPO stock from Salomon Smith Barney. In the bubble days, when IPOs of dot.coms often rocketed overnight in value, such allocations amounted to gifts—or payoffs, depending on your point of view.

The practice was called "spinning," and regular readers of the *Wall Street Journal* had a good giggle when the House probe was announced, because the paper had been writing about those IPO allocations as far back as 1997. The SEC and the NASD then said they were investigating the practice, but no measures had yet been taken to prevent it.

Was there a quid pro quo in the allocation of these hot IPO shares? The practice was widespread, and many executives whose companies were doing business with the investment banks were happy to cash in. "It's a black-and-white corporate bribery issue," said Steven Wallman, a recently departed SEC commissioner, in the *Wall Street Journal.*

Meg Whitman, the CEO of Ebay, was among many who didn't see it that way. Her explanation for making a quick $1.78 million on shares allocated to her by one of Ebay's investment bankers, Goldman Sachs, went like this: "While reasonable people can debate whether giving private banking clients preferred access to IPO shares is fair or whether policies regarding such transactions should be reformed, there is no question about the legality of this practice today." Her explanation, in a memo sent to Ebay's staff, amounted to this: It was legal, and everyone else was doing it, so I did it.

But some Ebay stockholders didn't see it that way. They thought that if lagniappes were being handed out by investment banks in return for business, the money ought to go to the company, not the CEO and fellow executives and directors. In one suit, filed by Rickey Broussard, the stockholder claimed "they caused harm to the company by using their positions of authority to advance their own personal interests at the expense of the company. They have misappropriated financial benefits, derived from EBay's relationship with Goldman, which rightfully belonged to Ebay."

Whitman, who soon joined the board of directors of Goldman, had to defend herself against that suit, and in the court of public opinion. In her memo to the staff, the Harvard MBA–degree holder also wrote that her $1.78 million gain she netted from spinning the IPO shares was "a small fraction of my total personal holdings on account with Goldman Sachs." Whitman ranked number 300 on the *Forbes* list of richest Americans in 2001, worth $708 million.

Why did she risk the assault on her integrity and that of the company that she has run so well? She certainly didn't need the money. Nor could she have been unaware of how unfair the practice is to small shareholders. Shades of Martha Stewart. Note: Whitman later resigned from the board of Goldman, Sachs.

At the center of the House's probe into spinning at Citigroup's SSB unit was the ubiquitous Jack Grubman once again. At another House committee hearing earlier in the month on WorldCom, Grubman had testified that he had actually attended WorldCom board meetings, which is unheard of for a mere analyst. Now House Committee Chairman Michael Oxley wanted to know who invited him to those meetings, and what was discussed. Some of those board members, as well as the CEO, Bernie Ebbers, and the CFO, Scott Sullivan, and his wife, Carla, had been awarded juicy IPO shares from SSB, on which they made quick profits.

Was Grubman doling out shares to reward WorldCom and other telecom executives in return for investment business? He had already been charged with selling out his research recommendations. It surely looked that way. July 22 had proven to be a very bad day for Grubman, for Citigroup, and for investors.

When the bell rang at 4 p.m. on the floor of the New York Stock Exchange, the Dow had dropped another 2.8 percent from Friday, closing at 7,784.58, its lowest point since October 1998.

At countless kitchen tables around the country that night, families looked at their shriveled 401(k) and other investments and shook their heads in despair. Millions of owners of S&P index funds had watched their portfolios drop 17 percent in value in only eleven trading days. Years of gains were gone. Out came the calculators and away went a lot of hopes and dreams. Retirement dates were pushed into the future. Vacations and trips were cancelled. Second thoughts were given to college for the kids. A lot of retirees faced going back to work, if they could find it.

In the ensuing days, despite a 488-point "dead cat" bounce the next day, there was yet more fallout from the corporate scandals.

Enronesque accounting tricks were revealed at El Paso Gas, another large and wounded energy giant. The whole energy sector was now suspect, and having a very rough time raising fresh capital.

The SEC reported it was looking into reports that AOL Time Warner may have inflated revenue in 2000 and 2001. AOL was accused of exaggerating revenue from online advertising sales. Already spooked by a $56-billion goodwill write-off early in the year, and dimming profit prospects because of the advertising slump, investors punished the stock even more. Shares dropped $2.60, or nearly 23 percent, to $8.70 on July 25.

Ironically, the company had just reported its very first quarterly profit since the merger. But the SEC probe terrified investors, who made the stock the most actively traded on the New York Stock Exchange the day of the announcement.

AOL Time Warner, the largest media conglomerate in the world, had slid beneath the important $10-a-share barrier. Many mutual funds and other large institutional investors will not buy stocks in the single digits.

Stockholders had watched Time Warner stock drop from a high of $92.25 a few weeks before merger in January 2000, to under $10, a loss of almost 90 percent.

Almost lost amidst all the accounting scandals were some terrible earnings reports from other corporate giants in trouble. AT&T posted a record loss of $12.7 billion in a single quarter. The main reason was a huge writedown for the sale of cable TV assets for far less than AT&T paid for them.

Chairman Michael Armstrong had been on a cable-buying binge, and spent more than $100 billion for cable assets. The idea was to offer customers TV, internet, and telephone service through cable. But Armstrong then decided to sell those assets to Comcast for only $52 billion. Armstrong was slated to become chairman of Comcast after leaving AT&T at the end of the year. The cable asset sale was certainly a nice way of making himself welcome at his new company.

The writedown let even more air out of the stock of AT&T, once deemed a refuge because of its stability and routine dividends. Many small investors had stayed with the company through all the turmoil of post-deregulation.

AT&T stock fell to $8.20 on July 24, its lowest level since 1988. In all, AT&T stock had dropped 67 percent during Armstrong's tenure. Not to worry, he had a nice, new job waiting for him.

Another big loser that day was Tyco International, the house that Dennis Kozlowski built. It posted a $2.32 billion loss for the third quarter. The stock dropped 10 percent, to $10.85. Since Jan. 1, the stock had shriveled by 80 percent. Rumors of a pending bankruptcy sent the shares down another 17 percent the next day.

A lot of small investors decided that they had seen enough. During the month of July, they dumped their mutual funds in record numbers.

When the final tally came in, redemptions of stock mutual funds for the month topped $52.6 billion—an all-time record. These were not transfers from one type of fund to another. The proceeds from their sales went into bank and money market accounts.

In the months that followed, investors kept on yanking money out of their stock mutual funds. After redeeming the record $52.6 billion in July, investors redeemed another $2.9 billion in August, $16.1 billion in September, and $7.7 billion in October. In June 2002, they had redeemed another $18 billion. So over the five-month period from June through October, while the corporate scandals filled the news, investors pulled a total of almost $100 billion out of stock funds, another all-time record.

The corporate scandals had succeeded in doing what the terrorists had failed to do on 9-11: destroying investor confidence in the stock market. Winning back that confidence could take years.

18

Sanford Weill: The Prince and the Banker

Banking establishments are more dangerous than standing armies.
—Thomas Jefferson

Prince Alwaleed bin Talal often spends part of his weekend camping out in the desert some forty miles north of Riyadh. But as befits a member of the Saudi royal family, and one of the world's richest men, he doesn't rough it in a pup tent.

He sits cross-legged against plush cushions under a huge fiberglass panoply big enough to cover a couple of tennis courts. His attendants and bodyguards and a clutch of supplicants are careful not to block the giant, flat-screen televisions scattered around the compound.

The prince channel surfs CNN, CNBC, Fox, and Bloomberg for news and financial information that is beamed in via satellite. Supplicants and visitors come and go as he nibbles from a low table crammed with delicacies, sips tea or Pepsi, works the phones, and chats with attendants and the occasional journalist who is invited to join him.

Bedouin leaders in tribal costumes sing his praises and beseech him for money and jobs, and are seldom refused. According to David Lynch, who wrote of his evening with the prince in *USA Today*, he gives away an estimated $100 million a year to his people—fruits from an investment portfolio in the tens of billions.

Prince Alwaleed is the largest non-U.S. stockholder in the world, who delights in being called the Middle East's Warren Buffett. He has major investments in News Corp., AOL, Apple, Motorola, Priceline, and other corporations. He also owns hotels from the Middle East to the U.S., including the Plaza in New York and the George V in Paris, as well a major slice of EuroDisney.

But his biggest holding of all is Citigroup, of which he owns about 15 percent, and he is its largest shareholder. At one time his investment was worth about half his fortune of $20 billion.

In the spring of 2002, when the first whiffs of trouble began emanating from Citigroup's Park Avenue headquarters, the stock fell to $42 a share, down from $58 in August 2000. Prince Alwaleed then told a *Wall Street Journal* reporter that the $42 price was "dirt cheap," and bought another $500 million worth of shares.

But by July 24, 2001, the stock had dropped to $23 amid more revelations and charges about Enron and WorldCom loans, and Jack Grubman's tainted research and IPO spinning. The piling on by regulators intensified worries that the bank was facing the loss of billions of dollars in loan losses, fines, and lawsuits that could take years to settle. Prince Alwaleed's stake had shrunk by at least $2 billion.

How had he become such a large shareholder? Alwaleed's relations with Citigroup go back to 1979, when he returned to Saudi Arabia after graduating from Menlo College, in the San Francisco Bay area. The twenty-two-year-old, who also attended Syracuse University, began speculating in the local real estate and stock markets, bankrolled with a $30,000 gift from his father—which he soon exhausted.

"I ran out of money immediately," he told CNBC. "So I had, ironically, to go to Citibank, in Riyadh, to borrow money." The bank turned him down at first, but once his father posted collateral, Alwaleed had $300,000 to play with. In a little over a decade, his Kingdom Holdings Trust had investments worth hundreds of millions, not strictly from investment gains, however. Like all Saudi royals, he was in a position to extract "commissions" from foreign companies that wanted to do business in his country. Elsewhere they're called bribes, but they are a mandatory cost of doing business in Saudi Arabia, where the royals take very good care of themselves. Alwaleed acknowledged that such "commissions" added significantly to his wealth.

There was a lot of construction going on in the country over the decade, and a lot of commissions had to be paid, and the prince got his share. His coffers were overflowing in February 1991, at the start of the Gulf War. When the shooting started, the U.S. market plunged and the CEO of Citigroup, John Reed, had a major problem on his hands. The bank's real estate portfolio was sinking fast as defaults mounted. Cash reserves dropped dangerously low. The bank was in danger of running out of money, which is not good for a bank.

"We were in serious trouble," Reed told CNBC. "And we clearly needed to raise capital."

Alwaleed's Kingdom Holding Co. had already been scooping up shares of the ailing bank to the tune of about $200 million. Reed figured that if the prince liked the company that much, he would give him the opportunity to really love it. He offered to sell the prince $590 million worth of bonds, convertible to common stock. The deal was made, and Alwaleed, who is a grandson of Saudi Arabia's founder, King Abdul-Aziz, wound up with 15 percent of the entire bank and became its largest shareholder.

"In the history of Citibank and Citicorp, it was one of the defining moments," Reed said. Relations between the U.S. and Saudi Arabia were then very cordial—U.S troops used Saudi Arabia as a staging area for the Gulf War. But a scandal surrounding the Bank of Credit and Commerce International cooled relations a bit. BCCI, which was controlled by wealthy investors in the Middle East, was part of a front to secretly buy and control U.S. banks. Alwaleed had nothing to do with BCCI, but the idea of a Saudi owning such a large chunk of Citicorp unnerved the Federal Reserve. (Never mind that the West had been getting rich on Saudi oil for generations.) The prince agreed to cut his ownership to 9.9 percent, and shed $364 million of the stock. Too bad for him. The Citicorp investment proved to be the best winner he ever had. A decade later, it was worth about $10 billion, not counting $1 billion he took out in 2000.

Another big investment by the prince did not turn out to be so successful, however. In 1994, Disney was having problems with the EuroDisney theme park outside Paris and Michael Eisner came calling. Alwaleed sank $345 million in the park, which never took off. "The problem was that we overestimated what Europeans were able to pay for a ticket and for a hotel room," Eisner told CNBC. "So our game plan was not as healthy as we anticipated." The value of Alwaleed's EuroDisney investment has slid over 40 percent. Another clunker in his portfolio was Planet Hollywood, into which he dumped $110 million. "Sometimes we get it wrong," he said.

Another thing that Alwaleed got wrong was the timing of his political advice. After the 9/11 terrorist attacks that murdered thousands of innocent people in New York and Washington, Alwaleed accompanied New York's Mayor Rudy Giuliani on an eight-hour visit to the rubble of the World Trade Center. He said he deplored al Qaeda's "criminal act" and wrote a check for $10 million for the Twin Towers Fund, to help the families of rescuers who were killed. But he also urged the U.S. "to reexamine its policies in the Middle East and adopt a more balanced stance toward the Palestinian cause."

Giuliani, a strong supporter of Israel, promptly returned the $10 million check (without checking with the intended recipients). The prince took it all in stride, however, and later told an Arab newspaper: "I am a Muslim, an Arab, a Saudi, and a nationalist. I am interested in my nation's causes and I condemn terrorism. I love

America, and the American is my friend—but the Palestinian is my brother."

Alwaleed added that he was holding Palestinian citizenship granted by President Yasser Arafat. "I have a Palestinian passport and I am proud of this," he told *Al-Watan*, an Arab daily newspaper.

It could not have been very pleasant for Sandy Weill, Citicorp's CEO and chairman and a major contributor to Jewish charities, to hear his biggest stockholder tell the U.S. what to do about Israel and brag about his Palestinian passport. But capitalism can make strange bedfellows. After all, it was the West that made the Saudi royals rich in the first place, and it was Citigroup that went to Alwaleed for financial support.

On the day the stock dropped to $23, Alwaleed called Weill, who tried to calm him with a little humor. "I guess you and I have lost a little money this week, your Highness," Weill said, according to Alwaleed. Weill's stake in the company had dropped $162 million in seven days.

The prince's stake had dropped a lot more than that, and he wasn't in a joking mood. "I think Sandy has to clarify the situation of Citibank much more aggressively," he told *Business Week*. But he made it clear he wasn't looking to sell. "This is not only the most profitable bank in the world, but it is also the cheapest," he said. Still, he wasn't offering to buy any more shares this time around.

Weill was facing the biggest crisis of his career. While the pressure had been building for some time, he now had to act fast to prevent even more severe damage to Citigroup and, even more important, to his own reputation. Weill was a billionaire by now, a power in politics, a philanthropist, a patron of the arts, and a fixture in New York society. Citigroup was too big, too profitable, and too powerful to be seriously hurt for long.

But Weill, at sixty-nine and at the pinnacle of a legendary career, feared he might not get another chance to have this ugly chapter fade into the background. There was even the possibility that the board might ask him to step down. Weill would do everything in his power to see that did not happen.

Clearly, he had three priorities: Get the stock up again; get the regulators off the company's back; and deal with "the Grubman issue." He wasted little time in taking action.

On July 25, the bank announced that it was speeding up its stock-repurchase program, and within days bought $2 billion worth of shares. Weill had authorization from the board to repurchase up to $5.5 billion in additional shares.

Next, Weill had to publicly answer the most serious charges that had been hurled at the bank. In a letter to Citigroup's employees, he denied that the bank had done anything wrong in making the controversial pre-payment loans to Enron.

He announced that the bank would be making significant changes in the way its analysts operated, to preclude conflicts of interest. The letter could have been entitled, "These are the things Jack Grubman and his crew have been doing for years, but we're not going to allow anymore."

Investment bankers would no longer be able to screen research reports or have any say in how analysts are paid. Analysts should be prevented by law from making sales calls with investment bankers, he suggested. And he said that Citigroup was taking immediate steps to adopt the SEC's new proposal for analysts "to certify" that they have not traded research recommendations for dollars.

In short, Weill was taking a preemptive strike at what the regulators were suggesting be made law.

The stock buyback and the reassurances of change—without admitting any wrongdoing—seemed to work. Within a week, the stock soon bounced back to the mid-$30 range. Although there were still a lot of problems to deal with, especially lawsuits, Weill seemed to have things under control. But by August 6, the stock began slipping again, and was down to $30. The next day Weill sent another memo, outlining more changes.

He announced that the company would be expensing options, and that a new governance board would be created. And he reiterated the company's policy of requiring senior management to hold on to 75 percent of any stock or stock options as long as they were with the company.

There was more, too. Weill addressed the issue of Enron-type loans. In short, there would be no more loans to companies hiding the debt from investors. (Though the memo did not admit Citigroup had ever done any such thing.)

Within weeks of that fateful July 22 bombardment, it appeared that Sandy Weill had managed to disarm the regulators, answer the critics, and send the stock back on its merry way. Earnings were still strong, it appeared that the crisis had peaked. Weill was winning the biggest fight of his life.

Of course there was still one dicey piece of business to deal with—Jack Grubman. On August 16, Grubman was asked to resign, and he agreed. He walked away with a severance package worth $32 million. That would not be the last Sandy Weill would hear of Jack Grubman, however.

The quickie, rags-to-riches version of Weill's career describes him as clawing his way out of poverty, a poor Brooklyn kid who overcame his humble origins to run one of the largest and most profitable financial institutions in the world. But his story is no hackneyed, Horatio Alger yarn. It is far more colorful and complicated, and even ironic. (For a complete biography, pick up a copy of *The King of Capital: Sandy Weill and the Making of Citigroup*, by Amey Stone and Mike Brewster.)

Weill may not have been born with a silver spoon in his mouth, or with a squadron of attendants to plump his cushions for him, but he was hardly underprivileged. His grandparents had the hard time, not him.

His maternal grandfather, Philip Kalika, fled the pogroms in Poland in the early 1900s and emigrated to New York where he eventually wound up in the garment business.

The "rag trade," as the garment business is still called on New

York's Seventh Avenue, was the first lowly rung on the economic ladder for many poor Jewish immigrants to the New World. They hustled pushcarts through the streets or worked long hours in sweatshops doing piece work for pennies. Kalika didn't stay on the bottom for long, and after only a few years owned his own dressmaking business. It thrived for decades in an industry where margins were as thin as a cheap cotton shirt. Kalika learned fast, and adapted quickly to changes in taste, materials, and manufacturing.

In 1919, he bought a large two-family home in Bensonhurst, then a pleasant, middle class neighborhood of single and two-family homes with big backyards and wide, leafy streets where you could play stickball without fear of getting run over.

It was home for the extended Kalika family. Weill grew up in that home, where his parents lived along with his grandparents and an uncle and aunt. Weill still keeps a photograph of the home in his office.

Sanford I. Weill was born, as they used to say in New York, "at the height of the Depression," on March 16, 1933. Unemployment stood at 25 percent, economic output had dropped by a third, and there had just been a run on the banks. Looking for scapegoats on whom to blame the financial mess the country was in, Congress naturally fingered the bankers in general and National City Bank in particular. NCB was then the largest bank in the country. Charles Mitchell, the president of the bank—the precursor of Citigroup—was hauled in front of a Senate committee and forced to resign. He was charged with income tax evasion by an ambitious young prosecutor from the New York District Attorney's office named Thomas E. Dewey (who later lost a presidential election to Harry Truman). Mitchell beat the tax evasion charges, but agreed to pay over $1 million in back taxes. For decades, the name Charlie Mitchell meant dirty, rotten banker.

Dozens of banks had failed after panicked depositors withdrew all their cash. To stem the panic, newly elected President Franklin D. Roosevelt ordered every bank in the country to close on March 6, 1933. The banks were reopened the day Weill was born. The day was historic for another reason, too. Prohibition ended, and low-alcohol beer and wine became legal.

But the banks would no longer be able to operate as they once had. That year Congress passed the Glass-Steagall Act, which divided banks into two distinct and separate categories: investment banks, which served the investment community; and commercial banks, which served depositors and borrowers. In effect, the Glass-Steagall Act prevented banks from taking depositors' money and investing it in the stock market. It made a lot of sense after the Crash of 1929, and the act endured for sixty-five years. But in 1998, Sandy Weill prevailed upon Congress to repeal that act so he could create Citigroup.

Weill's grandfather proved a far better businessman that Sandy's own dad, Max, called Mac. Bankrolled by his father-in-law, Mac opened a dressmaking business with his brother-in-law, but it sputtered. In 1944, Mac was indicted for price-gouging on dress materials he sold. The sum involved was a relatively small amount—about $8,000—but this was serious business during World War II, and Mac Weill was convicted, fined, and sentenced to three years in prison. He paid a $10,000 fine and the prison term was suspended. A year later, Mac moved the family to Miami to make a fresh start, but two years later returned to Brooklyn. But there was a lot of tension in the house in Flatbush where they moved. The parents fought; Sandy started to slip in his studies at public school.

The family decided to send him off to Peekskill Military Academy, not to discipline him so much as to get him out of a poisonous environment. The Weills finally divorced a few years later.

Located near West Point, Peekskill Military was something of a prep school for the U.S. Military Academy, and emulated its stringent military schedules and discipline. Weill fit right in at the school, despite the fact he had been an indifferent student and was distracted by his parents' deteriorating marriage. He said that the discipline and the success that he enjoyed there gave him a lot of confidence later.

He played the bass drum in the band, and did well enough in his studies that in his senior year he was elected to the National Honor Society, graduating third in his class. Never good at contact sports, Weill took to tennis and excelled in the game, winning the Westchester county schoolboy championship. He also adapted well to the military regimen, and was an officer during his junior and senior years. Only eight students were officers at any given time.

After graduating in 1951 he went on to Cornell to study engineering, but found it too demanding and switched his major to government. That gave him more time to play poker with his fraternity brothers at Alpha Epsilon Pi, and to become involved in student government and play on the college tennis team.

Cornell was one of the few Ivy League schools to have women students at the time, and Weill dated a few girls on campus but found the woman who would become his wife, Joan Mosher, back in his old neighborhood. She was an education major at Brooklyn College and despite her family's initial objections, she married him in 1955, after he finished college. The marriage has lasted almost half a century.

It was time to find a job, and with nothing specific in mind, Weill drifted to Wall Street, where there were always a lot of lousy paying jobs to be had, but some very good ones, too. He started off on the bottom rung, as a runner at Bear Stearns, and quickly caught on to the game: The more money that goes through your hands, the more you can keep. He got his broker's license and became a good salesman in a hurry. One of his colleagues was Alan "Ace" Greenberg, who is today chairman of Bear Stearns. "It was easy to see he was a winner," Greenberg later told *Money* magazine.

Weill fell in naturally with guys who also had success written all over them. In 1960, when Weill was twenty-seven, he and several chums chipped in a total of $200,000 to open their own brokerage business, called Carter, Berlind, Potoma and Weill. They would all go on to great success. Roger Berlind is the Tony award–winning producer of *Amadeus, City of Angels,* and twenty-three other Broadway plays; Arthur Carter is the publisher of the *New York Observer;* Marshall Cogan was owner of the 21 Club restaurant; and Arthur

Levitt, who joined the firm as a young salesman in 1963, became chairman of the Securities and Exchange Commission.

In his latest book, Levitt recalls those early days with fondness, but not much pride: "Our mandate was to grind out the gross and recruit new brokers with a proven knack for selling. But on the Wall Street I knew in the 1960s and 70s, the training of new brokers was almost nonexistent. Brokers were hired one day and put to work the next cold-calling customers. At all but a few firms, research was primitive."

Weill was the engine behind the small brokerage, but he itched to grow a lot bigger. When Hayden Stone, a much larger firm, was about to go under, he engineered a guppy-swallows-whale takeover. It was a bad decade for the market, which was stuck in a time warp. Other brokers began closing their doors, and Weill acquired Shearson Hamill, and then Loeb, Rhodes to form Shearson Loeb. He sold out to American Express for $1 billion in 1981.

Never one to underestimate his talents, Weill figured he would one day run the whole show as CEO, but now it was his turn to be stuck in a time warp. For four years he bided his time, waiting for a call that never came, and finally left American Express to start building his own financial services giant on his own. Improbably, he did it. In 1986, he bought a small consumer-loan business called Commercial Credit and for the next twelve years made a slew of shrewd acquisitions of brokerage houses, insurance companies, financial planners, and credit companies, combining operations and slashing costs. The result was Travelers Group, which included Salomon Smith Barney, Salomon Smith Barney Asset Management, Travelers Life & Annuity, Primerica Financial Services, Travelers Property Casualty Corp., and Commercial Credit.

But Weill wasn't finished. At age sixty-five, and already a wealthy and respected figure in New York and Washington circles, there were no more rungs on the ladder—just the top step. Weill stepped up to it.

He decided to merge Travelers Group with Citicorp. But there was one major problem: Such a merger would clearly be against the law. That old Glass-Steagall Act from 1933, as old as Weill's baby booties, stood in the way. The act specifically prohibited investment banks and commercial banks from doing business under the same umbrella, including that cute little red umbrella that was Travelers' logo. Another yellowing piece of legislation, the Bank Company Holding Act, also barred such a combination. Not to worry, Weill would worry about that later.

Even for Sandy Weill, who never met a president he didn't like, this was a brassy move. Operating at top speed, it would take a year at the minimum to get Congressional approval of legislation enabling such a merger. After all, it would mean striking down two laws that had served the nation well for many decades. Other than realizing Sandy Weill's dream of running the largest financial services company in the universe, there didn't seem any reason to change them.

It was still not a good idea to combine banks that take in depositors' cash and combine them with banks that underwrite dot.coms. But Weill called upon his Washington friends and and made his pitch. The Federal Reserve doesn't change laws, but it can alter rules. That's all Weill wanted—at first. (Weill became a director of the Federal Reserve Bank of New York in 2001.)

On April 6, 1998, Citicorp and Travelers Group announced the merger, which had a value of $140 billion and created the largest financial services company on the globe, serving over one hundred million customers in 100 countries around the world.

It was unclear then how the small customers of this new behemoth would fare after the merger, but elephants seldom worry about fleas.

The megadeal created a bank with assets of $700 billion, and net revenues of $50 billion. (It would become much larger after subsequent acquisitions.)

Stockholders loved the deal, especially since the shareholders of both companies would wind up with new stock without having to pay taxes on their existing shares. "Our ability to serve consumers, corporations, institutions and government agencies, domestic and foreign, will be without parallel," read the press release. "This is a combination whose time has come."

Exactly *why* the time had come for the creation of such a colossus was never pointed out. Was it Sandy Weill's recent sixty-fifth birthday, two weeks earlier?

And what about the laws preventing such a merger? On the third page of the press release were a few paragraphs that showed just how much power Sandy Weill had.

The Federal Reserve would allow the merged bank to operate for a two-year period, which could be extended for three more years, if necessary. Translation: Sandy Weill had a total of five years to get Congress off its duff and pass legislation allowing him to do what he just did.

The release boldly predicted that the legislation would come soon. "Citicorp and Travelers Group expect that current laws restricting bank holding companies . . . will change in the foreseeable future . . ."

In other words, the fix was in already. Sure enough, on November 12, 1999, President Clinton signed into law the Gramm-Leach-Bliley Act, which repealed the sixty-six-year-old Glass-Steagall Act prohibiting banks, securities firms, and insurance companies from affiliating. Done deal, almost. Weill still had one obstacle to clear before he could preside solo over the planet's largest financial institution. That obstacle was John Reed, who had been CEO of Citicorp, and with whom Weill had to share top dog status after the merger creating Citigroup. After the merger they were co-chairmen. An ugly power struggle was bound to ensue, and when the dust settled, Weill was alone atop the mountain. Reed resigned on February 28, 2000.

19

Jack Grubman: Analyze This

We have two classes of forecasters: Those who don't know and those who don't know they don't know.
—John Kenneth Galbraith

From his perspective, Jack Grubman had good reason to be bitter. He'd brought more money into Salomon Smith Barney than any single analyst, ever. He had helped raise billions for a vital industry that badly needed to spend billions. If the internet was the equivalent of the railroad in the late eighteenth century, telecom was the tracks.

Without new, high-speed pipes, there could be no cheap broadband, no cheap data and voice transmission. He had advised management, proposed mergers, even recruited talent for telecom giants.

He knew the telecommunications industry better than almost anyone, including most of the people who ran it. He was no numbers-crunching nerd who was terrified of asking tough questions of CEOs. By God, he *told* them what to do.

And now he was out on his ear and up to his large eyeballs in lawsuits. His career was finished, his reputation was shot, and prison was a possibility.

What in hell had he done wrong?

He got up in the morning and after his daily workout of one hundred pushups, had nowhere to go. There were no planes to catch, no clients to see or talk to, no research reports to write. He would spend most of his time with lawyers who were now on his own payroll, not Citigroup's. But the $2 million he got in his severance package for legal fees wouldn't last long at the current rate.

Maybe it would have been wiser if he'd clammed up at those televised hearings in Washington. He could have pleaded the Fifth Amendment and gone home. He would have lost his job, but he lost his job anyway.

He'd been lumped together with Bernie Ebbers and Scott Sullivan and Joseph Nacchio and Gary Winnick. Sure, he helped those guys raise billions for their companies. But he didn't cook any books, or haul away hundreds of millions in stock options, or borrow hundreds of millions from the corporate till. Yes, he made $20 million a year, but Jack Grubman earned it, he didn't steal it.

All Jack Grubman did was do his job. Why should he be ashamed of that?

No one saw the wall that the telecoms smacked into. Every industry has its reverses. Was anyone from AOL being attacked by regulators and hauled before congressional committees to be held up to ridicule on national TV? Those geniuses overestimated *advertising revenue*, for God's sake. Predicting ad revenue is a bunt compared to telecom growth. But AOL blew it and then they fudged the numbers. AOL stock dropped over 80 percent since the big merger.

Who could put a handle on future use of wireless, or broadband, or data or voice communication? Who would have dared to say that there was too much new capacity being added? Certainly no one in the industry. What was it that John Chambers, the CEO of Cisco, said in December 2000? "I have never been more optimistic about the future of our industry as a whole or of Cisco." Chambers was still predicting the industry would grow 50 percent a year. Chambers made $157 million that year, more than $300 million over five years, and he didn't have to defend himself before hostile committees on national TV. He wasn't facing fraud charges. He didn't have the press running after him every time he walked out of his apartment.

Cisco bragged about its great new system for tracking supply and demand for telecom gear. The new system was supposed to give Chambers pinpoint accuracy in his forecasts. How accurate was Chambers's prediction using that hot new model? Cisco stock dropped 88 percent in one year. Why wasn't he catching any heat?

And what about Philip Anschutz? He sold over $2 billion worth of Qwest stock before the company tanked. He never had to testify. And what about that Gary Winnick from Global Crossing? He was congratulated by the scalp hunters in Washington because he tossed $25 million back into his employees' 401(k) plans. Nice timing. He waited until he was on national TV, being grilled for walking away from his bankrupt company with $734 million. To Winnick, the $25 million was just a tip.

Why was the press all over Jack Grubman? They used to toss him bouquets.

The press tore Grubman apart for bad stock picking. But Jack Grubman never called himself a stock picker. His business card said Managing Director. He made it clear in *Business Week* and the *Wall Street Journal* years ago that he wore two hats, as a banker and as an analyst, and he saw no conflict in that. "What used to be a conflict is now synergy," he'd said. The publications quoted experts all over Wall Street who understood that. The old fashioned role of the analyst had changed. "The primary function of research analysts at top investment-banking houses is to promote the firm's investment-banking product," one of the experts said.

Sure, Grubman was bullish to the end on a lot of companies in telecom. But he had helped a lot of people make a lot of money along the way. Sure, when the sector imploded, and investors and lenders lost a staggering $2 trillion, he looked awfully bad. But all cheerleaders look silly when their teams lose. Grubman did more than cheer—he got out on the field and carried the ball. When his teams lost, he got booed off the field.

Business Week called him the King of Telecom, and that is what he was. He was no short-term stock picker. The statement he issued when he resigned summed it up: "While I regret that I, like many others, failed to predict the collapse of the telecommunications sector and I understand the disappointment and anger felt by investors as a result of that collapse, I am nevertheless proud of the work I, and analysts who worked with me, did."

On August 18, 2002, Jack Grubman swaggered out the door of Salomon with his head high. Whatever was going to happen to him would happen, and he wasn't going to cry about it. Tough guys don't cry no matter how hard the punches.

Jack Grubman always liked to make himself out as a tough guy. He had been an amateur boxer as a kid, encouraged by his father, Izzy, who was once a Golden Gloves champ who fought professionally for six years. On the wall of Jack's office was a big painting of the Jack Dempsey vs. Luis Firpo fight and a signed photograph of Muhammad Ali, along with a pair of boxing gloves. On Wall Street, if you are a "mutt" like Jack Grubman—a blue-collar guy in a blue-blood environment—the tougher you seem, the better.

It helped his tough-guy image to say that he was from South Philly, when in fact he grew up in Oxford Circle, in the city's northeast section. It was no bed of roses, but didn't sound as gritty as South Philly. As anyone who dealt with him knew, Jack Grubman was no shrinking violet. He didn't need to fib about coming from "Rocky's" neighborhood. But Jack had a tendency to b.s., which never left him.

His mother, Mildred, who worked in a department store, had big dreams for her only son. She'd had three miscarriages before he was born and when he finally made it into the world, she would see to it that he got the chance to make something important of his life. "She was someone who thought big thoughts," Grubman said. She liked Broadway shows and would go up to New York to catch them when she could. When Jack was growing up in the late fifties and sixties, one of the biggest hits on Broadway was *The Music Man*. An entire industry would one day dance to the tune that Jack Grubman played.

His dad, Izzy, worked for the city as a construction worker and later as an engineer. It was from him that Jack inherited a gift in math as well as a love of the boxing ring. Izzy could tell you the day of the week of any date in history, and still could at the age of eighty-two. In his heyday, he was strong enough to tear the Philadelphia Yellow Pages into eight pieces. Son Jack would later do the same thing with AT&T's stock.

Jack was a good student but no bookworm, making the National Honor Society twice at Northeast High School. In his senior year he won a national math award, but almost didn't graduate with his class because he cut so many math classes. His teacher wanted to flunk him for poor attendance but was talked out of it. While Grubman was in school, he played the clarinet in the band and joined the debating team, besides learning how to spar from his dad and doing some club boxing.

Math was his major at Boston U., where he graduated cum laude before earning a master's in probability theory at Columbia. Those credentials were hardly shabby. But he doctored his resume anyway, *Business Week* discovered, claiming a bogus degree from M.I.T. "It was a stupid mistake on my part," Grubman admitted. "At some point, I probably felt insecure, and it perpetuated itself."

In 1977 he began his working life at AT&T, and remained involved with the telecommunications industry the rest of his career. Although he had planned on becoming a math professor, once in the corporate rat race he felt compelled to prove himself. "I felt like I needed to be at the top of my game," he said. "I refuse to let anyone topple me. That's why I am so myopically focused."

He was assigned to do corporate planning for the company's eventual breakup in 1984 and also worked on analyzing demand in long-distance phone traffic. Early on, he showed that he was not one to take too much for granted. He challenged a computer model that was used to assess the results of rate increases on customer usage. He did his own calculations and determined that the computer model was based on faulty math so he stopped using it. He was proven right, and eventually the company scrapped the model. But the way he went about it was crude and didn't endear him to his bosses. Grubman didn't care; he'd made his point and wasn't concerned about whose noses got bent out of shape.

While working for AT&T he met his wife, Luann, and in 1985 went over to PaineWebber. His career as an analyst didn't get off to a great start when he initially flunked the Series 7 exam, which he had to pass.

He began analyzing the telephone industry, which had now been broken up into AT&T and the seven Baby Bells and a slew of upstarts. He worked long hours and dug through the numbers and his analysis was noticed. Once again, he called a spade a spade, despite who might get upset. In the early nineties, he issued a tough report on Sprint that irritated the CEO, William T. Esrey, enough to complain to Grubman's bosses at PaineWebber. Grubman was called on the carpet, but didn't back down, despite the fact that Sprint represented a lot of potential business for PaineWebber.

His work eventually caught the eye of Eduardo Mestre, head of mergers for Salomon Brothers, who asked Grubman to lunch one day to discuss a job offer. According to the *Wall Street Journal,* Mestre suggested the Yale Club, which is just across the street from Grand Central Station. If you have never been there, finding the ground floor entrance can be a little tricky.

When Grubman finally arrived at lunch, he knew a lucrative job offer was on the line, but started off by giving Mestre hell.

"He yelled at me for the wrong address," Mestre recalled.

His years at Salomon coincided with the rapid expansion of the telecommunications industry, and Grubman not only clocked it better than anyone in the business, he helped shape it. It was his view that the race belonged to the quick, and he thought that the small, aggressive companies could easily outmaneuver the industry giants, especially barnacle-encrusted AT&T. The newcomers weren't wedded to old technology or entrenched ideas, and rapidly built powerful new networks that big corporate customers flocked to at AT&T's expense.

In 1995, he cost his employer a fortune by downgrading AT&T from "buy" to "neutral," which in analyst parlance meant "dump the sucker." At the time, AT&T was spinning off Lucent Technologies, which included the famous Bell Labs operation. Not surprisingly, AT&T largely cut Salomon Smith Barney out of the IPO, which generated a total of over $100 million in investment banking fees.

Grubman had bucked the age-old practice on Wall Street of "you scratch my back and I'll scratch yours." It was a very gutsy call, and might have cost Grubman his job at other brokerage houses. Nonetheless, his downgrade of AT&T was right on the money. AT&T trailed its industry peers for the next few years, while the smaller, nimbler upstarts that Grubman favored were going through the roof. His credibility soared and so did his power. He became known as the industry "ax," the guy whom everyone in the business listened to. *Institutional Investor* named him the top analyst in the telecom field three years running. The publication's ratings are very important to analysts, whose reputations and compensation are at stake. The ratings are not based on an analyst's accuracy in picking stocks, but are determined by polling big institutional investors like pensions and mutual funds. These big money managers look beyond "buy" and "hold" ratings. They want hard numbers, which Grubman could provide. He was never reticent in sharing his views, and had information no one else did. He had become the industry's *consigliere*.

While beating up on AT&T, Grubman was touting competitors like WorldCom, Qwest, Global Crossing, Metromedia Fiber Networks, Level 3 Communications, and Winstar. In the "grow or merge" mood of the mid and late nineties, it wasn't clear whether these companies would be predators or bait, but it didn't matter. If

Grubman liked them, investors piled on. In late 1997, he started recommending Metromedia Fiber and it skyrocketed 500 percent in ten months. He recommended Qwest in May of 1998, and it doubled in eleven months. Global Crossing, which he touted starting in September of that year, rose 375 percent in six months.

"I'm sculpting the industry," he bragged to *Business Week.* "I get feedback from institutions and CEOs. It feeds on itself. It's a virtuous circle."

Grubman had become a star, and was earning serious money for himself and his firm. His $3.5 million salary was eye-popping enough, but would soon soar after Goldman Sachs tried to lure him away. According to Thomson Financial, in 1998 alone Salomon Smith Barney took in $343 million in fees from telecoms and was not about to let its rainmaker walk away. The firm bumped his salary to more than $20 million.

A year later Grubman bought a Manhattan duplex for $6.2 million for his wife and twins, a boy and a girl. At forty-six, Jack Grubman was at the very top of his profession. He was covering some forty telecoms with a combined market value of over $1 trillion, earning a fortune and taking crap from no one. Well, almost no one.

On November 30, 1999, Jack Grubman did the unthinkable—he upgraded his rating on AT&T from his long-standing "neutral" to "buy."

The change of heart set off b.s. detectors all over Wall Street. AT&T was on the verge of selling up to $10 billion worth of stock tied to its wireless business. The investment banking fees would be huge. Could there possibly be a connection? Was Grubman changing his tune so Salomon would get a big piece of that action?

Was there gambling in Rick's place? Shocking!

Adding to the suspicion was the fact that Sandy Weill was on the board of AT&T—and C. Michael Armstrong, chairman of AT&T since 1997, was on the board of Citigroup. How cozy.

The topper came when the *Wall Street Journal* reported that

Sandy Weill had called Grubman and "nudged him to give AT&T a fresh hearing." Armstrong had reportedly been asking Weill regularly to get Grubman to examine AT&T's new cable strategy.

In his report, Grubman said the reasons for the upgrade involved AT&T's plans to use cable TV lines to provide local telephone, high-speed data, and other broadband services to customers nationwide.

When questioned, Grubman kept a straight face. "Anyone who knows me knows that I call them as I see them," he said. "No one tells me what to do."

Well, practically no one. When the co-chairman of the board asks you to "give a fresh hearing" to something, you don't need a blueprint. But Grubman didn't set any speed records. It took him nine months to change his tune.

Naturally, all parties denied the report had any strings attached. "It's insulting to AT&T and to Grubman," said an AT&T spokeswoman. "We think Jack's report speaks for itself."

While the pros rolled their eyes, a lot of investors followed Grubman's advice. On the Monday after his "buy" report was issued and widely broadcast, AT&T stock was the most actively traded stock of the day, with a volume of over 32 million shares traded. It closed up $2.43 to $59.87. Salomon Smith Barney was later named as one of the lead underwriters on the AT&T Wireless sale and netted fees of nearly $45 million.

Almost a year later, on October 4, 2000, the stock closed at $29.75. Buyers had watched their investments get chopped in half.

Just a few days later, Grubman downgraded AT&T again, from a "buy" to "outperform." He said the only reason he didn't go even lower with his recommendation, to the dreaded "neutral," was because the stock had already dropped 53 percent from its fifty-two-week high. The stock dropped another 5.6 percent, to $27.25 after his report came out.

Despite the bad odor wafting from his earlier AT&T call, Grubman went about his business. He remained loyal to most of his pets like WorldCom, Qwest, Global Crossing, and Winstar. It was those bullish calls that got him into hot water later with regulators and prosecutors.

But in August 2002, after his resignation, that old AT&T business would resurface like Godzilla rising from ooze. Just as Sandy Weill was cobbling together a deal to make the regulators and prosecutors go away in return for paying a huge fine, Eliot Spitzer struck again. The politically ambitious New York attorney general came across some of Grubman's old e-mails from 1999. They were just what Spitzer was looking for—direct evidence to implicate not only Jack Grubman, but also the man at the top of the ladder, the chairman of Citigroup himself.

Spitzer had already taken center stage in the war against corporate malfeasance. He launched his lawsuits long before the SEC, the Justice Department, the NASD, and other state prosecutors acted. It was Spitzer whose name was first in the press.

Spitzer had already used internal e-mails to embarrass Merrill Lynch into settling charges of shading its research to accommodate investment banking clients. Henry Blodget, the Merrill Lynch analyst who had left behind the smoking e-mails, had already been fired. Merrill had to come up with $100 million to keep Spitzer happy. Blodgett had been flogging dot.coms in his research reports, while privately admitting that at least some were "pieces of shit." After the e-mails had appeared in the press, Merrill chose not to fight the charges and paid a $100 million fine instead. Merrill thought briefly of hiring Rudy Giuliani to defend itself against Spitzer, but wisely chose to settle instead. Giuliani vs. Spitzer could have been a great sideshow, but it wouldn't have done Merrill's reputation much good.

Spitzer had threatened criminal action if Merrill didn't agree to the settlement of the civil suit, which is ethically debatable, but practically effective. If you hold a gun to someone's head, they usually do what you want.

That settlement put Spitzer on the national map. The press called him a crusader, and "the Sheriff of Wall Street." In his race for reelection in 2002, Spitzer won a comfortable 66 percent of the vote.

It was clear that Spitzer had loftier political goals. At his post-election party, he announced, "We will pursue every abuse on Wall Street with or without Harvey Pitt." (Pitt was still chairman of the SEC, but resigned the next day.)

In personally targeting the nation's largest banker after a stock market collapse, Spitzer was following an old path. In 1933, another young New York prosecutor with an eye on high political office had also taken on the head of the biggest bank in the country. Thomas E. Dewey was chief assistant to the U.S. attorney in New York who brought tax evasion charges against Charles Mitchell, CEO of the National City Bank, the bank on which Citigroup was founded. Dewey lost that case, but had better luck later on prosecuting organized crime figures, most notably Lucky Luciano. Dewey was later elected governor of the state, and was the Republican candidate for president in 1944 and 1948, losing badly to Roosevelt the first time, but only narrowly to Harry S. Truman in forty-eight. The *Chicago Daily News* thought he'd won and ran a headline it would forever regret: "Dewey Wins!"

Dewey's career ended under a cloud. After World War II, Luciano accused him of having been "on the take" while in office and claimed to have paid him $90,000 for his ultimate release from prison and return to Sicily. When called to answer questions about Luciano's release before Senator Estes Kefauver, Dewey refused.

Spitzer thought he'd struck gold twice when he came across an e-mail Grubman had written to a friend that seemed to cook Sandy Weill's goose. Grubman bragged that he had changed his recommendation on AT&T not to snare investment banking fees, but rather to help his boss get rid of John Reed, who had been co-chairman at Citigroup.

The co-chairmen were involved in a bitter power struggle to see which one of them would stay atop Citigroup. Power sharing suited neither one of them, and the board had to decide which man to keep. Grubman wrote in his e-mail that he upgraded AT&T because Weill needed the support of the AT&T chairman, who was on Citigroup's board, in order to "nuke" Reed.

The e-mail made great copy, but didn't make a lot of sense. C. Michael Armstrong, AT&T's CEO, was a friend of Weill's, who had served on Sandy Weill's boards for years. Weill was also on the AT&T board. He already had Armstrong's support; he didn't have to butter him up by asking Grubman to make an upgrade.

Weill denied the allegation and then Grubman admitted, under oath, that he had invented the whole story. He said that he was just making himself sound more important than he really was, just to impress a friend.

Grubman, who lied about his resume, and who lied about being from South Philly, had lied in this e-mail, too. The furor died down, and Spitzer's smoking e-mail went up in flames.

The settlement talks went on, with Weill having already committed to substantial changes in the way Citigroup would do business in the future. But another smoking e-mail soon surfaced, and this one was a howler.

Here is what Grubman wrote:

> You know that everyone thinks I upgraded T for the lead in AWE. Nope. I used Sandy to get my kids into 92nd Street Y pre-school (which is harder than Harvard) and Sandy needed Armstrong's vote on our board to nuke Reed in showdown. Once coast was clear for both of us (i.e. Sandy victor and my kids confirmed) I went back to my normal negative self on T. Armstrong never knew that we both (Sandy and I) played him like a fiddle.

The media dined out on the story for days. The 92nd Street Y's pre-school is a pre-pre-Ivy track nursery for Upper East Side rich kids. It *is* harder to get into than Harvard, because the school stages a strange lottery that excludes most applicants. One day a year, and only one, the school opens the phones to parents to arrange appointments. So it's a dialathon contest. Parents use friends, relatives, business colleagues, anyone, to speed dial the school all day. Most parents never get through.

Jack Grubman could hardly be faulted for trying to get his twins into the elite school. But did he really downgrade AT&T to get Weill's support in getting the kids into the school? The twins were admitted—and Citigroup subsequently donated $1 million to the 92nd Street Y. It was all terribly embarrassing for Weill, as well as possibly illegal.

But he didn't take it lying down. Weill sent a memo to his staff denying he'd influenced Grubman in his upgrade. He also addressed the 92nd Street Y business: "Although my effort to help an employee's children is what led me to call the 92nd Street Y, the Y is a superb institution and our support is consistent with Citigroup's philanthropic efforts."

Weill had a case. What's wrong with helping an employee, if it is simply a matter of steering a donation? Citigroup gives away hundreds of millions a year to charities and other non-profit institutions like the 92nd Street Y, which has had a long cultural tradition in New York. It is certainly deserving. It was totally consistent that Weill would back the Y. He had always been a big donor to cultural endeavors.

It was all delicious stuff, but when the giggling stopped, the second of Eliot Spitzer's smoking e-mails really only pointed in one direction: Spitzer could prove a *quid*, but he couldn't prove a *quo*. There was still no direct evidence that Weill had told Grubman to change his call.

The *New York Times* had been rough on Weill, but he fought back.

In a letter to the editor written by Weill's PR person, she wrote that Weill had suggested a closer look at AT&T almost one year before Grubman's upgrade. She also pointed out that Weill himself was a significant AT&T shareholder before and after the upgrade—shares Mr. Weill still owned.

The furor subsided, and Sandy Weill is still head of the largest bank in the country. Lou Dobbs observed that the whole fiasco would have cost any other CEO in America his job, but Sandy Weill survived. You just don't mess with Sandy.

The press now turned on Eliot Spitzer. They questioned his ethics and his unbridled ambition. Spitzer was vulnerable. His background did not suggest that of your typical crusader.

Spitzer was born in the Riverdale section of the Bronx, an upper middle class community located on a sylvan sliver along the Hudson River. He went to Horace Mann, one of the best prep schools in the city, before going to Princeton and then Harvard Law School, where he was an editor of the *Harvard Review*.

He landed a plum position with Paul Weiss, Rifkin, Wharton and Garrison, a top law firm. But after a few years he left to become an assistant district attorney, a move that cost him several hundred thousand dollars a year in income. He made a name for himself prosecuting high-profile cases involving organized crime and political corruption.

He then went to Skadden, Arps, Slate, Meagher & Flom, where he defended executives accused of money laundering and securities fraud. In 1994, he ran for state attorney general and lost. He tried again in 1998 and succeeded in a dirty campaign in which he accused his opponent of accepting political donations from companies who did business with his office.

Forbes disclosed that Spitzer had his own problems concerning some political loans. The magazine also pointed out that Spitzer had invested money in a hedge fund run by James J. Cramer, and had profited from Cramer's IPO trading.

Spitzer's shining armor had been tarnished just as the final agreement that he had been seeking was about to be signed. In the end, Spitzer didn't get Weill, just as Dewey failed to get Charlie Mitchell. It's never easy to nail the banker.

On December 20, 2002, the nation's largest banking and brokerage firms agreed to pony up about $1.4 billion to settle conflict of interest charges. The largest fine—$400 million—was levied against

Citigroup, parent of Salomon Smith Barney. The others had to pay between $80 million and $200 million. The firms included Credit Suisse, First Boston, Bear Stearns, Deutsche Bank, Goldman Sachs, J.P. Morgan Chase, Lehman Brothers, Morgan, Stanley, and UBS Warburgh. Merrill Lynch had already paid a fine of $100 million.

The firms also promised to pay $450 million over five years to fund independent research for investors, and $85 million for investor education.

The settlement also insisted that the firms sever the ties between investment banking and research. Stock analysts' pay would no longer depend on the investment business they bring in. The firms would no longer be able to "spin" IPO shares to potential investment banking customers.

The corporate scandals of '02 had begun with the dazzling fireworks of Enron's crash, but ended with a whimper, behind closed doors.

20

Preventing More Fraud: Modest Proposals

*The punishment of wise men who refuse to take part
in the affairs of government is to live under the
government of unwise men.*
—Plato

Mr. B. was waiting for me just inside the lobby at the New York
Athletic Club. He'd agreed to an interview about the corporate scandals, and how they could be avoided in the future.

He popped out of his chair to greet me, though he was pushing
eighty and his face didn't lie about it. But he kept lean and fit and
still played a little handball once in a while. He'd just finished a gym
workout and his Colonel Sanders hair hadn't fully dried. He looked
like a wolfhound caught in the rain.

We took the elevator up to the bar and sat down at a quiet table
and ordered his usual, Glenlivet plain.

"You owe me something," I said, after we'd settled in.

"The last page of the article I wrote."

"Yes. I think you were getting to what should be done about options."

"We'll get to that," he said. "It's part of my prescription for preventing fraud like this from ever happening again. Investors lost trillions of dollars, although many of them don't even realize it. They know their stock funds are down, but they don't know why."

"Let's get started with the interview." I turned on the tape recorder and placed it on the table between us.

WGF: *A common thread can be found in many of these corporate collapses—AOL, Adelphia, Enron, WorldCom, Global Crossing, Tyco, and Qwest. The CEOs all had fortunes in stock options at stake.*

Mr.B: The CEOs of those companies paid more attention to the stock price than to the companies they were supposed to be running. That was their common act of fraud—gross negligence. They focused on their stock options, and screwed everyone else.

WGF: *So you would do away with stock options.*

Mr. B: No. Options make a lot of sense in a lot of companies, especially startups. And they make sense for a lot for employees. But they should not be offered to top management of large companies. Top managers should get compensated in stock, not options. The amount of stock they receive should be linked to performance. Plus, CEOs and other top managers would have to hold two-thirds of the stock they acquire until they leave the company.

WGF: *CEOs might not like that.*

Mr. B: They will learn to love it. They will have plenty at stake, but won't be such slaves to quarterly earnings. They won't have to worry about goosing the stock before their options expire. They will be able to think long term. If they perform well, they will still get very rich from the annual awards of stock.

WGF: *What would determine the amount of stock awarded to CEOs each year? The price of the stock?*

Mr. B: That would be one ingredient. But achieving performance goals would count more. Sometimes the price of a stock is way out of whack with what the company is really doing. The stock could be down, but if the CEO has achieved his goals, he should still be rewarded. Of course, those goals must be meaningful and realistic.

WGF: *Such as?*

Mr. B: Increasing market share on a competitor, for example. Or launching a new product or division. Or making an important acquisition or sale. Maybe avoiding a strike. The idea is to free the CEO to run the business, not spend all day with accountants and stock analysts.

WGF: *You mention analysts. The sell-side analysts did a lot to make the Class of '02 what they are today—ex-CEOs of collapsed companies.*

Mr. B: First, all analysts will have to use the same rating system, based on stars. They would rate the companies they cover by stars—one to five; the way Morningstar rates mutual funds. So a five-star rating would mean that the company is the best in its group, while no stars would indicate it is the worst. Analysts wouldn't be able to hide behind weasel words like "accumulate" or "underperform." The analysts themselves would also be awarded star ratings, based on the accuracy of their recommendations. The best analysts would rate five stars; the worst would get none.

WGF: *That should make their recommendations clearer, but it won't eliminate any conflicts they might have in rating clients.*

Mr. B: Let's face it. Those conflicts will probably never be eliminated. Sure, analysts will be segregated from the investment bankers, but the pressure will always be there to go gently on a client company. Analysts who do this will see their own ratings drop. Firms that make a habit of it will suffer in the overall ratings and lose customers.

WFG: *Who is going to pay for all this?*

Mr. B: The same people who are paying for it now—the institutions and other big traders. But good analysis is more important than ever on the retail level, too. There are a lot of individual investors who would pay more to use brokers whose analysts are rated the best.

WGF: *Are you saying that the full-service broker isn't dead?*

Mr. B: Investors who trusted their own judgment in the last bull market are not so sure of themselves now. Brokers who can provide them with good advice based on good research will win the hearts and wallets of a lot of insecure investors.

WFG: *So in your perfect world, you would curtail the use of stock options, and put the analysts on a star-rating system. What else would you do?*

Mr. B: Rate the boards of directors, too. Same star ratings. Criteria would include how the board is constituted—how many outsiders are on the board, for example. The boards that come closest to meeting governance guidelines will score the highest. The analysts can rate the boards as part of their routine research reports. I think board members would be very attentive to how they are rated. It reflects on their reputations.

WGF: *What else would you do with directors?*

Mr. B: Limit the number of boards they serve on. No director should serve on any more than three boards. As it is now, serving on a board takes up about one hundred hours a year of your time. If a member serves three boards, that is over three hundred hours. Even for a retired CEO, that is a lot of time. I would also limit the CEO to only one outside board. He is not being paid to help run another company. It goes without saying that the CEO should not be the chairman of the board. In any case, he cannot be allowed to control the nominating process.

The accounting committee has to get serious about looking at the books. You need very good people here, and they should be paid a lot more than other board members for their time. Fortunately, there is a lot of accounting talent for hire at our universities. I don't usually like academic types on boards, but we need them here.

WGF: *Should small, individual investors have direct representation on the board? There have been a few cases where investors have run for boards, and been elected.*

Mr. B: You don't need some crackpot with five shares on your board. But the talent pool for directors has got to be expanded. A handful of recruiters keeps on recycling the same people. Friends recommend friends. There has to be serious effort made at finding new, fresh faces.

WGF: *None of the remedies you are suggesting are draconian.*

Mr. B: No, but I have one more that would be very important to the health of our markets, as well as help foster honest behavior in the executive suite. I would eliminate or drastically cut the tax on dividends. It's a double tax anyway, as we know. The corporation pays taxes on its profits, and then the shareholders pay taxes on the profits if they are distributed as dividends. It is not only unfair, it has destabilized our markets.

WGF: *But investors say they don't want dividends. They would rather see the money reinvested in the company.*

Mr. B: That's no longer true. Recent surveys show the opposite. Cisco Systems asked its shareholders recently if they preferred a cash dividend, or a stock repurchase plan. The stock repurchase won, ten to one. But Cisco went one step further and asked stockholders what they would choose if the dividends were made tax-free. Over half of them said they would take the dividend.

Stockholders would prefer dividends, if it weren't for that ridiculous tax. Not all companies would want to pay out dividends of course. But those that do would see their stock benefit immediately. It would take on a premium, and it would become a lot less volatile. People who are receiving a decent dividend are less inclined to worry about the daily stock price. They will hold their shares longer. They will invest more, because they are getting a return that is tax-free, or close to it.

A consistent dividend also puts a nice floor on your stock. If the price drops and the dividend stays the same, investors will drive the price back up because the rate of return will be better.

It creates more capital formation, and it puts more money in the hands of consumers.

WGF: *What would the dividend rates be like?*

Mr. B: They wouldn't have to be high—roughly equivalent to a five-year bond. Nowadays, that's about 5 percent. It could be adjusted, of course.

WGF: *Won't that distribution of cash hamper a company's abilities to expand?*

Mr. B: No. In fact, paying regular dividends would probably improve its credit rating, making its cost of money cheaper. Look, not every company is going to want to do this. Lots of them cannot afford to. Investors won't ignore companies that don't pay dividends, but they will expect a lot more pop in the price of the stock.

WGF: *How will this help keep CEOs honest?*

Mr. B: It relieves a lot of the pressure of managing earnings. A bad quarter won't kill you, so you won't be as tempted to resort to questionable practices.

There's another element that is even more important. Shareholder involvement. When shareowners are collecting dividends, and in many cases relying on them for income, they pay close attention to the company and its management. They will become more vocal. More of them will read the financial statements and vote on proposals. They will feel as if they have a stake in the company.

Mr. B turned off the tape recorder and finished the last of his scotch. "No matter what anyone does," he said, "frauds, even major frauds, will happen again. The cycle now seems to be every ten or twelve years. There will always be people who will find a way to game the system for a while. We had the savings and loan crisis, the leveraged-buyout scandals, BCCI, and a lot of others and have survived. We'll survive this one, too."

Bibliography

Bernstein, Peter L. *Against the Gods: The Remarkable Story of Risk.* Hoboken, NJ: John Wiley, 1998.

Bogle, John C. *Common Sense on Mutual Funds*: New Imperatives for the Intelligent Investor. Hoboken, NJ: John Wiley, 2000.

Bruck, Connie. *Steve Ross and the Creation of Time Warner.* New York: Penguin, 1995.

Chancellor, Edward. *Devil Take the Hindmost: A History of Financial Speculation.* New York: Plume, 2000.

Cruver, Brian. *Anatomy of Greed: The Unshredded Truth from an Enron Insider.* New York: Carroll & Graf, 2002.

Evans, Harold, with Gail Buckland. *The American Century.* New York: Knopf, 1998.

Fusaro, Peter C., and Ross M. Miller. *What Went Wrong at Enron.* Hoboken, NJ: John Wiley, 2002.

Gerstner, Louis V. *Who Says Elephants Can't Dance?* New York: HarperCollins, 2002.

Levitt, Arthur, with Paula Dwyer. *Take On the Street: What Wall Street and Corporate America Don't Want You to Know, and What You Can Do to Fight Back.* New York: Knopf, 2002.

Lowenstein, Roger. *When Genius Failed. The Rise and Fall of Long-Term Capital Management.* New York: Randon House, 2000.

MacKay, Charles. *Extraordinary Popular Delusions and the Madness of Crowds* (1841). New York: Crown, 1995.

Motavalli, John. *Bamboozled at the Revolution.* New York: Viking Penguin, 2002.

Partnoy, Frank. *Fiasco; The Inside Story of a Wall Street Trader.* New York: Penguin Putnam, 1999.

Rowland, Mary. *A Commonsense Guide to Your 401(k).* New York: Bloomberg, 1997).

Schilit, Howard. *Financial Shenanigans.* New York: McGraw Hill, 2002.

Shiller, Robert J. *Irrational Exuberance.* Princeton, NJ: Princeton University Press, 2000.

Stone, Amey, and Mike Brewster. *King of Capital: Sandy Weill and the Making of Citigroup.* Hoboken, NJ: John Wiley, 2002.

Welch, Jack, with John A. Byrne. *Jack: Straight from the Gut.* New York: Warner Books, 2001.

Index

About the Author

William G. Flanagan has been a writer and editor for *Forbes, The Wall Street Journal, Business Week, Esquire,* and *New York.* He hosted *The Bill Flanagan Show* on WABC radio (a money call-in show) and acts as substitute host for Bob Brinker on *Moneytalk,* which is carried by over two hundred radio stations nationally. He was a regular on Lou Dobbs's *Moneyline* and has appeared on *Good Morning America, Today,* Fox News, and other national and local shows. He also had a bit part in the Woody Allen film *Radio Days.* He lives in New York.